98

THE INTERNATIONAL BANK

for Reconstruction and Development

1946–1953

Published for the INTERNATIONAL BANK

FOR RECONSTRUCTION AND DEVELOPMENT

By THE JOHNS HOPKINS PRESS: *Baltimore*, 1954

Foreword

This study of the International Bank for Reconstruction and Development, 1946-1953, has been prepared by the staff of the Bank. It consists of three parts. Part I is devoted to a discussion of the purposes, organization and financial structure of the Bank. Part II sets forth the major operational policies of the Bank and describes the general character of its operations. Part III is a country-by-country summary of Bank activities. In addition, the study includes 12 appendices containing, among other information, the Bank's Articles of Agreement and its financial statements as of December 31, 1953.

Unless otherwise indicated, all data in this study are given as of December 31, 1953.

Contents

PART I
Purposes, Organization and Financial Structure

PART II
Major Operational Policies and
General Character of Bank Operations

PART III
Country-by-Country Summary of Bank Activities

WESTERN HEMISPHERE

APPENDICES

Tables

Charts

PART I

Purposes, Organization
and Financial Structure

1

Origin, Nature and Functions

EARLY IN WORLD WAR II the economic and financial experts of the Allied Nations began to devote their energies to planning for the economic problems of the peace. They recognized that, if the peace were to be won, attention would have to be given not only to the immediate relief and physical reconstruction of economies disrupted by the war but also to "the expansion, by appropriate international and domestic measures, of production, employment, and the exchange and consumption of goods which are the material foundations of the liberty and welfare of all peoples. . . ."[1] Discussions were held on a variety of proposals that were intended to help realize these economic goals of the Allies.

Among these proposals, postwar monetary and financial plans had begun to be considered as early as 1941. From deliberations on these plans over the ensuing three years, the outlines of two complementary financial institutions emerged. The first—to become the International Monetary Fund—was to provide for international currency stability by helping to finance its members' temporary balance of payments deficits and by providing for the

[1] Article VII, Mutual Aid Agreement between the United States and Great Britain.

3

progressive elimination of exchange restrictions and the observance of accepted rules of international financial conduct. The second institution—to become the International Bank for Reconstruction and Development (popularly known as the World Bank)—was, as its name implies, to help finance the reconstruction and development of its member countries.

By the spring of 1944, after prolonged and intensive discussions between Treasury representatives of the United States and the United Kingdom and consultations with representatives of other countries, the proposals for these two organizations had reached an advanced stage. A United Nations Monetary and Financial Conference was accordingly convened. Following preliminary meetings at Atlantic City, the representatives of 44 nations assembled at Bretton Woods, New Hampshire, on July 1, 1944 and, three weeks later, completed final drafts of Articles of Agreement for the Fund and the Bank for submission to the various participating governments for their acceptance.

All of the nations which participated in the Bretton Woods Conference except the U. S. S. R., Liberia and New Zealand subsequently approved the charters of both the Fund and the Bank. The Articles of Agreement of the Bank were formally accepted by a majority of the participants by December 27, 1945. Six months later, on June 25, 1946, the Bank formally commenced operations.

Underlying Purpose and General Description

The participants at Bretton Woods realized that, at the conclusion of hostilities, there would be a pressing need for international capital to finance both the reconstruction of productive facilities destroyed by the war and an increase in productivity and living standards in the underdeveloped areas of the world. The requirements were recognized as being so great, and the risks so large, that private capital would be unable to fulfill them without some form of governmental guarantee. The Bretton

Woods Conference felt that the problem could best be solved by the creation of a new type of international investment institution which would be authorized to make or guarantee loans for productive reconstruction and development projects, both with its own capital funds and through the mobilization of private capital, and which would be provided with a financial structure under which the risks of such investment would be shared by all member governments roughly in accordance with their economic strength. This is the solution which was embodied in the Bank's Articles of Agreement.

The Articles establish the Bank as an intergovernmental institution, corporate in form, all of whose capital stock is owned by its member governments. The Bank's authorized capital is the equivalent of $10 billion, of which the equivalent of more than $9 billion has been subscribed. Only part of this, however, is required to be paid in and only a portion of what is so paid in is immediately available for lending. As is more fully described in Chapter 3, each member's total subscription is divided into three parts: (1) 2% of each member's subscription is payable in gold or U. S. dollars and is freely available for lending; (2) 18% of each subscription is payable in the local currency of the member and is available for lending only with the consent of that member; and (3) the remaining 80% of each subscription is not available for lending at all but is subject to call if and when required to meet the obligations of the Bank arising out of borrowings or guarantees.

This capital structure was designed to provide the Bank both with substantial loan resources from its own paid-in capital and with an even more sizeable guaranty fund, consisting of the unpaid 80% portion of all capital subscriptions, which would enable the Bank to mobilize private capital for international investment, either through the sale of Bank obligations to private investors or through Bank guarantees of private international credits. As the records of the Bretton Woods deliberations indicate, the emphasis from the beginning was not so much on what the Bank could lend directly out of its paid-in capital as on the concept of the Bank as providing a " safe bridge " over which private capital could move into the international field. Indeed, it is one of the unique features of the Bank that, although it is an intergovernmental organization, it must rely upon the private investment community for most of its financial resources.

The provision of guarantees to international lenders represented no innovation of itself; several loans to European governments in the early inter-war period, for example, carried the guarantee of other European governments. The new feature of the guarantee written into the Bank's charter was the sharing of the risk on an international basis, with each of the Bank's members, whether borrower or lender, responsible up to the amount of its capital subscription for the Bank's outstanding borrowings and guarantees. The amount of the risk thus guaranteed was limited, as a practical matter, by the charter requirement that the total amount of the loans made or guaranteed by the Bank was not to exceed 100% of its total unimpaired subscribed capital, reserves and surplus.

In drafting the provisions of the Articles of Agreement governing the use to which the Bank was to put the funds available to it, whether from its paid-in capital or from the sale of its obligations, the Bank's founders were acutely aware of the need to avoid the errors which had characterized much of the international lending of the past, and particularly during the inter-war period. Capital raised through sales of securities in foreign capital markets had frequently made little or no contribution to the productive capacity of the borrowers. Many of the loans had also been made at high interest rates and without reference to the ability of the borrowers to service new, or even existing, foreign debt. These lending practices were undoubtedly a contributing factor to the widespread defaults in the 1930's.

To avoid these errors of the past, the Bank's charter contains a number of protective provisions governing loans to be made or guaranteed by the Bank. These loans must be for productive purposes and, except in special circumstances, must be to finance the foreign exchange requirements of specific projects of reconstruction or development. The merits of all projects financed must be carefully studied and arrangements made designed to assure that the most useful and urgent projects are dealt with first. The borrower may be a member government, a political subdivision or a business, industrial or agricultural enterprise, but if the borrower is other than the government, the loan must be guaranteed by the member government in whose territories the project is located, or by its central bank or some comparable agency; in practice, the Bank has always obtained a government, as distinct from a central bank, guarantee. The Articles of Agreement enjoin the Bank to act " prudently " in making loans, paying due regard to the prospect that the borrower and, if the borrower is not a member, that the guarantor will be in a position to meet its obligations under the loan. The Bank is also specifically required to make arrangements to ensure that the proceeds of each loan are used only for the purposes for which the loan was granted, with due attention to considerations of economy and efficiency and without regard to political or other non-economic considerations.

The charter contains two other provisions governing the character of Bank lending which deserve mention at this point. The first is a prohibition against " tied " loans; that is, the Bank is to impose no conditions requiring the proceeds of its loans to be spent in the territories of any particular member or members. The second is a requirement that the Bank must be satisfied, before making or guaranteeing any loan, that in the prevailing market conditions the borrower would be unable to obtain the loan from private sources under reasonable conditions.

The Course of Bank Lending

Although the Articles of Agreement require the Bank to give " equitable consideration to projects for development and projects for reconstruction alike," it was contemplated at Bretton Woods that the initial emphasis of Bank activity would necessarily have to be on the urgent problems of reconstruction. And, in fact, the first loans of the Bank, made in 1947 and totalling $497 million, were in the nature of emergency assistance to four Western European countries to prevent a threatened interruption in the flow of their essential imports. These loans, by permitting the borrowing countries to sustain for a time the volume of imports necessary both for continued rehabilitation and operation of their productive facilities, helped to prevent a disastrous drop in production and possible economic collapse.

But even when these loans were granted, it was already apparent that the assumptions made at Bretton Woods about the require-ments for European recovery had been both too simple and too optimistic. The concept of Bretton Woods had been that the critical short-range relief needs of Europe after the war were to be met through donations by the United Nations Relief and Rehabilitation Administration (UNRRA), which had already been established; the external financing needed for more perma-nent recovery programs, to the extent that it could not be furnished from other sources, was to be supplied by loans from the Bank. Recovery was conceived of primarily in terms of the rebuilding of factories, mines, railroads, and other specific productive facilities.

By 1947 it had become clear that the physical devastation, disruption of trade and industrial and governmental dislocations caused by the war were far greater than had been envisaged at Bretton Woods. Unforeseen political conflicts accentuated the economic difficulties. As a result, the requirements for European recovery at the end of the UNRRA period involved much more than the reconstruction or modernization of specific productive facilities; there was also urgent need for financial aid to continue imports of food, fuel and raw materials which, for the time being, could come only from the dollar area. Despite substantial credits from the United States and Canada, European resources of dollar exchange had fallen to dangerously low levels by the end of 1946.

When it made its reconstruction loans in 1947, therefore, the Bank recognized that, important as this financing was to fill urgent immediate needs, the long-term requirements for European recovery were far too large for the Bank to meet with the resources at its command and, in fact, were far greater than the amount which the countries of Western Europe could afford to borrow with any reasonable prospect of being able to repay. At that time, the Marshall Plan proposals which eventuated in the European Recovery Program were already under consideration and the Bank gave them its full support.

When the European Recovery Program came into operation, the Bank turned its attention to its other major field of responsibility, the financing of productive projects in the less developed areas of the world. This has since been the principal area of concentration of Bank activities. Most of the Bank's development loans have been for basic facilities such as power, transportation, and irrigation and reclamation, which are a prerequisite for increased productivity in wide sectors of the borrowing countries' economies.

Up to December 31, 1953, the Bank had made 96 loans, aggregating the equivalent of almost $1.8 billion, in 28 member countries and three overseas dependencies. Of the amount lent, the equivalent of roughly $1 billion was for development projects located outside of Europe. A more detailed description of these lending activities is contained in Chapter 7 and, on a country-by-country basis, in Part III.

Issuance of Bank Obligations

The Bretton Woods Conference appears to have assumed that, by virtue of the guarantees of Bank obligations provided by its capital structure, the Bank would have ready access to the private investment market. The problem of marketing the Bank's securities, however, proved to be considerably more complicated than anticipated at Bretton Woods. Investors as a group knew little about the Bank or the resources behind Bank obligations; because of the experience of the inter-war years they were reluctant to engage in any investment which partook of the nature of foreign lending; and they were hesitant in any event about the purchase of unseasoned securities. Over and above this, at the time when the Bank commenced operations most institutional investors in the United States, who constituted by far the largest group of potential purchasers of Bank securities, were subject to state or federal laws which either prohibited or greatly restricted their purchase of Bank obligations. It was therefore necessary for the Bank, before it could raise money in the United States market, to undertake a widespread informational program and to make intensive efforts to obtain legislation qualifying its securities for institutional investment.

The marketing activities of the Bank are discussed in Chapter 9. As the discussion there shows, a reasonably broad market for Bank obligations has by now been created in the United States and $575 million of Bank dollar bonds are now outstanding, of which about $150 million are held by investors outside the United States. The Bank has also issued bonds in the capital markets of Canada, the United Kingdom and Switzerland in the currencies of those countries. Total Bank obligations, direct and guaranteed, outstanding on December 31, 1953, amounted to the equivalent of approximately $683 million.

Technical Assistance

As a result of the experience which it has accumulated in the development field, the Bank has been increasingly called upon to supplement its investment activities by providing advisory services of various kinds to its less developed member countries. This function was not stressed at Bretton Woods but, over the years, it has taken on increasing importance.

Some of these advisory services have been provided in connection with loan operations, including such matters as the determination of priorities among different projects, suggestions with respect to the technical plans for projects, and recommendations on administrative and organizational arrangements and on means for financing the local costs of projects. But increasingly the Bank has been called upon to assist its members in matters not specifically connected with loan proposals, particularly on the problem of development programming. In response to requests, the Bank has sent teams of experts to a number of countries to analyze their economies and to make recommendations designed to form the basis of long-term development programs. Members of the Bank's staff or consultants retained by the Bank have also helped a number of member countries on other important development problems, such as the establishment of programming and coordinating agencies, the formulation of major economic and financial policies, and the organization or expansion of local capital markets. A discussion of these technical assistance activities of the Bank is contained in Chapter 8.

2

Membership and Organization

Composition of Membership and Voting Rights

As of December 31, 1953, the Bank had 55 members (see Appendix D).[1] As already noted, only three of the 44 governments represented at Bretton Woods—the U. S. S. R., Liberia and New Zealand—have not become members, while 15 countries not represented at Bretton Woods have become members (Austria, Burma, Ceylon, Denmark, Finland, Germany, Italy, Japan, Jordan, Lebanon, Pakistan, Sweden, Syria, Thailand and Turkey).[2] After being a member since January 1946, Poland withdrew from the Bank in March 1950. For reasons described below, the membership of Czechoslovakia has been suspended.

Each member of the Bank has 250 votes plus one additional vote for each $100,000 share of capital stock subscribed by it. The shares and votes of the Bank's member countries are shown in Appendix I. The Articles provide that, with certain designated

[1] The same 55 governments are also members of the International Monetary Fund. Under the Articles of Agreement, membership in the Fund is a condition for admission to membership in the Bank.

[2] An application for membership from Indonesia was approved by the Board of Governors in September 1952, with a capital subscription of $110 million; Indonesia has until March 16, 1954, to accept membership. As of December 31, 1953, an application for membership from Israel was pending.

exceptions, all matters before the Bank are to be decided by a majority of votes cast.

Withdrawal and Suspension of Membership

Any member is entitled to withdraw from membership in the Bank at any time. Withdrawal is effective on the date when notice of withdrawal is received by the Bank.

Any member which fails to fulfill any of its obligations to the Bank may be suspended by decision of a majority of the Governors, exercising a majority of the total voting power. Unless a suspended member is restored to good standing within one year by a similar vote, its membership is automatically terminated.

When a government ceases to be a member, the Bank is required to arrange for the repurchase of its shares of capital stock. The shares must be repurchased at book value as part of the general settlement of accounts with the member. The government remains liable, however, for its direct obligations to the Bank as borrower or guarantor and for its contingent liabilities for losses or guarantees contracted by the Bank before the date it ceased to be a member to the extent that such losses exceed the amount of the reserve against losses existing on that date.[3] Poland is the only member to have withdrawn from membership.

Under the Articles of Agreement, any original member of the Bank whose metropolitan territories suffered from enemy occupation or hostilities during World War II had the right to postpone payment for five years of a portion of that part of its subscription payable in gold or United States dollars. Under these provisions, Czechoslovakia was allowed to postpone payment of $625,000 until June 25, 1951. In June 1951, Czechoslovakia claimed a further postponement of this amount, but the claim was rejected by the Executive Directors of the Bank. No payment

---

[3] In addition, on the conditions specified in Article VI, Sec. 4 (c) (iv), the former member remains liable on calls on the 80% portion of its subscription on account of obligations incurred before it ceased to be a member.

of the amount due having been made, the Board of Governors adopted a resolution in September 1953 suspending Czechoslovakia from membership effective at the close of business on December 31, 1953, unless it should pay the $625,000 before that time. Since the payment was not made by December 31, 1953, Czechoslovakia's membership was suspended as of the close of business on that date. It will be automatically terminated on December 31, 1954, unless in the meantime the Board of Governors votes to restore Czechoslovakia to good standing.[4]

Organizational Structure

The Bank's organization consists of:

a. A Board of Governors composed of one Governor and one Alternate Governor appointed by each member.

b. The Executive Directors, now 16 in number, of whom five are appointed by the five largest stockholders (the United States, the United Kingdom, France, China and India) and 11 are elected by the remaining members. Each Executive Director appoints an alternate with power to act for him in his absence.

c. The management, consisting of the President, who is elected by the Executive Directors, and the Vice President, other officers and an international staff appointed by the President. As of December 31, 1953, the staff numbered 434 persons of 31 different nationalities.

Board of Governors

Under the Articles of Agreement, all of the powers of the Bank are vested in the Board of Governors as representatives of the Bank's stockholders. However, with certain exceptions, the Board of Governors is authorized to delegate, and has in fact delegated,

---

[4] All other members who received a right to postpone payment until June 25, 1951, of a portion of their subscriptions payable in gold or United States dollars have made payment in full except China. China has made payments totaling $80,000 and has stated that it recognized its obligations to the Bank and would pay the balance of $2.92 million as soon as it was in a position to do so.

all of its powers to the Executive Directors. The exceptions include the admission of new members, the increase or decrease of the capital stock, the suspension of a member, decisions of appeals from interpretations of the Articles of Agreement made by the Executive Directors, approval of formal agreements with other international organizations, and decisions on distribution of the net income of the Bank and on the liquidation of the Bank.

The Board of Governors is required to meet once each year and it has become the practice to hold this annual meeting in September, jointly with the annual meeting of the Board of Governors of the International Monetary Fund. From the time the Bank commenced operations, there have been eight annual meetings, five of which have been held in Washington, D. C., the headquarters of the Bank, and the others in London, Paris and Mexico City. Since many members appoint as Governors of the Bank and Fund their Ministers of Finance, the heads of their Central Banks or others holding comparable positions, the annual meeting of the Board of Governors, although not often called upon to take significant formal action, has come to be regarded as an important occasion for informal exchanges of views, at a high level, on major international financial and monetary problems.

In cases where a decision by the Board of Governors has been required between regular annual meetings, as for example on the admission of new members, it has been obtained by telegraphic or mail vote. While special meetings of the Board of Governors are authorized, none has so far been called.

Members of the Board of Governors as of December 31, 1953 are listed in Appendix J.

Executive Directors

The Articles of Agreement provide that the Executive Directors shall be appointed or elected every two years. In accordance with normal business practice, the Directors are responsible for the

15

conduct of the general operations of the Bank. They have offices and hold their meetings at Bank headquarters. Their current practice is to meet regularly once a month, with special meetings called from time to time to handle specific items of business as they arise.

A majority of the Executive Directors, exercising 50% or more of the total voting power, constitutes a quorum. Each appointed Director casts the votes of the member appointing him and each elected Director casts the votes which counted toward his election. All the votes which a Director is entitled to cast must be cast as a unit and cannot be divided. For the preliminary consideration of certain policy matters, three standing committees of Executive Directors have been established, the members of which are appointed by the President. They are the Financial Policy Committee, the Membership Committee and the Pension Committee.

The duties and remuneration of the Executive Directors and their Alternates were the subject of study by a committee of the Board of Governors established at the Third Annual Meeting in 1948. The committee noted the major responsibilities assigned to the Executive Directors under the Articles of Agreement and stressed particularly the importance of their function in the formulation of Bank policy. It expressed the view, however, that it was not necessary for the discharge of those responsibilities that an Executive Director and his Alternate both serve on a full-time basis. The report recommended that, in the absence of special circumstances, a country or a group of countries should be represented generally by the Executive Director, with the Alternate appearing only occasionally, or by the Alternate, with the Executive Director normally appearing only at meetings or other times of special importance. The report further recommended that the compensation of Executive Directors and Alternates be based on the time actually devoted to Bank work.

The report of this committee was approved by the Governors at the Fifth Annual Meeting in 1950, and the recommendations contained in the report have since been followed. At present, only seven of the 16 Executive Directors serve on a full-time basis and only four of them have a full-time Alternate.

A list of the Executive Directors and Alternates as of December 31, 1953, together with a list of those who previously served in those capacities, appears as Appendix K.

Management and Staff

The President of the Bank is elected by the Executive Directors and acts as their Chairman; he has no vote except a deciding vote in case of an equal division. The President is chief of the operating staff of the Bank and, subject to the direction of the Executive Directors on questions of policy, is responsible for the conduct of the ordinary business of the Bank, the organization of its staff, and the appointment and dismissal of its officers and employees.

The Bank has had three Presidents, Mr. Eugene Meyer who served from June 18, 1946 to December 17, 1946, Mr. John J. McCloy who served from March 17, 1947 to June 30, 1949, and Mr. Eugene R. Black who has been serving since July 1, 1949. By action of the Executive Directors, the term of Mr. Black's service, which was due to expire on June 30, 1954, has been extended for an additional five years from that date.

In the discharge of their offices, the President, officers and staff of the Bank owe their duty entirely to the Bank and to no other authority. Under the Articles of Agreement, each member government has undertaken to respect the international character of this duty and to refrain from all attempts to influence any of the staff in the discharge of their official responsibilities.

In the conduct of the Bank's operations, the respective roles of the Executive Directors, on the one hand, and of the management and staff on the other have gradually evolved. As in the case of most corporate institutions, the management and staff carry on the actual operational activities of the Bank in accordance with general policies approved by the Executive Directors. Decision of the Executive Directors is required for all loans and bond issues, the annual budget, submission of reports to the Board of Governors and other matters involving policy issues. The Executive Directors normally take action upon recommendations by the management and do not generally concern themselves with matters of routine administration.

Organization of Staff

The senior management of the Bank consists of the President, the Vice President and the Assistant to the President. The Vice President is the deputy of the President and the general manager of the Bank. In the absence of both the President and the Vice President, the Assistant to the President acts as senior executive officer of the Bank.

The organization of the staff is outlined in the chart on the following page, which also shows the names of the principal officers of the Bank. The principal functions of the various Departments and Offices are as follows:

a. *Area Departments of Operations.* There are three area Departments of Operations, each of which is responsible for maintaining operational relationships with a particular geographical group of the Bank's member countries. These three Departments cover (1) Asia and Middle East; (2) Europe, Africa and Australasia; and (3) the Western Hemisphere. These Departments, with the assistance of other appropriate Departments, perform the following principal functions for the member countries within their respective areas: develop plans for loans, missions and related operations; examine loan applications and negotiate and administer loans; appraise development programs; follow economic developments in and assess creditworthiness of member countries; coordinate preparation of operational, economic and technical reports on loan operations; in consultation with the Technical Assistance and Liaison Staff, plan and direct technical assistance activities; and negotiate releases of 18% capital subscriptions.

Organization of Staff

As of December 31, 1953

INTERNATIONAL BANK FOR RECONSTRUCTION AND DEVELOPMENT

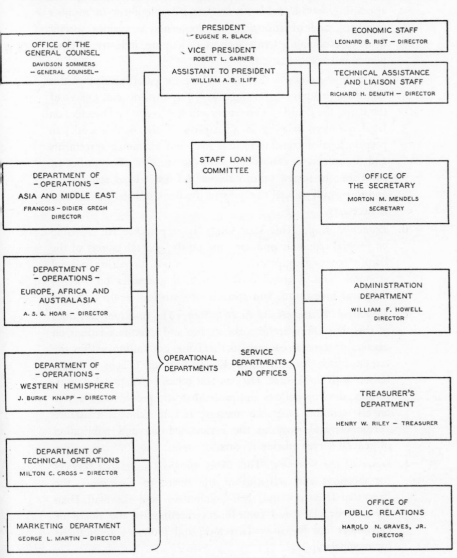

PRESIDENT
EUGENE R. BLACK

VICE PRESIDENT
ROBERT L. GARNER

ASSISTANT TO PRESIDENT
WILLIAM A. B. ILIFF

OFFICE OF THE
GENERAL COUNSEL
DAVIDSON SOMMERS
— GENERAL COUNSEL—

ECONOMIC STAFF
LEONARD B. RIST — DIRECTOR

TECHNICAL ASSISTANCE
AND LIAISON STAFF
RICHARD H. DEMUTH — DIRECTOR

STAFF LOAN
COMMITTEE

DEPARTMENT OF
— OPERATIONS —
ASIA AND MIDDLE EAST
FRANCOIS — DIDIER GREGH
DIRECTOR

OFFICE OF
THE SECRETARY
MORTON M. MENDELS
SECRETARY

DEPARTMENT OF
— OPERATIONS —
EUROPE, AFRICA AND
AUSTRALASIA
A. S. G. HOAR — DIRECTOR

ADMINISTRATION
DEPARTMENT
WILLIAM F. HOWELL
DIRECTOR

DEPARTMENT OF
— OPERATIONS —
WESTERN HEMISPHERE
J. BURKE KNAPP — DIRECTOR

OPERATIONAL
DEPARTMENTS

SERVICE
DEPARTMENTS
AND OFFICES

TREASURER'S
DEPARTMENT
HENRY W. RILEY — TREASURER

DEPARTMENT OF
TECHNICAL OPERATIONS
MILTON C. CROSS — DIRECTOR

MARKETING DEPARTMENT
GEORGE L. MARTIN — DIRECTOR

OFFICE OF
PUBLIC RELATIONS
HAROLD N. GRAVES, JR.
DIRECTOR

19

b. *Department of Technical Operations.* This Department has the function of assessing the merits of projects proposed to the Bank for financing and of following the progress of projects financed by the Bank. It is also responsible, in consultation with other appropriate Departments, for investigating and appraising specific fields of economic development in member countries, and of following developments in various specific fields of economic activity, such as agriculture, industry, mining, power and transportation.

c. *Office of the General Counsel.* The principal functions of this Office are to advise the management, Departments and Offices of the Bank, the Board of Governors and the Executive Directors on legal questions relating to all aspects of the Bank's work; to prepare legal documents such as loan and guarantee agreements and documents in connection with the issuance of securities by the Bank; to review other documents from a legal standpoint; and to furnish counsel to represent the Bank in legal proceedings if necessary.

d. *Economic Staff.* This staff Office is responsible for advising on general economic problems and on the general aspects of the Bank's economic approach to its operations, preparing general economic and financial studies, including studies on foreign debt and investment, and furnishing statistical services.

e. *Technical Assistance and Liaison Staff.* The principal functions of this staff Office are to make studies and recommendations on matters of general concern to the Bank not falling within the responsibilities of any other Department or Office; maintain liaison with the United Nations and other international organizations; develop policies and procedures and provide staff advice on all technical assistance matters; recruit technical assistance personnel; and assist in the review, editing and publication of general survey mission reports.

f. *Office of the Secretary.* This Office provides secretariat services for meetings and activities of the Board of Governors, the Executive Directors and their committees, and the Staff Loan Committee; plans and co-ordinates meetings of the Board of Governors and Executive Directors; and processes applications for membership.

g. *Administration Department.* The principal functions of this Department are to provide administrative services and supplies; review budget proposals and administer the Bank's administrative budget program; develop and operate a personnel program, including a training program; conduct internal audits; and administer the Staff Retirement Plan, the Bank's insurance program and the general files and records.

h. *Treasurer's Department.* The principal functions of this Department are to develop and execute financial procedures for the Bank; schedule cash requirements and provide for the collection, custody, investment and disbursement of Bank funds; handle questions relating to capital subscriptions and cooperate in arrangements for bond issues; maintain relations with member depositories and fiscal agents; examine and verify withdrawal applications of borrowers; maintain the Bank's accounting system; and prepare reports on the Bank's financial position.

i. *Marketing Department.* This Department develops and executes programs for the sale of Bank bonds and portfolio securities.

j. *Office of Public Relations.* This Office plans and carries out the Bank's public relations activities and is responsible for preparation of the Bank's Annual Report.

The principal instrumentality for achieving co-ordination of the conduct of Bank operations throughout all Departments and Offices is the Staff Loan Committee, whose function it is to consider and advise the President on all significant aspects of the Bank's work. The Staff Loan Committee is composed of the Vice President (Chairman), the Assistant to the President (Vice Chairman), the General Counsel, the Directors of the three Area Departments, the Director of the Department of Technical Operations, the Director of the Economic Staff, the Director of the Technical Assistance and Liaison Staff, the Treasurer and, when marketing matters are under consideration, the Director of Marketing.

Offices

The headquarters of the Bank are located at 1818 H Street, N. W., Washington, D. C. The Marketing Department has its office in New York City in the premises of the Federal Reserve Bank of New York. In addition, the Bank maintains a small European liaison office in Paris at 67 Rue de Lille. As of December 31, 1953, field representatives were stationed in Lebanon (accredited to Egypt, Iraq, Jordan, Lebanon and Syria), Nicaragua, Pakistan, Panama and Turkey.

Annual Report, Audit and Administrative Budget

The Bank publishes an annual report containing an audited statement of its accounts as of the close of its fiscal year on June 30. The Bank also publishes quarterly a summary statement of its financial position and a profit and loss statement showing the results of its operations. The Bank employs the firm of Price, Waterhouse & Co. as independent auditors.

Administrative expenses of the Bank are controlled through an administrative budget. This budget is prepared annually by the management after careful examination of the projected work program of each Department and Office; it is then presented to the Executive Directors for their review and approval. The management holds budget reviews regularly each quarter with the heads of the Departments and Offices to reappraise projected work programs, to review expenditures and, when necessary, to prepare modified budget estimates.

The administrative budget for the fiscal year ending June 30, 1954 and the administrative expenses incurred during the fiscal years ended June 30, 1952 and 1953 are outlined in Appendix H.

Advisory Council

The Articles of Agreement provide for an Advisory Council made up of representatives of banking, commercial, industrial, labor and agricultural interests, with as wide a national representation as possible, to meet at least once a year to advise the Bank on matters of general policy. The Bank's first Advisory Council, appointed in 1948, consisted of Sir Arthur Salter (United Kingdom), Chairman, and Messrs. E. E. Brown (United States), Herbert Hoover (United States), R. D. Harkness (Canada), Leon Jouhaux (France), Pedro Beltran (Peru), C. V. Raman (India), Lionel Robbins (United Kingdom), S. K. Alfred Sze (China) and Michal Kalecki (Poland). In accordance with the Articles, these members were appointed for a two-year term.

The Advisory Council held annual meetings at the Bank in 1948 and 1949. As a result of this experience, the Chairman of the Council advised the President of the Bank and the Board of Governors that, in his personal opinion, no Advisory Council appointed in accordance with the Articles of Agreement and entrusted with the function there defined was likely to have a value commensurate with its cost in time and money. A majority of the Bank's first Advisory Council expressed the same opinion.

In the light of the views thus expressed, the Executive Directors recommended to the Board of Governors in 1949 that the organization, selection, duties and all other matters relating to the Advisory Council be studied and that, pending completion of this study, the selection of new members of the Advisory Council be deferred. The Board of Governors approved this recommendation and no new members have since been appointed.

3

Financial Structure

Capitalization

The total authorized capital stock of the Bank is $10 billion in terms of United States dollars of the weight and fineness in effect on July 1, 1944. It is divided into 100,000 shares of the par value of $100,000 each. Total subscribed capital, as of December 31, 1953, was $9,038,500,000.

The capital subscription of each member is divided into three parts:

   a. 2% of each subscription is payable in gold or United States dollars, which may be used freely by the Bank in any of its operations.

   b. 18% of each subscription is payable in the currency of the subscribing member. These funds may be loaned only with the consent of the member whose currency is loaned.

   c. The remaining 80% of each subscription is not available to the Bank for lending but is subject to call if and when required by the Bank to meet its obligations on borrowings or on loans guaranteed by it. Payments on any such call must be made either in gold, U. S. dollars, or the currency required to discharge the obligations of the Bank for which the call is made.

Although no occasion has yet arisen for the Bank to contemplate any calls on the 80% portions of the capital subscriptions, they constitute assets of the Bank of which it is bound to avail itself when and to the extent necessary. The obligations of the members to make payment on such calls are independent of each other; in other words, a default by one or more members would not excuse any other member from its obligation to make payment. Calls on the 80% portion need not be deferred until the obligation has actually matured, but may be made sufficiently in advance of maturity to enable the Bank to meet the obligation as it comes due. No member may, of course, be required to pay more than the unpaid balance of its capital subscription. On the other hand, as pointed out in the previous Chapter, even withdrawal from membership does not relieve a government either from its direct obligations to the Bank or from its contingent liabilities (including its obligation to make payments of calls on the 80% portion of its subscription) for losses on loans or guarantees contracted by the Bank before it ceased to be a member.

Thus the 80% portions of the subscriptions constitute in effect a joint and several guarantee of the Bank's obligations by the Bank's members, with the members sharing proportionately in the risks of the Bank's loans and each member putting its own credit behind the Bank's obligations to the extent of its own 80% capital subscription.

Table 1 shows in summary form, as of December 31, 1953, the subscribed capital of the Bank expressed in United States currency.

Maintenance of Value of Subscriptions

The Articles of Agreement require each member to maintain the value of the Bank's currency derived from the 18% portion of that member's subscription to the Bank's capital stock if the par value of its currency is reduced or if the foreign exchange value of its currency depreciates to a significant extent in the member's territories. Similarly, if the par value of a member's currency is increased, the Bank is required to return to the member the increase in the value of such currency held by the Bank. From time to time, in appropriate cases, the Bank has received additional amounts of currency pursuant to this requirement.

TABLE 1

SUMMARY OF SUBSCRIBED CAPITAL AS OF DECEMBER 31, 1953

(In U.S. dollar equivalents. For full table and qualifying notes, see Appendix D.)

	United States Subscription	Subscriptions of Other Members	
Paid-in	In gold or U. S. dollars	In gold or U. S. dollars	In currencies of such members
2%	$ 63,500,000	$113,775,000	——
18%	571,500,000	——	$1,055,430,000
	$635,000,000	$113,775,000	$1,055,430,000
Subject to call	Payable in gold, U. S. dollars or the currency required to meet obligations for which call is made		
80%	$2,540,000,000	$4,690,800,000	

Sources of Funds for Lending Operations

The funds available to the Bank for lending come from four sources. The first, and during the early years of the Bank's operations the most important source consists of the payments made by members on account of their capital subscriptions to the Bank. The second source, and in the long run by far the largest, consists of borrowings by the Bank in various capital markets of the world. The third source consists of sales to investors of portions of the Bank's loan portfolio (both with and without the guarantee of the Bank) and of principal repayments to the Bank. The net earnings of the Bank constitute the fourth source of loanable funds.

a. *Capital Subscriptions.* The 2% of the subscription of all members which was payable in gold or U. S. dollars and which is freely available for lending amounted, as of December 31, 1953, to $177,275,000.[1]

As of the same date, the 18% local currency portions of the members' capital subscriptions aggregated the equivalent of about $1.627 billion; as already pointed out, these currencies are available for Bank lending only with the consent of the member concerned.[2] This consent provision was included in the Articles of Agreement primarily because it was foreseen that not all member countries would at all times be able to afford to export capital. To the extent that member countries can afford to release their 18% capital for Bank loans, the Bank has consistently maintained that it is inherent in their position as stockholders of the Bank that they should do so. And as economic conditions have improved, particularly in Western Europe, the response of the Bank's members to requests for 18% releases has been increasingly favorable.

The United States released all of the 18% portion of its capital subscription ($571.5 million) as early as April 1947. Subsequently, after making several partial releases, Canada also released the entire balance of its original 18% subscription (Can. $58.5 million). Releases of Western European currencies have aggregated the equivalent of $481.4 million of which $400.91 million have not been used and are subject to use only under certain specified conditions; of the amounts which have been used or allocated to loans, France has provided over half. Details of the Western European releases are shown in tabular form in the

---

[1] Payment of an additional $3,495,000 in this category, due June 25, 1951, had not been made as of December 31, 1953. See Note C in Appendix G.

[2] These local currencies are freely available for use, and have in fact been used, to defray local administrative expenses.

footnote.[3] A release equivalent to $2.8 million has been made by the Union of South Africa; all of this has been used or allocated for existing loans. Additional releases, aggregating the equivalent of about $33.4 million, have been made by 18 other members,[4] but these currencies have not thus far been usable because borrowers have not purchased goods in the releasing countries for Bank-financed projects and either the currencies released are inconvertible or, if convertible, their use has been restricted to local purchases.

b. *Sale of Bank Obligations.* The Bank has thus far sold its own obligations in an aggregate principal amount equivalent to approximately $769.8 million, of which the equivalent of approximately $653.5 million are now outstanding. These obligations and the methods by which they were marketed are described in Chapter 9. They may be broken down, by currencies, as shown on the next page (in U. S. dollar equivalents).

[3] Releases of Western European currencies:

	Used or allocated for loans	Available for lending in certain circumstances, but subject to consultation or other limitations	Unreleased	Total 18% Capital
Austria	$ 250,000	——	$ 8,750,000	$ 9,000,000
Belgium	4,500,000	$ 36,000,000	——	40,500,000
Denmark	1,450,000	10,790,000	——	12,240,000
France	34,550,000	59,950,000	——	94,500,000
Germany	3,100,000	56,300,000	——	59,400,000
Italy	5,538,000	26,862,000	——	32,400,000
Netherlands	2,000,000	47,500,000	——	49,500,000
Norway	620,000	8,380,000	——	9,000,000
Sweden	3,874,000	——	14,126,000	18,000,000
United Kingdom	24,609,000	155,128,000	54,263,000	234,000,000
	$80,491,000	$400,910,000	$77,139,000	$558,540,000

[4] Colombia, Costa Rica, Ecuador, El Salvador, Finland, Greece, Guatemala, Honduras, Iceland, India, Lebanon, Mexico, Pakistan, Paraguay, Philippines, Syria, Thailand and Yugoslavia.

	Original Amount Issued	Amount Outstanding
Payable in U. S. Dollars	$685,000,000	$575,000,000
" " Canadian Dollars	13,636,364	13,636,364
" " Pounds Sterling	14,000,000	14,000,000
" " Swiss Francs	57,126,235	50,843,513
Total:	$769,762,599	$653,479,877

c. *Portfolio Sales and Principal Repayments.* As of December 31, 1953, sales of portfolio assets, which are described in more detail in Chapter 9, aggregated the equivalent of about $84 million, of which about $55 million were with the Bank's guarantee and about $29 million were without guarantee. In addition, private investors have agreed to participate to the extent of roughly $1 million, without guarantee, in loans made by the Bank but not yet effective. Total principal repayments to the Bank have amounted to the equivalent of slightly more than $14.7 million.

d. *Net Earnings.* The growth of the Bank's net earnings is described in Chapter 7. As of December 31, 1953, aggregate net earnings, exclusive of commissions allocated to a special reserve (see page 31), amounted to the equivalent of approximately $86.6 million.[5]

Table 2 below shows the net funds obtained by the Bank for lending purposes, up to December 31, 1953, from all the foregoing sources. The Table does not include released 18% currencies which are not likely to be needed in the Bank's loan operations or which are not available for use without further approval by the member concerned.

[5] See note 6, page 31.

TABLE 2

AMOUNT AND SOURCES OF BANK'S LOAN FUNDS UP TO
DECEMBER 31, 1953

(*In U. S. dollar equivalents*)

2% portion of subscriptions of all members		$ 177,275,000
18% portion of subscriptions made available by:		
Canada	$ 53,356,000	
South Africa	2,800,000	
United States	571,500,000	
Western European members	80,491,000	708,147,000
Total available capital subscriptions		$ 885,422,000
Funds available from operations		87,500,000
Funds available from sale of bonds		653,479,877
" 18% " funds available from principal repayments or sales of loans in U. S. and Canadian dollars, Belgian francs and U. K. pounds sterling, which may be loaned again without further release		48,175,950
Other funds available from principal repayments or sales of loans		50,559,478
TOTAL:		$1,725,137,305

Resources behind Bank Obligations

Bonds issued by the Bank and its contingent liability on securities guaranteed by it are general unsecured obligations of the Bank. Apart from working capital held in cash and short-term investments and receivables on account of subscribed capital, the principal resources which back the Bank's obligations consist of its loan portfolio, special reserve and uncalled capital subscriptions.

Because of the Bank's paid-in capital, the face amount of the Bank's loan portfolio has, of course, always exceeded and is likely to continue to exceed the amount of the Bank's indebted-

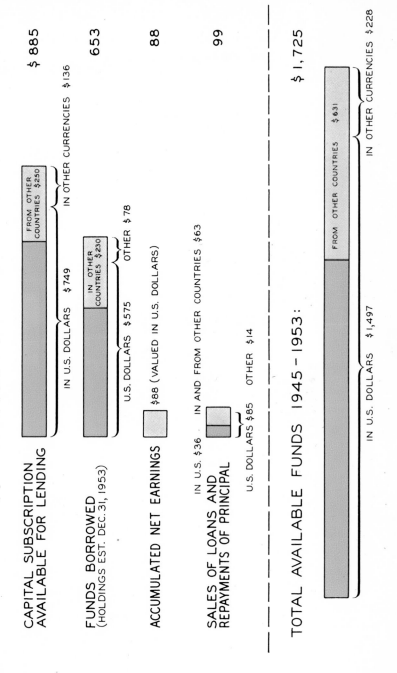

AMOUNT AND SOURCES OF BANK LOAN FUNDS

(Up to December 31, 1953, in equivalents of millions of U. S. dollars)

CAPITAL SUBSCRIPTION AVAILABLE FOR LENDING — $ 885

IN U.S. DOLLARS $749
FROM OTHER COUNTRIES $250
IN OTHER CURRENCIES $136

FUNDS BORROWED (HOLDINGS EST. DEC. 31, 1953) — 653

IN OTHER COUNTRIES $230
U.S. DOLLARS $575
OTHER $78

ACCUMULATED NET EARNINGS — 88

$88 (VALUED IN U.S. DOLLARS)

SALES OF LOANS AND REPAYMENTS OF PRINCIPAL — 99

IN U.S. $36   IN AND FROM OTHER COUNTRIES $63
U.S. DOLLARS $85   OTHER $14

TOTAL AVAILABLE FUNDS 1945 – 1953 : — $ 1,725

IN U.S. DOLLARS $1,497
FROM OTHER COUNTRIES $631
IN OTHER CURRENCIES $228

ness. In addition, the Bank has set up, as required by its Articles of Agreement, a special reserve fund, invested in liquid assets, which may be used only to meet the Bank's own obligations arising out of borrowings or guarantees. The Articles provide that, during the first 10 years of the Bank's operations, a commission of not less than 1% and not more than 1½% per annum must be charged on the outstanding portion of all loans made by the Bank out of borrowed funds and on all loans guaranteed by the Bank and that the commissions received are to be set aside in the special reserve; after 10 years, the rate of commission may be reduced or increased, as deemed advisable by the Bank in its discretion. The commission charge has been fixed to date at 1% and has been charged on all loans and guarantees, including loans made out of capital. As of December 31, 1953, the amount of the special reserve stood at just over $42.8 million.[6]

Besides the loan portfolio and special reserve, the Bank's obligations have behind them the Bank's unqualified right to call upon all member governments for the uncalled 80% portion of their capital subscriptions, aggregating the equivalent of over $7.23 billion (see page 26). The United States obligation alone is $2.54 billion; up to this amount, therefore, the Bank's obligations on its borrowings and on loans guaranteed by it are in effect covered by the full faith and credit of the United States.[7] It may be noted that, with the exception of such defaults as occurred in connection with World War I obligations, Canada, the United

---

[6] A supplemental reserve against losses on loans and guarantees has also been established on the books of the Bank to which the Bank's net earnings have been allocated; as of December 31, 1953, this supplemental reserve aggregated the equivalent of over $86.6 million. Funds allocated to the supplemental reserve are, however, used in Bank operations and are not, as in the case of the special reserve, segregated from the other assets of the Bank.

[7] Section 7 of the Bretton Woods Agreements Act (59 Stat. 512 et seq.; 22 U.S.C. 286 et seq.), which authorized United States membership in the Bank, gives the Secretary of the Treasury the authority, without further congressional action, to make payments on the United States subscription to the Bank as required from time to time and for that purpose to use as a public-debt transaction the proceeds of sale of certain government securities.

Kingdom, the other Commonwealth countries, the Scandinavian countries, Western Europe, and a number of other members whose capital subscriptions, with that of the United States, make up more than 85% of the total, have never failed to meet all contractual debt service.

The Articles of Agreement, as noted above, restrict the amount of loans and guarantees by the Bank to 100% of its unimpaired subscribed capital, reserves and surplus. The Bank, therefore, would have no reason, as a practical matter, to issue its obligations in an amount greater than those assets. In fact, however, the Bank's obligations are far from this maximum and are not likely to approach it in the foreseeable future. As already pointed out, as of December 31, 1953, the Bank's total funded debt amounted to the equivalent of about $653.5 million and its contingent liability on securities guaranteed by it amounted to the equivalent of about $29.1 million.

The following Table summarizes the resources behind the Bank's obligations:

TABLE 3

RESOURCES BEHIND BANK OBLIGATIONS AS OF DECEMBER 31, 1953
(In U. S. dollar equivalents)

Disbursed Loans Outstanding Held by Bank		$1,142,264,485
Uncalled 80% Subscriptions:		
United States	$2,540,000,000	
Other Members	4,690,800,000	
Total:		7,230,800,000
Receivable on Account of Subscribed Capital		
(other than from the United States)		889,964,042
Due from Banks and Other Depositories		125,150,989
Investment Securities		389,418,849
Special Reserve		42,800,070
Net Other Assets		8,698,096
Total Resources:		$9,829,096,531

4

Miscellaneous

Relationship with Other International Organizations

Formal relationships between the Bank and the United Nations are governed by an agreement approved by the Bank's Board of Governors in September 1947 and by the United Nations General Assembly in November 1947. The Bank is a specialized international agency within the meaning of Article 57 of the Charter of the United Nations. 'The agreement between the Bank and the United Nations specifically recognizes that " By reason of the nature of its international responsibilities and the terms of its Articles of Agreement, the Bank is, and is required to function as, an independent international organization." The agreement contains provisions governing such matters as reciprocal representation, consultation and exchange of information other than confidential material. It provides that no formal recommendation will be made by either organization to the other without reasonable prior consultation, and the United Nations specifically recognizes that " the action to be taken by the Bank on any loan is a matter to be determined by the independent exercise of the Bank's own judgment " and that " it would be sound policy [for the United Nations] to refrain from making recommendations

33

to the Bank with respect to particular loans or with respect to the terms or conditions of financing by the Bank."

At the working level, informal contact has been maintained by the Bank's staff with the United Nations Secretariat, particularly with the United Nations Technical Assistance Administration and the Department of Economic Affairs, in order to exchange information and to avoid duplication or conflict of work. Bank representatives attend meetings of various United Nations organs when matters of interest to the Bank are under discussion, including meetings of the General Assembly, the Economic and Social Council, and the regional economic commissions. The President of the Bank is a member of the Administrative Committee on Coordination, which is composed of the Secretary General of the United Nations and the heads of all the specialized agencies, and Bank staff members participate in the work of subsidiary bodies of that Committee. The Bank also participates in the work of the Technical Assistance Board, although it is not formally a member of the Board.

Mutually advantageous working relations have also been established with other specialized international organizations, particularly the International Monetary Fund, the Food and Agriculture Organization of the United Nations (FAO), the World Health Organization (WHO) and the United Nations Educational, Scientific and Cultural Organization (UNESCO). There is frequent informal consultation between the staffs of the Bank and Fund and members of the Fund staff have on occasion participated in Bank missions. In certain administrative fields, such as the maintenance of facilities used by both organizations and the establishment of staff pension and health programs, joint or cooperative arrangements have been made by the Bank and Fund. Close working relationships have been established with FAO, both through Bank attendance at many FAO meetings and through frequent staff contacts. FAO normally helps to recruit, assists in the briefing, and reviews the reports of the agricultural members of Bank general survey missions; in most cases FAO has also shared the costs of those mission members. In the case of two countries, Uruguay and Chile, joint Bank-FAO missions were organized to survey the agricultural sectors of the economy and to formulate recommendations for further development of agricultural production. When Bank general survey missions have included experts in the fields of public health and education, the Bank has received the help of WHO and UNESCO in recruiting appropriate personnel.

The Bank has been represented at the annual meetings of the Bank for International Settlements. And it has maintained liaison with the U. N. Economic Commissions for Europe, for Latin America, and for Asia and the Far East, the Organization of American States, the Organization for European Economic Co-operation and the Consultative Committee on Economic Development in South and Southeast Asia.

The Bank has also collaborated with FAO and the United Nations in sponsoring three training institutes, in Lahore, Santiago and Ankara, on the formulation and appraisal of economic development projects, and it has sponsored jointly with the Economic Commission for Latin America a seminar in Washington for discussion of methods and techniques of economic development planning.

Legal Status, Privileges and Immunities

The Articles of Agreement contain provisions which accord to the Bank, in the territories of each of its members, legal status and certain privileges and immunities. Each member government is required to take whatever action is necessary in its territories to make these provisions effective under its own law. The more important of these provisions of the Articles of Agreement may be summarized as follows:

a. *Legal Status.* The Bank has full juridical personality with capacity to make contracts, to acquire and dispose of property, and to sue and be sued.

b. *Judicial Process.* Actions may be brought against the Bank in the territories of any member in which the Bank has an office, has appointed an agent for accepting service or notice of process, or has issued or guaranteed securities, but no actions against the Bank may be brought by its members or persons acting for or deriving claims from its members.

c. *Privileges and Immunities.* The Governors and Executive Directors, and their Alternates, and the officers and employees of the Bank are immune from legal process for acts performed by them in their official capacity, except when the Bank waives such immunity. Unless they are local nationals, they are to be accorded by each member government the same immunities from immigration restrictions, alien registration requirements and national service obligations and the same treatment in respect of traveling facilities as are accorded to officials of comparable rank of other member governments.

The archives of the Bank are inviolable. The assets of the Bank are immune from seizure, attachment or execution prior to delivery of final judgment against it. The official communications of the Bank are to be accorded by each member the same treatment accorded to official communications of other members.

The Bank, its assets, property, income, and its authorized operations and transactions are immune from all taxation and from all customs duties. The Bank is also immune from liability for the collection or payment of any tax or duty.

No tax is to be levied on or in respect of salaries paid by the Bank to Executive Directors, Alternates or employees of the Bank who are not local nationals.[1] No tax is to be levied on any security

---

[1] Whether or not a local national is taxed on his Bank salary depends upon the laws of his own country. Since the laws of different members vary in this respect, the burden of taxation is unequal. To assure equality of real salaries received by its staff, therefore, the Bank fixes salaries on a net-of-tax basis. If an employee

issued by the Bank which discriminates against that security solely because it is issued by the Bank, nor is any such tax to be levied if its sole jurisdictional basis is the place or currency in which the security is issued, made payable or paid, or the location of any office of the Bank.

is required by his government to pay taxes on his Bank compensation, the Bank pays him an amount in addition to his net-of-tax salary designed to cover such taxes. In computing the amount of this additional payment, it is assumed that the employee's gross salary (net-of-tax salary plus tax reimbursement) is his only income.

PART II

Major Operational Policies
and General Character
of Bank Operations

5

Major Operational Policies

THIS CHAPTER DESCRIBES the major operational policies of the Bank as they have evolved to date. These policies relate largely to the methods and standards by which the Bank seeks to determine, in the case of any member country, how much it can prudently lend, for what purposes its loans should be made, what types of loan are most likely to achieve those purposes, and the conditions which need to be established to assure that the Bank's financing will in fact be effective. Although most of the policies described in this Chapter derive directly or indirectly from general provisions of the Articles of Agreement, they are examined here from the standpoint of the specific content they have received as they have actually been applied in the solution of practical operating problems. It should be emphasized that the Bank is operating in a complicated and largely new field, and in an economic environment which is constantly changing. This circumstance has required, and will continue to require, that the Bank keep its policies flexible.

Assessment of Repayment Prospects

In making or guaranteeing a loan the Bank is obliged under its Articles of Agreement to pay " due regard to the prospects

41

that the borrower, and, if the borrower is not a member, that the guarantor, will be in position to meet its obligations under the loan "; the Articles further enjoin the Bank to act " prudently " in the interests both of the borrowing country and of the members as a whole. Even apart from this provision of the charter, it would be implicit in the concept of the Bank as a continuing institution, designed to operate on a sound business basis and with funds borrowed in the private market, that it should make loans only where there are reasonable prospects of repayment.

This does not mean, of course, that the Bank adopts the standards of the market place in determining how much it can lend to individual countries. On the contrary, as already noted, one of the principal purposes of creating the Bank was to have an agency which could accept the special risks inherent in international investment in cases where, by reason of those risks, private investors were unwilling or unable to act unaided. For example, so long as the danger of a third world war remains, the Bank must accept this risk if it is to achieve the purposes envisaged in its Articles of Agreement. Similarly, the Bank has to accept the risk of a recurrence of a world-wide depression of the type experienced in the 1930's; in fact, for the long term the Bank adopts for operational purposes the assumption that production, income and trade in the world as a whole will continue to expand. But the Bank's responsibility to accept special risks of this type affecting the creditworthiness of its borrowers as a whole does not relieve it of the obligation to make an objective economic appraisal of the amount of external debt which each prospective borrowing country can reasonably be expected to service, these special risks aside, and to keep its loans within the limits of creditworthiness so determined.

The assessment of repayment prospects involves an exercise of judgment after consideration of a multitude of factors. The availability of natural resources and the existing productive plant within the country are the obvious starting points, but equally

GROWTH OF THE BANK

(Cumulative totals expressed in millions of U. S. dollars)

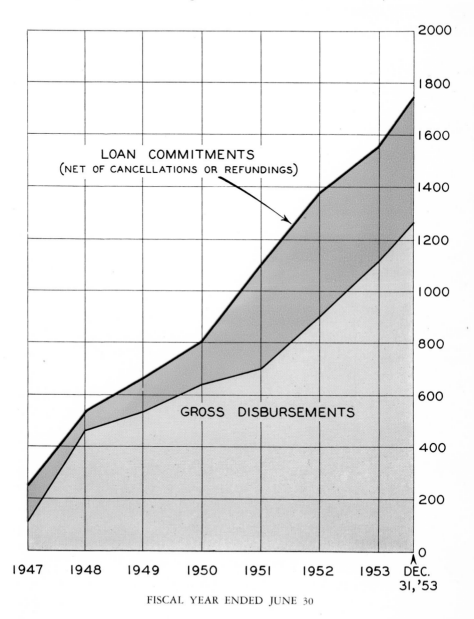

FISCAL YEAR ENDED JUNE 30

GROWTH OF THE BANK

(Cumulative totals expressed in millions of U. S. dollars)

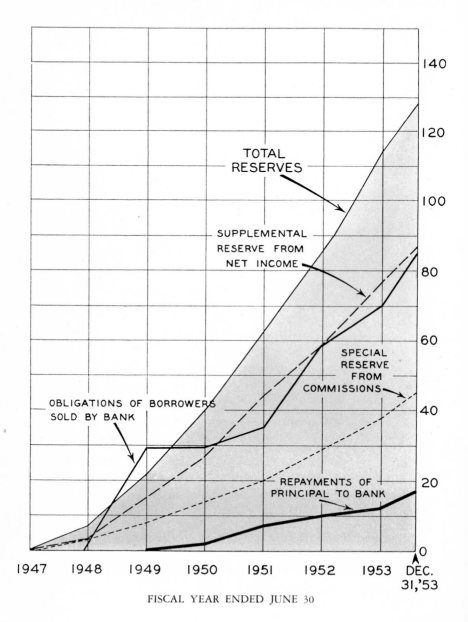

FISCAL YEAR ENDED JUNE 30

important is the capacity of the country concerned to exploit its resources and operate its productive facilities effectively. This involves, among other things, an evaluation of the effectiveness both of the government administration and of the important private enterprises operating within the country, the availability of managerial, supervisory and technical skills, the types of investment which are proposed to be undertaken both with domestic resources and with funds borrowed from the Bank, and the economic and financial policies which are likely to be followed, particularly insofar as they affect the levels of consumption and of domestic savings and the flow of foreign private capital. The probable impact of all these factors upon the country's future balance of payments position must then be assessed in the light of such considerations as the likely course of prices for the country's principal exports and imports, the stability of export markets, the essentiality of imports, and the effect of population increases. Moreover, in a world of inconvertible currencies, it is not sufficient simply to consider how much over-all foreign debt the borrower can service; it must also be determined in what currencies such a service obligation can be met.

Complicating judgment in every case is the fact that creditworthiness is not determined by economic forces alone; within fairly wide limits, it is determined, too, by the intangible factor of the country's traditional attitude towards its foreign debts. A country which shows a willingness to maintain debt service at the expense, if necessary, of short-term domestic interests is plainly a better credit risk than a country, even with a potentially somewhat stronger economy, which does not treat its foreign obligations with equal seriousness and which may therefore be unwilling, in times of stringency, to make sacrifices in consumption standards to maintain debt service. In this connection, the past debt record of the country is significant. To be sure, events have sometimes made defaults inevitable, but in such cases the attitude of the country to its obligations, and the sort of settlement it has made or offered to its creditors, are valuable guides in judging credit for future loans. The Bank is convinced that its loans are likely to be most effective, and repayment prospects therefore brightest, where the government evidences a serious and courageous approach to its economic and financial problems and regards the maintenance of both internal stability and external credit as important means of promoting the country's long-term development.

The Specific Project Provision

Underlying many of the Bank's lending policies is the provision of the Articles of Agreement requiring that "loans made or guaranteed by the Bank shall, except in special circumstances, be for the purpose of specific projects of reconstruction or development."

The objective of this provision is simply to assure that Bank loans will be used for productive purposes. In effect, the only requirement which it imposes is that, before a loan is granted, there shall be a clear agreement both on the types of goods and services for which the proceeds of the loan are to be expended and on the uses to which those goods and services are to be put. Without such specification it would be impossible for the Bank to judge whether or to what extent a loan is likely to be effective in raising the level of production.

In the early days of Bank operations, there was considerable criticism of the specific project approach, but the criticism was almost always based on the assumption that the Bank examines the merits of particular projects in isolation, without reference to their relation to the over-all development needs of the borrowing country. In fact the Bank does precisely the opposite. As is more fully explained below, the Bank seeks in the case of each borrowing country to determine what are the appropriate investment priorities and then to adapt its program of financial assistance to meet the priority needs. Consistently with this approach the

Bank has encouraged its members to formulate long-term development programs and has provided a number of them with substantial technical assistance for this purpose. The existence of such a program, particularly in countries whose investment requirements are large in relation to their available financial resources, greatly facilitates the task of determining which projects are of the highest priority in the light of their prospective contribution to the program as a whole.

Once a determination has been made of the most urgent needs of any member country, the only safeguard by which the Bank can assure that its resources are in fact used to meet those needs is to require, before granting a loan, that an agreement be reached with the borrower on the precise purposes of the loan, whether it be for a single project or for a program of related projects. If the Bank were to make loans for unspecified purposes or for vague development programs which have not been worked out in terms of the specific projects by which the objectives of the program are to be achieved, there would be danger that the Bank's resources would be used either for projects which are economically or technically unsound or are of a low priority nature, or for economically unjustified consumer goods imports.

This danger is by no means hypothetical. Many projects presented to the Bank, particularly in the earlier years of its operation, have been in far from satisfactory form. In many cases there have been inadequate or incorrect cost estimates; there have also frequently been deficiencies in the technical plans or proposed financial or administrative arrangements. During the course of discussions between the Bank and the borrower, it has often been possible to work out modifications of a project to reduce its cost, to increase its technical efficiency or to improve its financial or organizational features. And occasionally a substitute project or one conceived on a somewhat larger scale has been found to be more useful or more economic than the one originally proposed.

There are special cases, of course, where detailed project

investigations are neither necessary nor feasible. The early reconstruction loans to France, Denmark and the Netherlands, for example, were designed to meet emergency needs of those countries for foreign funds to finance a large variety of imports essential to the rehabilitation and continued operation of their industries. Because those needs affected so many different sectors of the economy, because it was so urgent to assist in meeting the needs in order to prevent a disastrous decline in production, and because the Bank had satisfied itself that the goods financed by the loans were to be used for essential and productive purposes, the Bank was willing to make the necessary financing available without detailed examination of the specific projects in connection with which the goods were to be employed. As these loans indicate, the specific project provision is not interpreted as committing the Bank to a single inflexible lending technique to be applied without regard to the actual needs of a given situation. It is rather a lending policy which, in the opinion of the Bank, is desirable in the vast majority of cases to assure that member countries use their limited capacity for foreign indebtedness to the best advantage.

Selection and Analysis of Projects

The available resources of every country, including its capacity to borrow abroad, are limited. To the extent that those resources are devoted to particular investment projects, other projects may have to be abandoned or delayed. To be of maximum effectiveness, therefore, Bank investment must be devoted to those undertakings which will contribute most to strengthening the economy of the borrowing country.

In practice, the Bank seeks to accomplish this objective by investigating the over-all economic position of the borrowing country, with particular reference to its investment expenditures and the relation of individual projects to the country's actual development needs. This investigation may reveal, first, that some projects which have not been submitted to the Bank and for which financing has not otherwise been arranged nevertheless merit a high priority; and, second, that a number of those submitted to the Bank, while worthy of consideration, are of relatively low priority. The Bank expresses its views accordingly in its discussions with the authorities of the country concerned, emphasizing its preference for financing the projects that seem most urgently required and advising postponement of those that appear less immediately important to the country's development.

The Bank has found that there is no single test by which the relative urgency and productivity of various alternative projects can be judged. The situation in each country must be considered on its own merits. In every case, however, the Bank's general approach to the problem is the same: it seeks first to determine what are or should be the important goals of a proper investment program and then to gauge the relative priority of the various projects by the extent of their contribution to those goals.

Where the project under consideration involves a revenue-producing facility, such as a power system, railroad or manufacturing plant, which is intended to be self-liquidating in terms of local currency, the Bank wishes of course to satisfy itself, before granting a loan, that the enterprise is soundly conceived to achieve that objective. But the relative profitability of different projects is frequently not a proper test of their relative contribution to a country's development. In many cases, certain basic investments in public utilities, transportation and ports, flood control, reclamation, irrigation and similar projects are required before other investments in more immediately profitable activities can be undertaken. The indirect benefits properly attributable to these basic investments may be very great even though the direct earnings of the activities, at least in the short run, are not high or may even be nonexistent. For example, a highway system, unless it involves toll roads, yields no direct revenue but it may foster all kinds of industrial and agricultural activity. Similarly, flood control, irrigation or land reclamation projects may often be among the most useful and most urgent investments to be undertaken, even though, if their cost is paid out of general tax revenues rather than from water charges or other direct assessments, they provide no direct financial return.

As a matter of general policy, derived implicitly from the Articles of Agreement, the Bank concentrates its lending on projects designed to contribute directly to productive capacity and normally does not finance community projects of a primarily social character, such as sewage, street-paving, water supplies, housing, and health and education facilities. Although projects of this latter type are plainly basic to the development of any country, the Bank believes that its loans, which normally finance only a small part of the total investment expenditures of the borrowing country, can most effectively be applied in the more directly productive sectors of the economy.

Determination of the economic priority of the project is, of course, only a first step. The Bank also needs to assure itself that the technical, financial and administrative plans for the project are satisfactory. Determination on this point often involves investigation, study and negotiation over a broad field. The Bank wishes to be satisfied that the engineering plans have been competently drawn, that the project is suitably designed (and not unnecessarily elaborate) for the function it is intended to perform, and that construction will be entrusted to competent hands and will be properly supervised. It wishes to be satisfied, too, that cost estimates are reasonably accurate and that the financial structure of the enterprise is appropriate for the type of venture involved. The arrangements for securing the remainder of the capital not supplied by the Bank are also carefully scrutinized to determine their adequacy to assure prompt completion of the project. If the planning or proposed arrangements appear unsatisfactory in any of these respects, the Bank seeks to help the borrower work out suitable modifications.

The Bank places particular stress upon the assurance of adequate management for the project—a problem of substantial difficulty in the case of many underdeveloped countries where managerial and administrative experience is often extremely limited. Because proper management is so often the key to the success of projects presented for Bank financing, it is the practice of the Bank, in those cases where adequate local managerial skills are not available, to suggest that the borrowing country look abroad for organizations or individuals qualified to run the enterprise, at least during the initial stages, and to provide appropriate management training to local personnel. Where this type of arrangement is agreed to by the borrowing country, the Bank, upon request, frequently helps the borrower to find a qualified organization or individual for the task. But irrespective of whether management is to be entrusted to local or foreign hands, the Bank always seeks to satisfy itself, before advancing funds for the project, that the project will in fact be operated properly.

In this connection, the Bank has frequently insisted, in the case of government projects, that their operation be entrusted to a quasi-autonomous authority, or in some other fashion be insulated from political pressures and the rigidities of government administrative procedures. In a number of cases, the Bank's help has been sought and given in the establishment and staffing of quasi-independent operating authorities of this sort.

Management considerations are also an important factor in the Bank's reluctance to finance government-owned projects in the field of competitive industry. In the case of government-owned industries, management is apt to lack incentive to exercise initiative and to keep operations at maximum efficiency; moreover, the government, being government and having objectives other than the commercial success of a particular industrial enterprise, may subordinate the interests of the enterprise to extraneous considerations and may therefore interfere with the management's

49

independence by exerting political influence on appointments or policies. For these reasons, and because of the many other claims upon public funds for projects unattractive to private capital, the Bank believes that, to the greatest extent practicable, the field of competitive industry should be left to private enterprise. Although the Bank has no absolute bar against loans to government-owned industries in cases where private capital is not available, it will undertake such financing only if satisfied, after thorough examination, that the government's participation will not in fact interfere with efficient operation or have an unduly deterrent effect upon the expansion of private initiative and enterprises in the same or other fields.

The Bank recognizes, of course, that by financing one particular investment project, it may be releasing for some other investment activity resources already available to the borrower. This is a principal reason why the Bank seeks to consult with its member countries not only concerning the merits of projects for which loans are requested but concerning the country's projected investment expenditures as a whole. The fact that the ultimate effect of its loans may be to release resources for other uses is not, however, regarded by the Bank as in any way relieving it from the obligation of satisfying itself that the particular projects it finances are economically and technically sound and are of a high priority nature. As has already been noted, the Bank's project investigations have frequently resulted in more effective utilization of the resources of both the Bank and of its borrowers. Furthermore, as the underdeveloped countries have become more generally familiar with the Bank's method of investigating projects and with the criteria it applies to their suitability for finance, they have tended gradually to apply the same standards to the investment projects which they finance from their own resources.

Types of Expenditures Financed

It is the Bank's established practice not to finance the whole cost of any project or program. The Bank's normal lending takes the form of loans in foreign exchange to finance that part of the cost of the project or program representing the requirements for imported goods and services. Most countries will have within a reasonable time direct import requirements for productive projects or programs of a type suitable for Bank financing in an amount as large as, or larger than, the probable capacity of the country to service foreign debt. In such cases the use of Bank loans to cover only these direct import needs meets the development financing requirements of the borrower and, at the same time, assures that the foreign exchange furnished by the Bank will be used for directly productive purposes. Moreover, the policy of requiring such countries to meet local currency expenditures without drawing upon their limited external creditworthiness is a practical way of assuring that they will mobilize their own resources to meet a substantial part of the cost of projects or programs which the Bank is helping to finance.

The situation is different in the case of those countries, primarily capital equipment producing countries, whose direct foreign exchange requirements for imported capital goods for investment projects or programs suitable for Bank financing are small in relation to their creditworthiness. Such countries may not have sufficient genuine savings of their own to provide all the capital required for productive projects or programs of high priority and financing them by credit creation might jeopardize monetary stability. In such cases, the Bank is willing to consider loans of foreign exchange to finance a portion of the local expenditures in connection with projects or programs of a type otherwise qualified for Bank financing, although, as in the case of direct import loans, the borrowing country itself will normally be expected to provide the major part of the cost. Only a few local expenditure loans have been made by the Bank to meet cases like this and they are regarded as an exception to the normal pattern of Bank lending.[1]

Methods of Procurement under Bank Loans

The Articles of Agreement prohibit the Bank from tying the use of the proceeds of any loan to expenditures in any particular country. At the same time, the Articles require the Bank to ensure that the proceeds " are used only for the purposes for which the loan was granted, with due attention to considerations of economy and efficiency." Thus Bank borrowers are free to use the proceeds of their loans in making purchases anywhere they wish, provided only that they observe a proper standard of economy and efficiency.

The Bank, however, attaches great importance in its own interest as well as that of the borrowing country to the procurement of the goods needed for any Bank-financed project in the cheapest possible market consistent with satisfactory performance. Moreover, as a cooperative international institution among whose principal purposes is promotion of the " long-range balanced growth of international trade," the Bank wishes all of its member countries to have a fair opportunity to supply goods which are financed by Bank loans. To this end, the Bank encourages its borrowers to resort to procurement on a competitive international basis, unless this procedure is clearly inappropriate. In some cases, in order to make sure that maximum benefit is obtained from this system of procurement, the Bank advises, or even requires, its borrower to employ a qualified consultant to assist in determining the qualifications of bidders, in preparing specifications and in analyzing the relative merits of bids.

---

[1] In addition to loans of foreign exchange, the Bank's Articles of Agreement permit it, in exceptional circumstances, to make a loan in the borrower's own currency to cover the local costs of a project, regardless of their effect upon foreign exchange requirements, provided the local currency cannot be raised by the borrower on reasonable terms. However, the Bank has not yet been presented with a case where financing of this nature has seemed appropriate.

Circumstances will, however, frequently arise where international bidding on a competitive basis may not be appropriate and where the borrower is able to advance cogent reasons for making his purchases in some particular market: for example, familiarity of the operating organization with certain types of equipment, the desire to standardize equipment in order to avoid complications in maintenance and spare parts control, and the availability of dealers' maintenance and service facilities for specific types of equipment. Moreover, it sometimes happens that part of the equipment for a project will already have been ordered before a Bank loan has actually been made, or that the equipment required is available only in one market or group of markets.

Even where, for good and sufficient reason, international competition has not been developed in the bidding for the supply of equipment, the Bank satisfies itself before making disbursements under the loan that the equipment is suitable for the project and that the terms of the purchase are reasonable.

The Bank never proposes that a borrower should place a contract with a designated supplier or that competition should be restricted to a designated group of suppliers. Nor does the Bank furnish lists of suppliers to its borrowers. Decision as to which suppliers should be invited to bid and to which of them the contract is to be awarded is the responsibility of the borrower, subject only to the ability of the borrower to satisfy the Bank as to the suitability of the goods and the reasonableness of the terms of purchase.

Economic and Financial Policies of Borrowing Country

It happens not infrequently that the Bank's examination of general economic conditions in the borrowing country reveals the existence of economic or financial practices or policies which so adversely affect the financial and monetary stability of the country that, if continued, they would endanger both the productive purposes and the repayment prospects of any Bank loan. In

53

such cases, it is the policy of the Bank to require, as a condition to Bank financing, that the borrowing country institute measures designed to restore stability to its economy. The Bank does not, of course, insist that all remedial measures which may appear necessary in the case of any given country be completed before that country may qualify for a loan. On the other hand, the Bank is not normally willing to rely simply on a representation by the government that such remedial measures will in due course be taken. The Bank's position is midway between these extremes; it requires concrete evidence that the government is actually taking appropriate steps to establish stability, but, once given such evidence, it is usually willing to make a loan concurrently with the execution of the measures adopted.

The Bank has taken a similar position in the case of those member countries whose credit was or is impaired by the existence of an unsettled default on their outstanding foreign obligations. The Bank is obligated, under its Articles of Agreement, to encourage international investment for the development of the productive resources of its members. It has, therefore, a direct interest in the creation and maintenance of satisfactory relations between its member countries and their external creditors. Accordingly, the Bank's normal practice is to inform loan applicants who are in default on foreign obligations that the Bank will be unable to assist them unless and until they take appropriate steps to reach a fair and equitable settlement of their debts. It may be added that the Bank has been greatly encouraged by the progress made by its member countries in recent years in clearing up default situations (see pages 114-115).

There are other types of governmental policies, too, which may so adversely affect the borrowing country's debt-servicing capacity, or the future prospects of a particular project presented for financing, that they serve as a deterrent or a bar to Bank lending. Use of scarce foreign exchange resources to effect a shift of ownership of public utilities or other enterprises from foreign private interests to government hands, if done for political rather than economic reasons, is one example. Another is the adoption of rate policies for utilities, whether publicly or privately owned, which are so restrictive that the utilities cannot operate, and maintain and expand their facilities, on a sound business basis. The Bank believes that, to the extent that it can use its influence to prevent diversion of investment resources to low priority uses, which is often the effect of nationalization measures, or to prevent distortion of the economy through the kind of subsidies involved in unjustifiably low utility rates, it is serving the best interests of its member countries.

It must be remembered that governments, however conscientious, are apt to be subject to political pressure to emphasize short-run objectives which promise immediate advantage rather than policies designed primarily for the long-run development of their countries, particularly where long-range policies entail some sacrifice of immediate benefits or adversely affect important local interests. In this type of situation, the Bank's insistence upon appropriate economic and financial measures to create a favorable environment for development over the long term has not infrequently provided a countervailing influence of some considerable significance.

Continuing Relationship with Borrowers

It is the Bank's practice to maintain a close relationship with its borrowers throughout the life of each loan. There are two main aspects to this continuing relationship. First, the Bank checks to assure that loan funds are expended only for authorized goods or services and closely follows the progress of the projects. Second, the Bank keeps in touch during the entire life of the loan with economic and financial developments in the borrowing country through information submitted by the government, periodic visits to the country by Bank officials, and consultation and exchange of views with the government's representatives.

The objective of the Bank's check on the progress of the

55

projects is to bring to light at the earliest possible moment those difficulties, technical, administrative, financial and the like, which frequently arise, particularly in the execution of large-scale construction programs, and which cannot be foreseen at the time a loan is made. Early knowledge of the existence or the prospect of such difficulties puts the Bank in a position to discuss the best solution with the borrower in good time. In this manner, a number of difficulties which might have hindered the successful accomplishment of various projects have been averted or overcome.

Similar considerations motivate the Bank in giving continuing attention throughout the life of each loan to the general economic and financial conditions in the borrowing country. One objective is, of course, to ensure that the maintenance of service on Bank loans is not jeopardized by the emergence of conditions which might reasonably be prevented. But the Bank also has a broader objective in view. By keeping closely in touch with the progress of its members, the Bank hopes to be of some assistance to them in meeting important economic problems. The member countries, in turn, are able to discuss their plans for investment well in advance and to obtain an early indication of the Bank's opinion. On both sides this tends to facilitate subsequent financing from the Bank or, in the long run, from any other source.

Promotion of Local Private Enterprise

In its efforts to stimulate development, the Bank places special stress upon the growth and expansion of the private sector of the economy. A great many loans of the Bank are designed, either directly or indirectly, to stimulate private investment, and the importance of private enterprise, particularly in directly productive pursuits, has consistently been emphasized by Bank general survey missions.

Bank loans directly to private enterprises have been limited by the requirement of the Articles that any such loan must be guaranteed by the government or by the central bank or its equivalent. This has discouraged private borrowers who fear that a governmental guarantee might lead to interference by the government in the conduct of their business. Governments, for their part, have hesitated to place their guarantee on loans for private projects, however useful, for fear of being charged with favoring one private firm over another, or with favoring private projects over public ones. Nonetheless, by the end of 1953, loans made directly to private borrowers amounted to the equivalent of approximately $200 million. In addition, many of the loans made to governments or public bodies have in fact been used to help privately-owned companies. In some cases the proceeds were re-lent to industry; that was true, for example, of the three loans made to the Bank of Finland in 1949 and 1952, which were used for the benefit of electric power companies and wood products enterprises. In other cases, the Bank's loans provided foreign exchange which was then purchased by private industry with local currency and used to pay for imports. A large part of the proceeds of the reconstruction loans in France, the Netherlands and Luxembourg was distributed in this manner, and the same is true of the Bank's loans to Australia in 1950 and 1952.

Moreover, in a number of countries, the Bank has instigated or encouraged the establishment of a development bank to make loans for private industrial projects and has given a credit to the development bank to enable it to meet the foreign exchange requirements of its borrowers. Whenever practicable, the Bank has also sought to ensure that private investors provide the equity capital for, and control the operation of, the development bank itself. Particularly in the case of Turkey these efforts of the Bank have had very encouraging results.

The greater part of the Bank's contribution to the promotion of local private enterprise is less direct but not for that reason the less important. As has already been indicated, most of the Bank's loans are for basic utilities—highways, railroads, power facilities,

57

irrigation and reclamation projects and the like—which are an essential condition for the growth of private enterprise. Where these utility services are provided by a private company, the Bank lends directly to the company with the government's guarantee; where, as is more often the case, the utility facilities are publicly owned and operated, the Bank's loans are made to the government or to a governmental agency. But whether the loan is to a public or private borrower, the resulting expansion of utility services, particularly of power and transportation, is a prerequisite to the development of private initiative in industrial, agricultural, mining and all other directly productive undertakings.

It is the Bank's policy when considering a loan, whether to a public agency or to a private company with a government guarantee, to take care that, in its judgment, the government's position as borrower or guarantor will not either exercise, on balance, a deterrent influence on the investment of private capital in productive ventures or interfere with the management's ability to operate the enterprise efficiently. The Bank encourages its member governments to seek, to the extent feasible, to attract private participation in all revenue-producing projects proposed for Bank financing; and even when private funds are not immediately forthcoming, the Bank tries to assure that the capital structure of the project is such as to facilitate subsequent private investment in the venture.

The Bank has also frequently taken steps to encourage a more favorable climate for private business, both domestic and foreign. This aspect of the Bank's activities is discussed in Chapter 10, which summarizes the various means by which the Bank has sought to stimulate private international investment.

6

Procedures for Making
and Administering Loans

THE PROCEDURES FOLLOWED by the Bank in making and administering loans necessarily vary considerably from case to case, for their effectiveness depends largely on their adaptability to the variety of situations with which the Bank has to deal. Differences in the conditions and experience of the countries in which the projects are located, in the extent to which the Bank has become familiar with them, and in the projects themselves, all affect the character not only of the investigation made of each loan application but also of the subsequent administration of each loan. No two applications or loans are handled in exactly the same way. Nevertheless, over the course of the Bank's history, certain basic standards governing these phases of the Bank's operations have been developed. These are described in the present Chapter.

Exploratory Discussions and Preliminary Investigation

Wherever possible, the Bank prefers to have informal exploratory discussions with prospective borrowers before a formal loan request is filed. These discussions enable the Bank to determine whether the project to be financed is of a type which the Bank can consider and to indicate to the prospective borrower what kinds of information the Bank must have concerning economic conditions in the borrowing country and concerning the project. If the prospective borrower is not a member government, the Bank requires, before starting any serious investigation, an indication from the government that it will guarantee a loan for the project. Often, if the prospective borrower is a member government, its initial approach consists of an indication of its general development aims and a tentative inquiry as to the possibility, extent and conditions of Bank assistance. Such inquiries often lead to an invitation to the Bank to study the government's investment program with a view to possible Bank financing for a portion of it.

In general, the actual processing of a loan request falls into two parts: a preliminary one, in which the Bank reviews the economic situation and prospects of the borrowing country and the relation of the project under consideration to its economic needs and potentialities, and then a more technical and critical examination of the engineering, financial and other aspects of the project and of the appropriate conditions for a loan. These two stages of investigation may proceed more or less concurrently or they may be successive, depending on the circumstances.

The main object of the preliminary investigation is to satisfy the Bank that the borrower can repay the loan and that the project will make a significant contribution to the economy of the borrowing country. If the project is in a country with which the Bank has had no previous experience, the Bank seeks to acquire a comprehensive picture of the structure and development of the economy. It therefore begins its study with such fundamentals as a review of the country's agricultural, mineral and industrial resources, the state of basic facilities such as transport and power, the amount and quality of manpower resources, the pattern of external trade and payments, and the condition of internal finances, particularly the budget and currency position. If the Bank has previously made a loan in the country or has otherwise become familiar with its economy, this preliminary review is dispensed with and the inquiry is confined to an intensive study of recent economic developments and prospects.

In either case, the object of the economic investigation is to determine (1) whether the country needs and can effectively use an addition to its investment resources and, if so, how much and at what rate; (2) the extent to which and the currencies in which the country can afford to service additional foreign indebtedness, and whether the Bank can lend these amounts without undue risk; (3) the development requirements of the country, the order of priority of the various fields of investment, the fields in which Bank financing can make the greatest contribution, and the place in these priorities of the particular project under consideration; and (4) whether the economic and financial policies of the government are well adapted to the needs of the country or whether some modification of those policies would remove obstacles to the development process or strengthen the country's balance of payments position.

Although the Bank is precluded by its charter from making or denying loans to achieve political objectives, it cannot ignore conditions of political instability or uncertainty which may directly affect the economic and financial prospects of the borrower. An examination of the political situation, to the extent that it may bear upon the soundness of the proposed loan, is therefore also included in the initial investigation.

On the basis of this preliminary study, the Bank can usually form at least a provisional judgment as to whether or not the borrower can effectively use and will be able to repay additional foreign debt. The Bank can thus decide in principle whether a loan should be granted and, if so, whether the particular project under consideration is appropriate for Bank financing. If the entire investment program of the government has been submitted to the Bank for study, it can at this point indicate which projects within the program it believes should be given precedence.

Project Examination and Determination of Loan Conditions

If the preliminary investigation has led the Bank to a favorable conclusion with regard to repayment prospects and the appropriateness of a particular project, the second and more detailed investigation begins. Staff technicians or consultants are called upon to make a thorough examination of the technical plans for the project. A similar examination is made of the plans for financing that part of the cost of the project which is not expected to be met out of the Bank's loan. If a marketing problem is involved, it may be necessary to check the market survey made by the borrower or, if none has been made, to assist the borrower in making one. It is also necessary to examine in detail and sometimes to suggest revisions in the administrative and managerial arrangements proposed by the borrower to carry out and operate the project; in a number of cases, the Bank has found it essential to insist upon the employment of consulting engineers to supervise the construction of projects or upon the establishment of quasi-autonomous authorities to operate public facilities. If a revenue-producing enterprise, public or private, is the prospective borrower, the past record of that enterprise is closely scrutinized. Technicians assess the financial return on the goods or services the project will produce and the economic benefits which the country is expected to derive from its execution.

At this stage, too, the Bank staff may work out specific recommendations for strengthening the economic and financial policies of the member government. As the previous Chapter has shown, the adoption of such recommendations may sometimes become a condition for Bank financing.

Methods of Investigation

Much of the work of these two investigations takes place in the Bank's home office. Here the Bank studies all available information about the country and the project. In addition to its own files, the Bank takes advantage of the large reservoir of source material which is made available to it by many other institutions, national and international, public and private. Information from all these sources is supplemented by information specifically requested from the borrower.

No study in the Bank's home office, however, can yield the benefits of an on-the-spot investigation. At some stage of the processing of a loan, therefore, the Bank usually sends a mission to the borrowing country to familiarize itself at first hand with the project and with economic conditions. The composition of the mission and its responsibilities depend entirely on the task at hand. It may consist of just one or two persons or half a dozen persons of various qualifications. The mission members are normally drawn from the Bank staff but, since the Bank cannot possibly keep on its permanent staff experts in each of the many fields which it may be called upon to examine, it frequently employs independent consultants for specific short-term assignments or borrows technical experts for this purpose from member governments, other international agencies or private firms.

Formal Negotiations

If the second, technical phase of the investigation results in a satisfactory report on the project, the Bank advises the borrower that it is ready to begin formal negotiations for a loan. As the Bank's experience has broadened and as its members have grown familiar with the provisions of the Bank's loan and guarantee agreements, it has become possible in most cases to complete formal negotiations quite quickly. Although some contractual provisions generally need to be fashioned to meet the particular case, most of them have become standard, for they are based on the requirements of the Articles of Agreement and on policies which the Bank applies without discrimination to all its borrowers.

Negotiations are carried out, on behalf of the Bank, by its management and staff but the Executive Directors are kept abreast of the major problems arising in the course of discussions with the borrower, as they were informed of the main results of the investigations which led up to the negotiations. When agreement has been reached on the project and on the terms and conditions of the loan, the loan and guarantee agreements and all supporting documentation are presented to the Executive Directors, together with the recommendation of the President, for their approval.[1]

After the signing of the loan agreement a period of several months normally elapses before the agreement becomes effective. The effectiveness of the agreement generally depends upon the fulfillment of certain prescribed conditions, the most common of which requires the borrowing country to take whatever legislative action may be necessary to make the loan or guarantee agreement binding upon it. Where such legislative authority already exists, the period between the date when the agreement is signed and the date when it becomes effective is generally somewhat shorter. Disbursements are made under the loan only after the agreement has become effective.

Administration

The administration of the loan covers the direct supervision of disbursements, a continuing scrutiny of the execution and later the operation of the project, and a continuing review of the economic and financial conditions of the borrower and of the country in which the project is located. These continue throughout the life of the loan until it has been fully paid.

The first purpose of the administration of a loan is to assure,

---

[1] The President's recommendation to the Executive Directors is accompanied by the report of a special committee set up in accordance with the Articles of Agreement. This committee, which consists of designated Bank officials and an expert selected by the Governor representing the member in whose territory the project is located, certifies that, after careful study of the loan proposal, it finds that the project to be financed comes within the purposes of the Bank, is in the interests of the member country concerned and of the members of the Bank as a whole, and accordingly merits the financial assistance of the Bank.

in the interests of both the borrower and the Bank, that the proceeds of the loan are used, in an economical manner, for the purposes for which they were intended. To this end the Bank disburses funds under its normal project loans only as expenditures are incurred for specified goods and services. This is a requirement not only of the Bank's Articles of Agreement but of sound business procedure. By means of this procedure and the reporting system mentioned below, it is possible to follow each item financed by the Bank, from the determination of specifications and the placement of an order, to delivery of the item and its actual use in the project.

In almost every case disbursements are made by the Bank on the basis of documentary evidence showing that the goods or services to be financed are covered by the loan agreement, that they are reasonable in cost and of proper quality, and that payment has been or will have to be made for them. The evidence required is based on normal banking procedures and every effort is made to avoid unnecessary work for the borrower or his commercial banker.

Administration of a loan cannot stop with the supervision of the use of the loan proceeds. A generator financed by the Bank serves its purpose only when installed in a powerhouse built by local labor paid with domestic currency from the borrower's resources. Accordingly, to be sure that the project is being carried out efficiently and on time, the Bank must observe the whole process of construction. It does so by requiring records to be kept and regular periodic reports to be submitted on the progress of the entire project. Such reports must cover progress on the work of engineering survey, specification and design, progress in placing contracts for goods and services and in their manufacture and delivery, progress in physical construction, and the course of expenditure on the project. Both physical progress and actual expenditures must be shown in relation to original work schedules and cost estimates. The form and detail of the reports vary from case to case, but must be sufficient to meet the minimum requirements of the Bank. Those minimum requirements are no more than any prudent business man or manager needs in controlling his own affairs.

Reports from the borrower are supplemented by periodic visits to the project by Bank staff. On such visits, Bank personnel examine the site of the project and the work being done, scrutinize the accounts of the borrower, observe the use and maintenance of goods and equipment purchased with the loan proceeds, and assess the competence of the management and administration of the project. As a result of such reports and tours of inspection, problems arising in the course of construction are discussed and solutions jointly explored. Changes in the specifications of the project or in construction schedules are sometimes found necessary and are mutually agreed upon. Sometimes, too, changing financial conditions increase wages and prices so that the cost of the project grows beyond the amount originally estimated; in such cases, the borrower and the Bank usually consult on the measures that need to be taken to assure completion of the project.

Concurrently with its observation of the progress of the project, the Bank keeps abreast of economic and political developments in the borrowing country, both through periodic staff visits and through regular economic and financial reports from the government. In addition, the government is required under the loan agreement to advise the Bank of any major development which might endanger the execution of the project or interfere with the service or repayment of the loan.

The borrowing member's reports and the Bank's own inspections become the basis of a periodic Loan Administration Report presented both to the Bank's Executive Directors and to the member. The purpose of these reports is not only to keep the Executive Directors and the member governments informed of the progress of a particular project and loan. They may make specific recommendations to the borrowing country for improvements in the execution and operation of Bank-financed projects, and they sometimes serve as a basis on which the Bank can discuss with a member government the existence or the probable emergence of factors which might unfavorably affect the country's external credit standing. These reports also afford a useful background against which the Bank can determine its future policy towards the member country, whether in connection with additional loans or in the field of technical assistance.

7

Lending Activities
and Financial Results

General

As of December 31, 1953, total Bank loan commitments, in United States dollars and other currencies, aggregated the equivalent of approximately $1.781 billion. Of this amount, approximately $31 million has been refunded or canceled at the request of the borrowers; the net total of commitments made by the Bank from the beginning of its operations to date is therefore roughly $1.75 billion. In all, 96 loans have been made to governments, government agencies or private borrowers in 28 member countries and three overseas dependencies. These loans have financed more than 400 different projects. Table 4 on the following page shows a classification of the Bank's lending by country and geographical area.

Disbursements on Bank loans through December 31, 1953 aggregated the equivalent of approximately $1.236 billion. While U. S. dollars were used for most of these disbursements, 13 other currencies have also been utilized (for details, see page 80).

European Lending

As already noted, the Bank's first loans were made in advance of the European Recovery Program to help in the postwar reconstruction of four countries of Western Europe. The first borrower was the Credit National of France, a semi-public corporation to which the Bank lent $250 million in May 1947. In August of the same year, the Bank lent the Netherlands $195 million, Denmark $40 million and Luxembourg $12 million.

TABLE 4

GEOGRAPHICAL DISTRIBUTION OF LOANS AS OF DECEMBER 31, 1953
(In U. S. dollar equivalents net of cancellations and refundings)

Country	Number of Loans	Amount	
EUROPE			
Belgium	2	$ 46,000,000	
Denmark	1	40,000,000	
Finland	4	38,081,000	
France	1	250,000,000	
Iceland	5	5,914,000	
Italy	2	20,000,000	
Luxembourg	1	11,762,000	
Netherlands	9	221,452,000	
Turkey	5	59,600,000	
Yugoslavia	3	60,700,000	
	33		$ 753,509,000
WESTERN HEMISPHERE			
Brazil	9	175,300,000	
Chile	4	37,300,000	
Colombia	7	69,305,000	
El Salvador	1	12,545,000	
Mexico	5	80,328,000	
Nicaragua	5	9,197,000	
Panama	2	1,490,000	
Paraguay	1	5,000,000	
Peru	2	3,800,000	
Uruguay	1	33,000,000	
	37		427,265,000
AUSTRALASIA			
Australia	2	150,000,000	
	2		150,000,000

ASIA AND THE MIDDLE EAST

India	5	109,800,000	
Iraq	1	12,800,000	
Japan	3	40,200,000	
Pakistan	2	30,450,000	
Thailand	3	25,400,000	
	14		218,650,000

AFRICA

Belgian Congo	1	40,000,000	
Ethiopia	3	8,500,000	
Northern Rhodesia	1	14,000,000	
Southern Rhodesia	1	28,000,000	
Union of South Africa	4	110,000,000	
	10		200,500,000
Total Loans:	96	*Total Amount:*	$1,749,924,000

The proceeds of the loans to France, the Netherlands and Denmark were used to purchase imports for many different sectors of the economy—especially manufacturing, agriculture, transportation and the generation of electric power. The goods purchased came almost exclusively from the United States, and consisted about equally of raw materials (primarily petroleum, cotton, coal and lumber) and of finished goods (ranging from factory and farm machinery to railway locomotives, ships and structural steel). The loan to Luxembourg was designed primarily to help restore the production of steel, which is the backbone of that country's economy, and for the railways.

Although the Bank continued operations on the Continent after the European Recovery Program was adopted in April 1948, its lending was on a restricted scale. In contrast to the 1947 reconstruction loans aggregating $497 million, Bank loans to European member countries in the ensuing six years totaled the equivalent of roughly $264 million, excluding loans for dependent overseas territories. A number of these later loans were for projects complementary to undertakings being financed under the European Recovery Program; this was the case with Bank-financed projects in Belgium, Iceland, the Netherlands and Turkey. In Turkey, for example, ERP funds paid for tractors to increase farm production, especially of wheat, and helped bear the cost of constructing farm-to-market roads; Bank loans were made for grain storage installations and for the improvement of Turkish ports, through which wheat and other farm products move to world markets.

It was characteristic of most of these later loans to Europe that they were for projects designed to add to, and not merely restore, Europe's productive plant. Examples are the two Turkish loans, made in 1950 and 1953, to provide medium- and long-term credit for industry; the loan made to Belgium in 1951 to help her bear the cost of a 10-year program for developing the Belgian Congo; the loans to Finland, in 1949 and 1952, for the expansion of electric power and of the wood products industries; and the two Italian loans, made in 1951 and 1953, to support a 12-year program for the development of southern Italy and the islands of Sardinia and Sicily.

Development Lending

Beginning in 1948, the emphasis of Bank lending has been on the long-term financing of productive projects in the less developed countries, lying for the most part outside Europe and North America. Here the Bank found itself faced with problems very different from those involved in European reconstruction. The task was not simply to restore missing components to economies which were already mature; the underdeveloped countries needed still to build the foundations on which modern economies depend: electric power systems, roads, railroads, ports, irrigation works and the like. At the same time, the underdeveloped countries had relatively few leaders in business or government able to plan investment; they were greatly hampered by a shortage of technicians and administrators able to design and carry out projects; and they had only a limited ability to muster even the modest resources of local capital which were available for the kind of long-term investment on which steady and continuous economic

71

development depends. It was obvious that the Bank would not be able to move as quickly in the field of development financing as it had in the field of reconstruction.

The Bank's first development loans were made to Latin America, commencing in 1948, and total Bank investment in Latin America is now greater than in any other underdeveloped area. Ten of the American Republics have received loans, aggregating the equivalent of almost $447 million. Brazil, with loans of just over $175 million, has borrowed more money from the Bank than any other underdeveloped country.

The Bank's first loan in Asia was made in 1949 (to India); its first loans in the Middle East (to Iraq), Australia (to the Commonwealth Government) and Africa (to Ethiopia), were made in 1950. Of these areas, Asia and the Middle East together have received loans aggregating the equivalent of over $222 million, with India accounting for nearly half the total; countries in Africa have borrowed the equivalent of about $200 million, with the Union of South Africa accounting for somewhat more than half; and Australia has borrowed $150 million.

Purposes of Bank Loans

Table 5 on the following page shows the specific purposes for which the Bank's post-reconstruction loans have been made. The figures demonstrate the emphasis which the Bank has put on projects, particularly in the fields of power and transportation, designed to have a generally stimulating effect on production of all kinds, as distinguished from facilities designed for the production of specific end goods. Projects of the latter type, it should be noted, are more likely to attract private capital than basic facilities of the type financed by the Bank, which usually require large outlays of capital and provide only modest returns over a protracted period.

To date, the Bank has lent the equivalent of $492 million to increase supplies of electric power; apart from the reconstruction

TABLE 5

Loans Classified by Purpose and Area as of December 31, 1953
(*In millions of U. S. dollars, net of cancellations and refundings*)

Purpose	Area					
	Total	Asia and Middle East	Africa	Australasia	Europe	Western Hemisphere
GRAND TOTAL	1,750	218	201	150	754	427
RECONSTRUCTION LOANS						
Total (France, The Netherlands, Denmark, Luxembourg)	497	—	—	—	497	—
OTHER LOANS						
Total	1,253	218	201	150	257	427
Electric Power (machinery, equipment and construction materials)	492	68	88	30	35	271
Transportation	304	67	69	39	35	94
Railroads: locomotives, rolling stock, rails, shop and station equipment	193	63	61	16	3	50
Shipping: vessels and marine equipment	12	—	—	—	12	—
Airlines: planes and equipment	14	—	—	7	7	—
Roads: building machinery and equipment	64	—	7	16	—	41
Ports: docks, loading and dredging machinery and harbor craft	21	4	1	—	13	3
Communications (telephone and telegraph equipment and supplies)	26	—	2	—	—	24
Agriculture and Forestry	152	51	—	54	29	18
Mechanization: general farm machinery and equipment	60	—	—	44	2	14
Irrigation and flood control: construction equipment and materials	60	41	—	5	13	1
Land improvement: machinery, construction equipment & materials	20	10	—	5	3	2
Grain storage: construction materials	5	—	—	—	4	1
Timber production: machinery and vehicles	7	—	—	—	7	—
Industry	169	32	—	27	90	20
Manufacturing machinery	146	32	—	20	74	20
Mining equipment	23	—	—	7	16	—
General Development	110	—	42	—	68	—
Development banks	20	—	2	—	18	—
General development plans	90	—	40	—	50	—

credits, this is the largest single category of Bank lending. Power projects have been financed in 17 different countries: Australia, Belgium, Brazil, Chile, Colombia, El Salvador, Finland, Iceland, India, Japan, Mexico, Nicaragua, Southern Rhodesia, the Union of South Africa, Uruguay, Turkey and Yugoslavia. Assistance in the development of electric power in Latin America, which has absorbed about two thirds of Bank lending in that area, has been particularly significant. In Mexico, for example, projects assisted by Bank loans will by 1956 add 70% to the generating capacity that existed when the Bank engaged in its first Mexican power financing in 1949.

The Bank's post-reconstruction loans for transportation amount to the equivalent of $304 million. The first of these loans was made in 1949 to finance the purchase of locomotives and spare parts for the Indian Railways. Bank funds have since been committed for the purchase of locomotives or rolling stock for railways in Australia, Brazil, Pakistan, the Rhodesias, the Union of South Africa and Yugoslavia, for repair shop equipment in Colombia, Thailand and the Union of South Africa, and for the construction of new railways in Colombia and the Rhodesias.

In addition, the Bank has committed $64 million for the purchase of equipment and services for the improvement or construction of motor roads. It has made two loans, totaling almost $31 million, for this purpose in Colombia, and has provided other funds for highway improvement in Australia, Brazil, Ethiopia and Nicaragua. Bank loans have also provided funds for port improvements in Peru, Turkey, Thailand, the Union of South Africa and Yugoslavia, for commercial aircraft and ships for Netherlands fleets, and for aircraft in Australia.

Only relatively minor amounts have thus far been lent for communications projects. Individual loans made in Brazil and Uruguay primarily for power installations included lesser amounts for equipment to expand telephone services; a loan made to

Ethiopia to modernize telecommunications has not yet become effective.

The Bank's lending in direct support of agricultural development projects amounts to $152 million, including a small amount for forestry. Of this $152 million, the greater part represents investment in basic agricultural development—irrigation, flood control and land clearance. The Bank has made loans for these purposes in Australia, Chile, India, Iraq, Pakistan and Thailand. In addition, it has financed the importation of tractors and farm implements in Australia, Colombia, Chile, Nicaragua, Panama, Paraguay, Peru and Yugoslavia. In most instances, the agricultural projects aided by the Bank formed a relatively small part of wider programs aimed at expansion of agricultural production and the improvement of productivity. Agriculture has also benefited substantially by a number of other Bank loans, particularly those for power, railroad, highway and port facilities.

Post-reconstruction loans aggregating $169 million have been made for industrial projects in seven countries: Australia, Belgium, Chile, Finland, India, the Netherlands and Yugoslavia. They include two loans made directly to private industry: $31.5 million to a steel manufacturer in India and $20 million to a manufacturer of paper products in Chile. The remaining industrial loans were made to governments or governmental financing institutions for use by manufacturing and mining enterprises, for the most part privately owned, including steel, coal and other mineral ventures in Australia, steel manufacturing in Belgium, wood products industries in Finland, and a wide variety of industrial undertakings in the Netherlands and of industrial and mining projects in Yugoslavia.

Loans aggregating the equivalent of another $20 million have been made to development banks to be used by them very largely in connection with private industrial credits. Two loans, each the equivalent of $9 million, have been made to the privately-owned Industrial Development Bank of Turkey for this purpose.

A $2 million loan to the government-owned Development Bank of Ethiopia, while available for either agricultural or industrial projects, has up to now been used primarily for small industries processing agricultural products.

The final category of Bank loans shown in Table 5 consists of credits amounting to the equivalent of $90 million, made to support programs of economic development in the Belgian Congo and in southern Italy. The Bank lent the Congo $40 million for imports needed in the first years of a 10-year program; in that case the Bank's disbursements on the loan, instead of being tied to specific imports, were geared instead to the general rate of expenditure on the program, and in particular to expenditures made by the Office des Transports Coloniaux for the improvement of transportation in the Congo. At the same time, the Bank lent $30 million to Belgium to cover part of the indirect foreign exchange costs occasioned by her support of the Congo program.

The Bank's two loans in Italy, each of $10 million, were intended, like the loan to Belgium, to cover indirect foreign exchange costs, arising in this case from a 12-year program for the development of southern Italy. In the case of both Italian loans, the loan contracts provided that the lira counterpart of the dollars loaned would be utilized for purposes to be agreed by the Government and the Bank.

Distribution of Expenditures under Bank Loans

In the early years of its operations, Bank loans were used almost exclusively for purchases in the United States. Europe at that time did not have available significant amounts of capital goods for export to other continents; on the contrary, the European countries themselves needed capital equipment from the United States. Accordingly, most of the loan applications filed with the Bank were designed to secure financing for essential goods which the borrowers needed to import from the United States. As European productive capacity recovered, this situation has gradu-

CUMULATIVE LOAN DISBURSEMENTS

To December 31, 1953

(Expressed in millions of U. S. dollars)

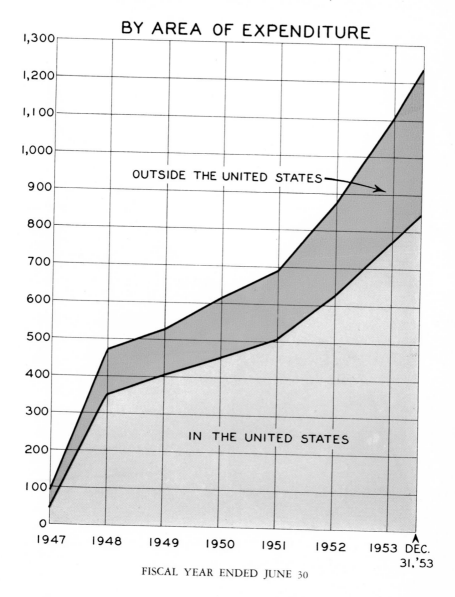

BY AREA OF EXPENDITURE

OUTSIDE THE UNITED STATES

IN THE UNITED STATES

1947 1948 1949 1950 1951 1952 1953 DEC.
31,'53

FISCAL YEAR ENDED JUNE 30

CUMULATIVE LOAN DISBURSEMENTS

To December 31, 1953

(Expressed in millions of U. S. dollars)

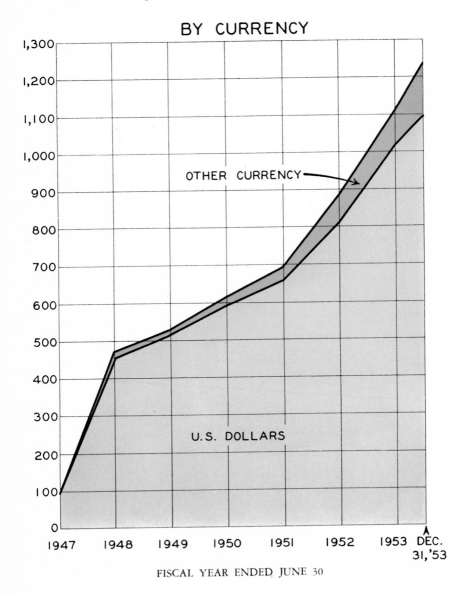

BY CURRENCY

OTHER CURRENCY

U.S. DOLLARS

1947   1948   1949   1950   1951   1952   1953 DEC. 31,'53

FISCAL YEAR ENDED JUNE 30

ally changed and borrowers from the Bank are now obtaining more of the goods they need from sources of supply outside the United States.

Table 6 shows cumulatively by years the geographical distribution of expenditures under Bank loans and the accompanying charts show cumulative loan disbursements both by area of expenditure and by currencies used.

TABLE 6

DISTRIBUTION OF EXPENDITURES UNDER LOANS

(*In millions of U. S. dollars*)

Area of Expenditure	To July 1950	%	To July 1951	%	To July 1952	%	To July 1953	%	To Jan. 1954	%
United States	$452.2	73.7	$505.6	73.1	$626.2	71.4	$ 770.3	69.8	$ 844.7	68.3
Europe	66.7	10.9	78.2	11.3	125.0	14.3	193.2	17.5	246.0	19.9
Canada	34.8	5.6	45.5	6.6	61.7	7.0	71.4	6.5	76.1	6.2
Latin America	55.5	9.1	57.5	8.3	58.4	6.7	61.0	5.5	61.7	5.0
Africa	2.2	0.3	2.2	0.3	2.3	0.3	4.0	0.4	4.3	0.3
Middle East	1.9	0.3	1.9	0.3	2.1	0.3	2.2	0.2	2.3	0.2
Asia	.7	0.1	.8	0.1	.8	—	1.2	0.1	1.2	0.1
	$614.0		$691.7		$876.5		$1,103.3		$1,236.3	

Currency Problems

It is the Bank's general practice, except in the unusual case of a local expenditure loan (see page 53) to provide its borrowers with whatever currencies they need to pay for goods and services under their loans. For example, if a borrower buys in the United Kingdom equipment covered by a Bank loan, the Bank normally supplies the borrower with sterling, while if the purchase is made in France, the borrower normally receives French francs.

The Bank may furnish the particular currency needed by the borrower either out of its own holdings in that currency or by purchasing it with other currency which it holds. In the first case, the loan is repayable in the currency furnished to the borrower; in the second case, the loan is repayable in the currency used by the Bank to buy the currency furnished to the borrower.

77

Table 7 shows the distribution among different currencies of disbursements by the Bank through December 31, 1953 and also the amounts repayable in these different currencies. The "disbursed" column indicates the amounts of the different currencies actually furnished to borrowers under Bank loans; it does not necessarily represent total purchases in the country whose currency

TABLE 7

DISTRIBUTION OF DISBURSEMENTS AND REPAYMENT OBLIGATIONS AMONG CURRENCIES

(In U. S. dollar equivalents)

Currency	Disbursed	Repayable
Austrian schillings	$ 226,542	$ 226,542
Belgian francs	31,581,184	5,007,882
Canadian dollars	55,699,108	51,507,857
Danish kroner	1,388,232	1,104,190
French francs	16,537,566	15,234,365
German marks	10,988,181	—
Italian lire	4,441,060	2,862,412
Netherlands guilders	3,059,530	584,094
Norwegian kroner	197,946	113,729
South African pounds	2,115,580	2,115,580
Swedish kronor	4,921,004	940,115
Swiss francs	21,039,773	42,532,632
United Kingdom pounds	85,718,634	16,395,685
United States dollars	998,390,394	1,097,679,651
TOTAL:	$1,236,304,734	$1,236,304,734

is indicated. The "repayable" column shows the amounts of the different currencies used by the Bank to make these disbursements.

Currency considerations affect Bank lending in several ways. So long as major currencies remain inconvertible, the Bank has to gauge the amount of its lending to any member country in any currency on the basis of the member's creditworthiness in that currency. Many countries, for example, are better able to service loans in European currencies than in U. S. dollars; yet the availability to the Bank of currencies other than dollars has been very limited. In such cases, the amount of dollars which the Bank can lend is limited by the country's creditworthiness in dollars, while the amount which the Bank can lend in European currencies, if it can lend them at all, depends largely upon the extent of the willingness of its European members to release a portion of their 18% capital subscriptions for the loan. In order to conserve its European currencies for loans to countries whose creditworthiness in dollars is small, the Bank follows the policy of using only dollars in loans to countries, such as most of the American Republics, whose foreign exchange earnings are primarily in dollars, irrespective of where the goods financed by the Bank are to be purchased.

To the extent that European currencies available to the Bank are convertible, the Bank, of course, takes advantage of that fact. For example, since Yugoslavia is in a better position to service debt in Swiss francs than in U. S. dollars, the Bank has financed purchases by Yugoslavia in the United States by buying U. S. dollars with Swiss francs. Similarly, the Bank has made cross-purchases of currencies convertible within the European Payments Union; it has used pounds sterling, for example, to finance purchases in Germany.

Term, Interest Rate and Other Charges

The Bank normally makes medium- or long-term loans, with the principal amortized over the life of the loan and with the final maturity coming due after five years or more. The length of Bank loans to final maturity is shown in Table 8.

The Bank has made only two loans with a final maturity of less than five years.[1] These were two-year credits made in 1951

---

[1] A one-year loan of $10 million was made to the Comision Federal de Electricidad and Nacional Financiera of Mexico in January 1949 for relending to the Mexican Light and Power Co., Ltd., pending that Company's reorganization. However, that loan was refunded, as originally intended, out of a $26 million 25-year loan made the next year to the reorganized Company.

in Finland and Yugoslavia for equipment to increase the production of timber for export to Western Europe. Only one loan—the 30-year $250 million reconstruction credit to France—has been for more than 25 years.

In establishing the length of its loans, the Bank has generally followed the principle that the term should not be longer than the anticipated life of the equipment being financed. Loans made

TABLE 8

TERM OF LOANS

Length	Amount
Less than 10 years	$ 68,800,000
10–14 years	112,400,000
15–19 years	268,100,000
20–24 years	282,400,000
25 years	799,400,000
30 years	250,000,000

for very heavy equipment—for example, power installations—have customarily been made for terms of from 20 to 25 years. Loans made for less durable equipment, such as farm machinery, have often been made for around seven years.

The loan contracts provide for repayment of principal in semi-annual instalments designed to amortize the loan completely by final maturity. The borrower is normally given a period of grace ranging from two to five years before the first instalment comes due; the length of the period of grace, which is applicable only to principal and not to interest payments, is generally determined by the time estimated to be necessary to bring the project into operation. In formulating the amortization schedule, which is either on a level or gradually increasing basis, the Bank takes into account maturities on other debts of the borrower so as to avoid, to the extent practicable, any unduly heavy service burden in any given year or years.

Interest and other charges on Bank loans have been on a nondiscriminatory basis, without distinction among borrowers. Since the Bank's lending has thus far been mostly in dollars, the basic component in the interest rate on any given loan, whether made with funds derived from capital subscriptions or the sale of Bank obligations, has been the estimated cost to the Bank, at the time the loan is made, of borrowing money for a comparable term in the United States capital market. In addition, as noted in Chapter 3, the Bank charges on all loans a commission of 1% for the purpose of creating a special reserve against losses. Finally, the Bank has included in the interest charge a small fraction out of which administrative costs are paid and a contribution made to reserves. These three components—the estimated cost of borrowing to the Bank, the commission and the fraction for administrative costs—make up the total interest rate on each loan.

Changes in the cost of borrowing in the United States have occasioned fluctuations in interest charges. The reconstruction loans of 1947 carried interest at 4¼%. The rate on loans of 20 years or more rose in the following year to 4½%. It then fell gradually until it reached 4% in 1950. From 1951 onward, there was a hardening of money rates in the United States market; the interest on long-term loans accordingly rose to 4⅞% in 1952 and to 5% in 1953. Interest charges on loans of shorter term have, of course, been somewhat lower.

The full interest rate is charged only on that part of the loan which has actually been disbursed. To compensate the Bank to some extent for the cost of holding funds at the disposal of the borrower, a commitment charge is made on the undisbursed portions of a loan. In the case of the Bank's early loans, this charge was originally set at 1½%, but in 1950, the Bank reduced it to ¾ of 1% both for new loans and for the undisbursed portions of existing loans.

Financial Results of Operations

The Bank has not had any defaults in payments of interest and principal on its loans. As of December 31, 1953, it had accumulated reserves equivalent to almost $130 million. The special reserve, derived from loan commissions, amounted to the equivalent of nearly $43 million. Accumulated net earnings, placed in a supplemental reserve against losses on loans and guarantees, amounted to the equivalent of just under $87 million. In addition, the Bank received repayments of principal from borrowers aggregating the equivalent of more than $14.7 million and the equivalent of roughly an additional $30 million principal amount of loans sold by the Bank from its portfolio has matured or the Bank has received advice of prepayment by the respective borrowers.

The Bank's fiscal year runs from July 1 to June 30. The Bank entered its first full fiscal year of operations on July 1, 1946 with a deficit of slightly over $125,000, and during the year spent approximately $940,000 more than it earned. In the following fiscal years, income exceeded expenditures by increasing amounts. Net earnings, excluding income from loan commissions allocated to the special reserve, rose from the equivalent of approximately $4.09 million in fiscal 1948 to the equivalent of nearly $18.49 million in fiscal 1953, and for the first six months of fiscal 1954 amounted to the equivalent of approximately $10.12 million.

Gross income, consisting principally of income from loan charges and earnings on investment of the Bank's liquid assets, rose from the equivalent of approximately $1.23 million in fiscal 1947 to the equivalent of over $52.93 million in fiscal 1953, and for the first six months of fiscal 1954 amounted to the equivalent of about $29.49 million. Annual allocations to the special reserve rose during the same period from approximately $33,000 to about $9.55 million, and for the first six months of fiscal 1954 amounted to roughly $5.56 million. Annual expenditures, including regular

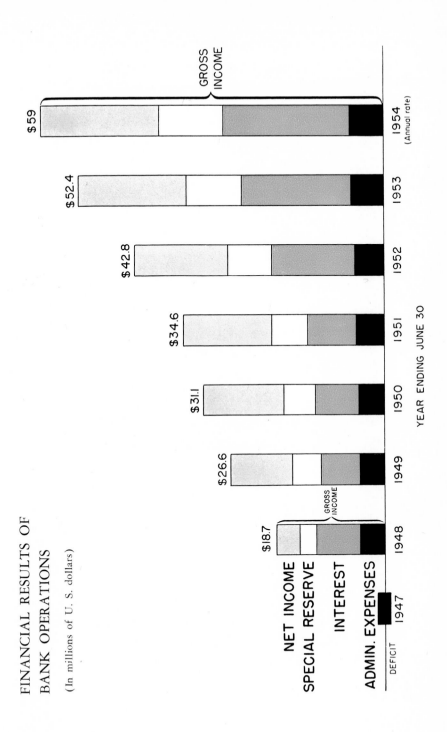

FINANCIAL RESULTS OF
BANK OPERATIONS

(In millions of U. S. dollars)

GROSS
INCOME

$59

$52.4

$42.8

$34.6

$31.1

$26.6

$18.7

GROSS
INCOME

NET INCOME

SPECIAL RESERVE

INTEREST

ADMIN. EXPENSES

DEFICIT 1947

1948   1949   1950   1951   1952   1953   1954
(Annual rate)

YEAR ENDING JUNE 30

administrative outlays, payments of bond interest, and expenses for bond issuance, rose from the equivalent of nearly $2.14 million to the equivalent of about $24.35 million, and for the first six months of fiscal 1954 amounted to about $13.81 million.

The Bank's income and expenses are shown from fiscal 1947 to date in Table 9 below:

TABLE 9

INCOME AND EXPENSES

(In millions of U. S. dollars)

Fiscal Year	Gross Income	Allocations to Special Reserve	Expenditures Admin.	Interest & Other	Net Income
1947	$ 1.23	$ .03	$2.08	$ .06	$ .94 (deficit)
1948	18.70	3.05	4.05	7.51	4.09
1949	26.57	4.99	4.07	6.90	10.61
1950	31.13	5.66	4.37	7.40	13.70
1951	34.59	6.39	4.84	8.20	15.16
1952	42.75	7.56	5.14	14.18	15.87
1953	52.39	9.55	5.72	18.63	18.49
1954 (6 mos.)	29.49	5.56	2.93	10.88	10.12

8

Technical Assistance

EVER SINCE THE BANK entered the field of development lending, it has found itself called upon to give technical aid or advice to member governments on matters relating to loan operations. Sometimes this aid has consisted of helping a member government to define priorities among different projects. Sometimes it has consisted of advice by Bank technicians as to desirable modifications in the technical plans for a project designed to reduce its cost, to make it more efficient, or to adapt it better to a country's needs. And sometimes it has consisted of suggestions as to administrative or organizational arrangements for a project or as to plans for its financing, including the raising of local capital.

Increasingly, however, the Bank has been asked to provide advisory services on a broader scale and on matters not connected with immediate loan proposals, and it is with services of this type that the present Chapter deals. Although the requests to the Bank for such services have covered a wide variety of problems, the Bank has sought to confine its activities primarily to those fields where, by reason of its character as a development financing institution and of the operational experience gained by its staff, it could appropriately be considered as having particular qualifications to undertake the assignment. Application of this standard has led to an emphasis, although by no means an exclusive concentration, in the Bank's technical assistance program on the problems of development programming and the mobilization of local capital.

Assistance in Development Programming

The Bank's concern with development programming grew directly out of its operational experience. During the early years, applications for development loans filed with the Bank not infrequently consisted simply of lists of projects which the member government had under consideration, without any indication of the relative priority of the various projects, the relation between them or their place in the development pattern being worked out for the country as a whole. A good deal of the time and attention of the Bank's staff was necessarily devoted, therefore, to helping member governments determine priorities among the different projects they had in mind and sometimes to suggesting additional projects in fields which appeared to have been overlooked or insufficiently emphasized. Missions sent by the Bank to its underdeveloped member countries confirmed the inadequacy of development programming efforts in a great many cases and pointed to the consequent risk that scarce investment resources might be misapplied. They noted, with few exceptions, the absence of any effective government agency charged with taking an over-all look at the economy and appraising proposed projects within the framework of a consciously formulated development pattern.

It was against the background of this experience that the Bank decided, in 1949, to comply with a request of the Government of Colombia to organize a general survey mission to analyze the Colombian economy and to make recommendations on the basis of which the Government could formulate a long-term development program. The mission to Colombia was in the nature of an experiment, but its results were sufficiently encouraging to convince the Bank that this type of assistance could, in appropriate cases, do much to stimulate development.

Up to the present time, the Bank has organized general survey missions to the following countries, always upon request of the governments concerned:

Country	Date of Organization
Colombia	1949
Turkey	1950
Guatemala	1950
Cuba	1950
Iraq	1951
Ceylon	1951
Surinam	1951
Jamaica	1952
British Guiana	1953
Nigeria	1953

General survey missions are now being organized to go to Malaya and Syria early in 1954.

The terms of reference of each survey mission have varied in accordance with the particular needs of the country to which it was sent, but the basic purposes have been the same. In general terms, these missions are intended to survey the development potentialities and problems of the countries to which they go and then to make recommendations designed to assist the governments in formulating long-term development programs. The emphasis is on three points. The first is to estimate in a rough order of magnitude the amount of investment which a country can appropriately undertake with the resources at its command. The second is to recommend priorities for public investment among the important sectors of the economy and among types of undertakings within each sector, after taking into account estimated private investment requirements. The third is to suggest economic and financial policies and administrative measures necessary to assure success of the development program. In addition, the missions frequently find themselves in a position to make a number of important technical recommendations designed to improve productivity in various sectors of the economy.

The size and composition of the missions have been determined in the light of the requirements of the particular economies surveyed. The smallest group consisted of six experts and the largest of 16; the average has tended to be from 10 to 12. Besides the mission chief, the groups have normally included two or three economists and experts in the fields of agriculture, industry, transportation and power. In addition, as appropriate, experts on mining, water resources, forestry, education, public health, and housing and community planning have been appointed. All of the experts for the missions have been recruited on an international basis; nationals of 17 different countries have served as mission members, with one group including as many as eight different nationalities.

The Bank has received the assistance of many other organizations in this aspect of its work. The Food and Agriculture Organization of the United Nations has furnished agricultural experts for most of the missions and has in many cases shared the costs of those experts. The International Monetary Fund has also occasionally provided the services of a staff member. Public health experts have been recruited in cooperation with the World Health Organization and educational experts in cooperation with the United Nations Educational, Scientific and Cultural Organization. Experts have also been seconded by various member governments, as well as by the U. S. Federal Reserve Board and the Federal Reserve Bank of New York.

In each case, one or more members of the Bank's staff have participated in order to provide the mission with the experience already gained by the Bank in this type of work and to provide for continuity in relationships between the Bank and the particular country concerned. In fact, the tendency has been to use Bank staff members for the economic posts on the mission, and frequently for the post of mission chief as well, and to rely on outside consultants primarily in specialized technical fields.

It has been the Bank's general policy that the costs of general survey missions should be shared by the Bank and the government concerned. The Bank is convinced of the desirability of asking the recipient government to defray a substantial part of the cost, both in fairness to the other stockholders of the Bank and as an indication of the government's seriousness of purpose in requesting the Bank's help. The practice has been for the Bank to pay the salaries of its own staff attached to the missions, half the salaries of outside consultants, and all travelling and living expenses of the mission outside of the country concerned. The government pays the other half of the consultants' salaries and all local expenses while the mission is in the country.

The end product of the work of the mission, as such, is a report containing the mission's analysis and recommendations, prepared in such form that it can be utilized not only by technicians but by all intelligent elements of the community as the basis for consideration of a national development program. To this end, arrangements are made for translation of the report into the language of the country concerned and for its publication within that country. An English version of each report is also published for the Bank by the Johns Hopkins Press of Baltimore, Maryland.

The reports make no attempt to formulate a detailed blueprint for the development of the country's economy; quite apart from the desirability of flexibility and ample scope for individual initiative, the development process is too complicated, and the factual data too inadequate and inaccurate to make such blueprinting practicable. The objective of the mission reports is rather to set forth feasible development targets, to recommend the amount of investment, and directions of public investment, necessary to achieve those targets over a period of years, and to advise the government on those major economic, financial and administrative problems which must be satisfactorily solved if the recommended investment program is to be effective. A serious effort is made in all the reports to avoid, on the one hand, such a proliferation of recommendations on small technical details that the broad development pattern envisaged by the mission is obscured, and, on the other hand, recommendations of such a broad general character that they provide an inadequate guide to action.

The contents of the report are the responsibility of the chief of the mission, and the Bank always makes clear in transmitting the report that the views expressed are those of the mission rather than positive recommendations of the Bank as an institution. Nonetheless, the Bank's staff keeps closely in touch with the progress of the mission and carefully reviews its work, with a view both to making constructive suggestions and to enabling the Bank to satisfy itself that the report, on the whole, has been competently prepared and lays the foundations of a sound development program.

The recommendations of a general survey mission are, of course, of practical value only in so far as they are incorporated by the government of the recipient country into its own indigenous program and that program is then implemented. The Bank has consistently urged, therefore, that the report of the mission be widely disseminated throughout the country, that the recommendations be subjected to careful study and to such modification as the responsible authorities deem necessary, and that some continuing agency be established to keep under constant review and periodically to revise whatever program may eventually emerge from consideration of the report. In several cases, the Bank has provided the services of staff members or consultants to help member governments both in their study of mission recommendations and in the implementation phase.

In one case, the Bank provided development programming assistance through the use of a different technique from that of the general survey mission. In response to a request from the

Government of Nicaragua for Bank help in the formulation of a development program, the Bank assigned two members of its staff, an economist and an engineer, to spend a year in Nicaragua working directly with the government, not only on drawing up a program but on actually putting it into effect. During the course of this work, arrangements were made with the assistance of the Bank's representatives for other experts in various specialized fields to come to Nicaragua for short periods of time under the auspices of the Bank, the Fund, FAO and other organizations. At the end of the first year, a report was prepared by the Bank's representatives setting forth the program which they had worked out in cooperation with the Nicaraguan authorities. The Bank thereafter agreed to maintain a representative in the country for a further period to help in the initial stages of the program's operation.

Somewhat more limited programming assistance has been given to Mexico, Chile and Uruguay. In the case of Mexico, an arrangement was made between the government and the Bank to establish a joint working party, consisting of two Mexican and two Bank economists, to assess the major long-term trends in the Mexican economy with particular reference to Mexico's ability to absorb additional foreign investment. The report of this working party, which has been published both by the government in Spanish and by the Bank in English, covers much of the same ground, and has served many of the same purposes as the usual survey mission report. In the case of both Chile and Uruguay, the Bank joined with FAO in sponsoring missions to analyze the agricultural sectors of those countries' economies and to formulate recommendations for the further development of agricultural production.

Although the Bank's activities in the field of development programming are still too recent for full evaluation of their effectiveness, the results to date are encouraging. For example, in Colombia the government established, at the suggestion of the Bank, a nonpartisan Economic Development Committee to make a thorough study of the report of the Bank's mission and to recommend what action should be taken on the proposals contained in that report. This resulted in a number of steps being taken by the government to check inflation, relax foreign exchange controls, strengthen the Central Bank, and liberalize policies regarding the import and export of capital. A National Planning Council was then established to carry on the work of development programming and a Bank staff member, on leave of absence, has been serving as the Council's top planning adviser; a Bank-nominated economist has also been appointed as the Council's fiscal adviser. An extensive program to reorganize and rehabilitate the railroads, drawn up by engineering consultants employed by the government in cooperation with the Bank, is now being carried out with the aid of a Bank loan. The Bank has also made two loans to support an extensive program for rehabilitating and maintaining the Colombian highway system and has advised on the organization and staffing of a new highway maintenance service.

Considerable action has resulted from the assistance rendered to Nicaragua. The government has accepted the program recommended by the Bank's representatives as the basis for its future economic policy; it has organized a National Economic Council to coordinate the government's economic activities and to supervise execution of the program; legislation has been enacted establishing a National Development Institute to promote the growth of industry and agriculture; a Budget Bureau has been organized and budgets prepared providing for a marked increase in development expenditures; an income tax law has been passed; customs duties and the general tax structure are being studied and revised; substantial foreign obligations have been prepaid; the mining laws and power development policy have been revised; and a consultant nominated by the Bank has been employed by the government to assist in improving operation of the railroad.

Similarly, the Government of Ceylon is engaged in an intensive study of the Bank's mission report on its economy. A Planning Committee of the Cabinet, assisted by a Planning Secretariat, has been established substantially as recommended by the mission. And mission recommendations have been taken into account in connection with government decisions on the initiation or continuance of a number of industrial projects. Legislation is also under preparation for the establishment of a development financing institution suggested by the mission.

In Jamaica, the government has announced its adoption in principle of the main recommendations of the Bank mission and is taking steps to implement them. The Government of Uruguay has requested a loan to carry out part of the program recommended by the mission to that country. And in Iraq, recent development budgets indicate that governmental thinking has been substantially influenced by the investment recommendations of the mission to that country.

Other Technical Assistance

In March 1952, the Governments of India and Pakistan accepted an invitation from the President of the Bank to send engineers to the Bank to study, together with Bank engineers, possible technical measures to increase the supplies of water available from the Indus system of rivers for purposes of economic development. The working party, since its first meeting in May 1952, has been collecting data and making technical studies regarding the characteristics of the river system, the historic manner of its use and the facilities required to permit additional uses. The function of the working party is to work out a plan by which the supplies of water effectively available to each country can be increased substantially.

The major concentration of the rest of the Bank's technical assistance program has been in connection with problems of mobilizing local capital. In several countries, including Iceland, Turkey, Panama, Ethiopia and Nicaragua, development financing institutions have been established, or existing institutions reorganized, with the aid of consultants employed or recommended by the Bank or of Bank staff members; and Bank loans have sometimes been made to help in the financing of such institutions. In connection with a Bank loan to El Salvador in 1949 to finance the foreign exchange costs of a major hydroelectric project on the Rio Lempa, the Bank lent the services of its then Director of Marketing to advise the Salvadorian authorities on the issuance of bonds within the country to finance the local currency costs of the project. Similarly, at the request of the Philippine Government, the Bank's Director of Marketing visited Manila in 1952 to advise on the development of a government bond market. Assistance of the same general nature has been provided by Bank consultants to Cuba and Colombia.

In recent years, the Bank has received an increasing number of requests to nominate experts for employment directly by member governments in such positions as economic or financial adviser, head of a development bank or central bank, or adviser to a governmental planning agency. Sometimes, as in the case of the Honduran Development Bank, the Colombian Planning Office and the Turkish Industrial Development Bank, the Bank has given staff members leaves of absence, or permitted them to resign, to accept positions of this sort; sometimes it has sought to recruit qualified outside experts. Other technical assistance activities have been too varied to permit convenient summarization. They have included the provision of advice to several countries on fiscal problems, the study by Bank experts, or by experts recommended by the Bank, of the problems of particular industries, and advice on major economic and financial policies. The principal activities of this type undertaken by the Bank are included in the country-by-country description of Bank operations contained in Part III.

Training Programs

Another type of service furnished by the Bank, closely allied in purpose to the technical assistance activities just described, has consisted of training programs designed primarily to give officials of member countries information about the Bank and its policies and methods, a better understanding of economic development problems and techniques, and particular knowledge of various phases of financial administration.

The Bank's General Training Program, now entering its sixth year, is its major training activity. Including the 1954 class recently selected, 47 young men and women from 40 countries, mostly junior career officials, have participated or are participating in this program. During each course, which lasts 11 months, the participants attend lectures and discussions on such subjects as economics of development, balance of payments, national income accounting, project preparation and analysis, private foreign investment and International Bank policies and procedures. The trainees make case studies of development experience in different countries and of the possible application of that experience to their own countries. One week is devoted to a visit to the Tennessee Valley Authority, and another is spent visiting securities exchanges and financial institutions in New York. Short courses in national income accounting at the Department of Commerce and in balance of payments analysis at the International Monetary Fund are included. Balancing this academic work, the trainees are assigned to various departments of the Bank for several months in order that they may work closely with Bank staff members on practical operating problems.

In addition to this General Training Program, the Bank over the past three years has provided individually specialized training for 24 more senior officials from 11 different countries. These officials usually remain about six months and obtain training in the general work of the Bank, the preparation of projects for

Bank financing, and various aspects of public administration, such as budgeting, tax administration and central bank administration. In making arrangements for this type of training the Bank has sought and received the cooperation of many agencies of the United States Government, the Canadian Government, state and local governments in the United States, and a number of private financial institutions.

9

Marketing of Bank Securities

As of December 31, 1953, the total of direct and guaranteed obligations of the Bank outstanding was equivalent to nearly $682.6 million. In all, 14 public issues of Bank securities have been marketed since the start of operations—eight in the United States, four in Switzerland and one each in Canada and the United Kingdom—and two additional Swiss issues were sold at private sale.

This Chapter is devoted to a discussion, not only of the bonds which have been issued and the methods which have been employed to issue them, but also of some of the more important policy considerations which have affected Bank marketing activities. The Chapter also contains a discussion of portfolio sales and loan participations.

Policy Considerations

At Bretton Woods, it was generally contemplated that the major part of the Bank's operations would take the form of guarantees by the Bank of loans made by private investors, rather than of direct borrowing and lending by the Bank. In practice, the operations of the Bank have not developed in that direction, except to the extent, noted later in this Chapter, that it sells part of its loans with its guarantee. There are a number of reasons for this. In the first place, when the Bank started operations its own credit had not yet been established and, as a consequence, it was believed likely that loans guaranteed by the Bank would sell in the market at varying interest rates, depending on the credit of the borrowing country. This would have reflected adversely on the credit of the Bank. Moreover, since securities guaranteed by the Bank would not have been as readily marketable as direct obligations of the Bank, use of the guarantee technique would have increased the cost of money to the Bank's members. In addition, the Bank found that private investors showed very little interest in this type of transaction. Consequently, the Bank concluded that the practical course to follow was to concentrate on selling its own bonds in the market and using the proceeds for direct Bank loans.

The scale and timing of the Bank's marketing activities have generally been determined by the scope of its lending operations. The Bank originally followed the highly conservative practice of having on hand funds available for disbursement equal to at least 100% of all loan commitments, even though disbursements under the loans were expected to stretch over three or four years. As the market for the Bank's bonds became better established, this requirement was somewhat relaxed but the Bank still maintains the practice of keeping on hand funds sufficient to cover at least a year's estimated disbursements.

Because of the difficulties involved in introducing a new security to the market, the Bank decided at an early date that it would not be desirable to wait, before floating an initial issue in any member country, until the 18% portion of that country's capital subscription had been fully utilized. This policy was designed to enable the Bank to take advantage of any favorable opportunity to prepare the various securities markets for Bank issues and to establish Bank obligations in those markets. Except for these initial issues, however, the Bank has followed the general principle

97

of borrowing only those amounts needed for a reasonable period ahead of the several currencies required for its lending operations.

The United States market has been and in all likelihood will for many years continue to be the major source of Bank funds (see page 103). Nonetheless, it has consistently been the Bank's policy to develop as broad an international market as practicable for its obligations. The more non-dollar currencies, useful in Bank lending, which the Bank can raise, the greater will be its ability to satisfy the financial requirements of its borrowers. Moreover, as a continuing international lender which must go to the market periodically to finance its operations, it is important to the Bank that it should be able to tap as many sources of capital as possible and should not be unduly dependent on any one source. The creation of a broad demand for Bank obligations, both dollar and non-dollar, by investors outside the United States strengthens the position of the Bank's outstanding securities and facilitates future borrowing operations, whether in dollar or non-dollar currencies.

The Bank believes that the advantages to be gained from selling obligations in markets outside the United States are sufficient to justify, if necessary, paying somewhat higher interest charges than would be required for the sale of dollar obligations. Although in the case of all the issues sold outside the United States, except the last two Swiss issues, the interest rates were higher than the rates prevailing at the time in the United States, the differentials were not unduly large and the amounts sold were sufficiently small in relation to outstanding dollar issues as not significantly to affect the average cost of money to the Bank. The Bank has not given serious consideration to borrowing in markets where the discrepancy in interest levels has been very wide.

The United States Market

When the Bank first contemplated selling an issue of bonds in the United States market, it found itself confronted with two obstacles of major proportions. The first was the general attitude of the investment community which was almost completely unfamiliar with the Bank and the character of its obligations and which viewed with considerable mistrust any investment partaking of the nature of foreign lending. In order to overcome this obstacle, the Bank was required to engage in an intensive and continuing informational program, designed to familiarize investors throughout the United States with the nature and functions of the Bank, its financial structure and its methods of operation.

In the second place, investments by institutional investors in the United States, such as savings and commercial banks, insurance companies and trusts, which constitute by far the largest group of potential purchasers of the Bank's securities, are strictly regulated by the laws of the several states and, in certain instances, by federal law. When the Bank started operations in June 1946, there were only a few states where institutional investors could legally invest in the Bank's securities and thus most of the important channels of investment in the United States were closed to the Bank. This situation existed not because of any intentional design to limit investment in the Bank's securities but because the framers of the various legal investment laws did not have in mind a new type of institution such as the Bank.

Accordingly, in 1947 the Bank undertook a wide program to qualify its securities for institutional investment in the United States. This program met with considerable success; the Bank has succeeded in obtaining legislation or administrative rulings permitting the Bank's bonds to be bought by the principal classes of institutional investors in practically all the states having large aggregations of institutional funds. As of December 31, 1953, the Bank's bonds were, subject to various statutory and administrative qualifications of general application, legal investments for commercial banks in 45 states and the District of Columbia, for savings banks in 27 states and the District of Columbia,[1] for life insurance companies in 40 states, for non-life insurance companies in 37 states, and for trust funds in 36 states and the District of Columbia.

In addition to this action by the states, federal action was necessary in order to permit the national banks to assist in the marketing of Bank issues. When the Bank commenced operations, the national banks were prohibited under the National Bank Act from underwriting and dealing in the Bank's bonds, although they were permitted to underwrite and deal in United States Government, state and municipal bonds. Moreover, while government bonds were accorded exemptions under the Securities Act of 1933 and the Securities Exchange Act of 1934, these exemptions were not extended to Bank bonds which, instead, were placed in essentially the same category as private corporate obligations.

The Bank's marketing activities were greatly facilitated, therefore, when the United States Congress, in 1949, enacted legislation (Public Law 142—81st Cong.; Act of June 29, 1949) amending the National Bank Act and the Bretton Woods Agreements Act to deal with this situation. The amendment to the National Bank Act permits national banks and state member banks of the Federal Reserve System to deal in and underwrite securities issued by the Bank up to 10% of their unimpaired paid-in capital stock and unimpaired surplus, provided those securities are at the time eligible for purchase by national banks for their own account. Pursuant to a ruling by the U. S. Comptroller of the Currency, Bank bonds are eligible for purchase by national banks for their own account up to 10% of their capital and surplus and are also eligible as security for U. S. Government deposits. The amendment to the Bretton Woods Agreements Act exempts securities issued or guaranteed by the Bank from certain provisions of the Securities Act of 1933 and the Securities Exchange Act of 1934,

---

[1] Only 36 states have separate savings banks.

in effect according them the same general treatment under those Acts as U. S. Government, state and municipal bonds.[2]

As a result of this legislation United States banks have played a substantial role in the distribution of the Bank's bonds both as underwriters and distributors. In addition to participating in the initial distribution of the Bank's bonds, certain of the larger banks have also dealt in the bonds, thus helping to broaden the market for them.

United States Issues

Pertinent data about the eight public issues which the Bank has sold in the United States are shown in Table 10 below; as indicated at a later point (see page 111), substantial amounts of these dollar bonds are held by investors outside the United States.

The bonds have become well seasoned and are now generally regarded as investments of high quality. All issues are rated " AA " or the equivalent by the three largest bond rating services in the United States, except that two issues are rated " AAA " by one of these services. The market action of the bonds has compared very favorably, not only with high grade corporate bonds, but also with United States Government bonds.

The Bank has marketed its bonds in the United States in a number of different ways, adjusting its selling techniques from

---

[2] The legislation calls for the Bank to file with the Securities and Exchange Commission such reports with respect to its securities as the Commission determines to be appropriate in view of the official character of the Bank and its operations and to be necessary in the public interest or for the protection of investors; requires the Securities and Exchange Commission and the National Advisory Council on International Monetary and Financial Problems to file periodic reports with the Congress as to the effect of the Act on the Bank's operation and permits the Securities and Exchange Commission, acting in consultation with the National Advisory Council, to suspend the exemption granted the Bank's obligations from the Securities Acts. Under rules promulgated by the Commission, reports are required in connection with each public issue by the Bank in the United States. These reports are designed to make available at the Commission information similar to that which would have to be included in a registration statement filed under the Securities Act of 1933.

time to time on the basis of its experience. The initial issues offered in 1947 were sold on an agency basis through approximately 1,700 security dealers; the next issue was sold early in 1950 through competitive bidding to a group of commercial banks and investment banking firms; and for the two issues sold in 1951,

TABLE 10

BOND ISSUES IN THE UNITED STATES

Date	Description of Issue
July 15, 1947	$150,000,000, Twenty-Five-Year 3% Bonds, due July 15, 1972.
July 15, 1947	$100,000,000, Ten-Year 2¼% Bonds, due July 15, 1957, refunded in 1950.
February 15, 1950	$100,000,000, 2% Serial Bonds of 1950, due 1952-1962, used to refund the 1947 issue of the same amount.
March 1, 1951	$50,000,000, 3% Twenty-Five-Year Bonds of 1951, due March 1, 1976.
October 1, 1951	$100,000,000, 3¼% Thirty-Year Bonds of 1951, due October 1, 1981.
May 15, 1952	$50,000,000, 3⅜% Twenty-Three-Year Bonds of 1952, due May 15, 1975.
October 15, 1952	$60,000,000, 3½% Nineteen-Year Bonds of 1952, due 1971.
October 1, 1953	$75,000,000, 3% Three-Year Bonds of 1953, due 1956.

the agency method was again used but with a much smaller number of participating banks and investment firms.

In order to achieve greater continuity, to induce a more active sales effort, and to develop an increasingly broader market for Bank obligations, the Bank adopted in 1952 the technique of a direct negotiated underwriting, a technique which has been employed in all subsequent issues. The underwriting was done by a nation-wide syndicate of large investment banking firms, commercial banks and dealers headed by Morgan Stanley & Co.

and The First Boston Corporation. The syndicate, in turn, organized a selling group consisting of a large number of investment dealers throughout the United States to facilitate the distribution.

In connection with the $75 million issue of the Bank's Three-Year Bonds in September 1953, a part of the issue, for the first time in a Bank dollar bond offering, was sold through an underwriter outside the United States, a Dutch banking group headed by the Netherlands Trading Society, which in turn sold a part of the bonds underwritten by it through public subscription. A part of the same issue was also sold through banking groups not acting as underwriters in Switzerland, the United Kingdom, Belgium and Sweden.

The Federal Reserve Bank of New York has been designated as fiscal agent for the Bank in connection with each of its bond issues in the United States. As such, the Federal Reserve Bank handles payments of principal and interest, registration, transfer and exchanges of bonds, and other miscellaneous fiscal functions.

Swiss Issues

The Bank now has outstanding five issues in Switzerland totalling Sw. fr. 218.5 million, equivalent to about $50.8 million. Four of these issues were sold to the public by a syndicate of leading Swiss banks headed by the Swiss Bank Corporation, the Credit Suisse and the Union Bank of Switzerland; two other issues were sold at private sale but one of these has since been refunded. Except for a 2½% serial bond issue due from 1954 to 1956, the maturities of the bonds range from 10 to 15 years and the interest rate is 3½%.

Although not a member of the Bank, Switzerland has entered into an agreement with the Bank which recognizes its international personality and legal capacity and grants it facilities which correspond in large part to those which the Bank enjoys in the territories of its members. This has facilitated the Bank's marketing operations in Switzerland by clarifying its legal status there and by according it certain tax and other benefits.

United Kingdom Issue

The Bank has sold one public issue in the London market, an issue of 20-year bonds bearing interest at 3½%; the total amount of the issue was £5 million, equivalent to $14 million. This issue was sold in 1951 to a London syndicate of banking firms composed of Baring Brothers & Co., Ltd., Hambros Bank, Ltd., Lazard Brothers & Co., Ltd., Morgan Grenfell & Co., Ltd., N. M. Rothschild & Sons, and J. Henry Schroder & Co. The securities were, in turn, publicly offered throughout the United Kingdom by a large group of dealers. Baring Brothers & Co., Ltd., is fiscal agent for the issue. Various legal and administrative rulings were made to facilitate the marketing. In addition, special legislation was enacted by the United Kingdom exempting transfers of the securities from United Kingdom stamp duty. Since this stamp duty is a relatively substantial item, the exemption was of particular benefit in the marketing of the securities.

Canadian Issue

The Bank has sold one public issue in Canada, an issue of Can. $15 million, 10-year 4% bonds. It was sold in 1952 by a Canadian syndicate of investment dealers and charter banks, headed by the Dominion Securities Corp. Limited, A. E. Ames & Co., Limited, and Wood, Gundy & Company, Limited. The Bank of Canada is fiscal agent for the issue. The marketing of the issue entailed essentially the same preparation, although in more limited scope, as the first United States issue. Rulings were obtained in various provinces of Canada facilitating the sale of the bonds. In addition, special legislation enacted by the Canadian Government in 1947 permitted insurance companies to invest in Bank obligations.

Action by Other Countries

In addition to the action taken by the governments of those countries in which the Bank has sold issues, a number of other governments have taken various steps to broaden the market for Bank bonds in their territories. The Netherlands Government, for example, has facilitated the introduction of Bank bonds in the Amsterdam market by exempting from requisitioning Netherlands Trustee Certificates issued against certain bonds of the Bank. As a result these Trustee Certificates have been listed on the Amsterdam Stock Exchange and purchases of Bank bonds have been made in the United States market for the account of Netherlands investors, who exchange the bonds for Trustee Certificates. The French Government has authorized the listing on the Paris Bourse of various bond issues of the Bank. French foreign exchange regulations permit residents of France to purchase the bonds in the United States with dollars acquired through the sale of other dollar securities in the United States. Bonds so acquired are officially traded on the Paris Bourse and may be purchased directly against French francs. In Turkey, the Ministry of Finance has registered the Bank's bonds on the Istanbul Stock Exchange, according them the privileges and registration fee exemptions accorded to Turkish state obligations. Australia and Canada have taken action to make the bonds permissible investments for insurance companies and South Africa has made them eligible for investment by commercial banks. Chile, Cuba, Colombia and Mexico have classified the bonds as legal investments for banks and other financial institutions and have permitted those institutions to invest part of their foreign exchange reserves in Bank bonds.

Various of the Bank's issues are now listed on securities exchanges in the following cities outside the United States: London, Paris, Amsterdam, Brussels, Antwerp, Luxembourg, Zurich, Basle, Geneva, Lausanne, Berne and Mexico City.

Type of Bond Sold by Bank

All bonds issued by the Bank are its direct obligations. None of them is backed by pledge of assets. The bonds contain a provision to the effect that, with a minor exception, the Bank will not pledge any of its assets to secure other debt unless the bonds share *pro rata* in such pledge. The bonds state, as required by the Articles of Agreement, that they are not an obligation of any government.

All of the issues, except the Swiss issues and two United States issues, contain sinking fund provisions obligating the Bank to purchase or redeem bonds for sinking fund purposes in varying amounts during the life of the particular issue. Each issue, except one United States issue, is subject to redemption prior to maturity at the option of the Bank upon varying conditions.

Holders of Bank bonds do not, as such, enjoy any general exemption from tax on the interest paid to them on the bonds. Under the Articles, as noted in Chapter 4, the bonds and the interest thereon are not subject to any tax (1) which discriminates against the bonds solely because they are issued by the Bank, or (2) the sole jurisdictional basis for which is the place or currency in which the bonds are issued, made payable or paid, or the location of any office or place of business maintained by the Bank. Also, under the Articles, the Bank is not under any obligation to withhold or pay any tax on the interest on the bonds.

As regards United States taxation, the United States Treasury Department has ruled that interest on bonds issued by the Bank is exempt from United States income taxes, including withholding taxes, if paid to an individual who is not a national or resident of the United States, or to a corporation organized under the laws of a country other than the United States, whether or not such corporation is engaged in trade or business in the United States, unless the corporation is a life insurance company and the interest is attributable, within the meaning of the United States

Internal Revenue Code, to the company's insurance business in the United States. Comparable tax rulings have also been made in certain other member countries where the question has arisen because of the sale of Bank bonds in those countries.

Portfolio Sales and Loan Participations

From time to time the Bank has replenished its funds by selling portions of loans from its portfolio, with or without its guarantee. While these transactions have not been substantial in comparison with the Bank's public issues, they have proved a useful adjunct to the Bank's direct borrowing operations. In addition, the Bank has been able from time to time to arrange for private investors to participate with the Bank in making loans.

Portfolio sales and loan participations have taken a variety of different forms, each designed to suit the particular circumstances involved. In most cases, the portfolio sale, whether with or without guarantee, has been arranged for subsequent to the making of the loan sold. The purchasers have generally been institutional investors, primarily banks and insurance companies, both in the United States and in other countries. Most of the sales have been of early maturities.

In several cases, however, the Bank has sold obligations of its borrowers as part of the original loan transaction. For example, in 1948 the Bank made a $12 million 10-year loan to four Dutch shipping companies, receiving notes in that amount from the shipping companies. The Bank then sold, as part of the same transaction, $8.1 million of those notes, with the Bank's guarantee, to a group of 10 United States commercial and savings banks. The notes sold consisted of all those maturing in the first six years and part of those maturing in the seventh year. Later, the balance of the notes were sold to similar accounts. In a comparable transaction, the Bank sold to a group of private banks and an insurance company in the United States, with its guarantee, bonds representing the $16 million loan which it made to the Kingdom of Belgium in 1949.[3]

In several cases private interests have directly participated with the Bank in making loans. For example, in connection with the loans of $40 million made in 1953 for three Japanese power companies, two contractors supplying equipment to the power companies, Westinghouse Electric International Company and International General Electric Company, participated in the loans to the extent of approximately $6 million. A similar arrangement was made in connection with the loan in 1952 of $7 million to K. L. M., the Royal Dutch Airlines. In that case the Chase National Bank of the City of New York participated to the extent of 50% of the loan. In both instances, the private interests took the early maturities.

A different type of arrangement was made in connection with the 1951 loans of $50 million in the Union of South Africa. In that case a group of eight United States commercial banks, in addition to extending an existing $20 million revolving credit, made a new $10 million loan to the Union of South Africa concurrently with the Bank's loans. The Bank adjusted the maturities on its loans so as to permit the private banks to take the earlier maturities. Thus, in effect, the Bank loans and the private financing constituted one credit transaction to meet the Union's capital requirements.

Table 11 below shows the total amount of loans sold and agreed to be sold by the Bank, with and without its guarantee:

---

[3] When portfolio sales are made with the Bank's guarantee, the Bank continues to collect from the borrower the 1% commission charged on all loans for purposes of the special reserve. When such sales are made without guarantee, the Bank ceases to collect the commission and as a matter of practice gives the borrower the advantage up to 1% of the differential, if any, between the rate of interest provided for in the loan contract and the rate of interest at which the notes representing the loan are sold by the Bank.

TABLE 11

LOANS SOLD AND AGREED TO BE SOLD

(*In U. S. dollar equivalents*)

	Total principal amount sold and agreed to be sold	Amount matured or retired before maturity
With guarantee	$54,875,844	$25,757,901
Without guarantee	29,177,194 *	4,287,154
	$84,053,038	$30,045,055

---

* Arrangements have been made to sell an additional $997,000 after the loan involved becomes effective.

Holders of Bank Obligations

Of the total of direct and guaranteed obligations of the Bank outstanding on December 31, 1953, equivalent to approximately $682.6 million, investors in the United States were estimated to hold about $443 million, or roughly 65%, distributed approximately as follows: life insurance companies, 19%; savings banks, 19%; pension and trust funds, 20%; commercial banks and other investors, 7%.

Investors outside the United States have in recent years purchased progressively larger amounts of Bank obligations. In 1953, for example, they purchased the great majority of all guaranteed obligations sold by the Bank, in addition to acquiring substantial additional amounts of the Bank's own bonds. It is noteworthy that, of the $75 million issue of the Bank's Three-Year Bonds sold in September 1953, more than $40 million were sold to investors outside the United States: $20 million to central banks and special funds in 12 countries; $10 million in Switzerland; $5 million in the Netherlands; $3.5 million in the United Kingdom; and $1 million each in Belgium and Sweden.

It is estimated that investors outside the United States now hold about 35% of the Bank's direct and guaranteed obligations, or the equivalent of about $240 million. Of this amount, these investors held about $150 million of the Bank's direct dollar bonds, about $13 million of dollar obligations guaranteed by the Bank, and about $77 million of the Bank's bonds payable in currencies other than dollars. These investors include central banks in 17 countries.

Table 12 below shows the estimated distribution of holdings of the Bank's direct and guaranteed obligations:

TABLE 12

ESTIMATED DISTRIBUTION OF BANK OBLIGATIONS

(*In U. S. dollar equivalents*)

United States	Amount	% of Total
Savings Banks	$132.5	19.4
Pension and Trust Funds	133.0	19.5
Life Insurance Companies	131.0	19.2
Commercial banks and others	46.5	6.8
	$443.0	64.9
Investors Outside the United States	239.6	35.1
TOTAL:	$682.6	100.0

10

Bank Activities in Support of
Private International Investment

General

One of the major purposes of the Bank, as stated in its Articles of Agreement, is to promote private international investment. In a sense, all of the Bank's lending activities may be regarded as promoting such investment, since as already noted, the Bank's loan funds have been derived in large and increasing measure from placing its own securities in the private capital markets of its member countries. Bank action in making the portfolio sales and in arranging for the loan participations described in the preceding Chapter has also had the effect of mobilizing private savings for international investment.

Quite apart from the source of its funds, most of the Bank's loans for the expansion of basic public utility facilities have served to help either in removing obstacles to or creating new productive opportunities for private capital, both foreign and domestic. Since most of these facilities are still under construction or have only recently been completed, it is not yet possible to undertake a broad survey of their effect in opening up investment opportunities for private capital. Nevertheless, there is every reason to believe that the effects have already been substantial and will be increasingly significant. For example, the Bank loans in the Rhodesias and the Belgian Congo for the expansion of transportation and power are obviously promoting a continuation of the private capital inflows which have recently been playing such a large part in the development of those areas. Similarly, the power facilities which the Bank is helping to finance throughout Latin America have doubtless contributed significantly to the process of industrialization which is now gaining momentum there, financed in part by private foreign enterprises.

In a number of ways, too, the Bank has sought to improve the general climate for foreign private investment. For one thing, as has already been indicated, the influence of the Bank has frequently been exerted to encourage borrowing countries to adopt economic and financial policies conducive to development, such as measures to achieve economic and monetary stability and to remove unnecessary or discriminatory exchange restrictions. Moreover, the Bank takes into account, in connection with the consideration of loan applications, the willingness of the borrowing country to provide fair treatment to investors and to rehabilitate its credit standing where that may be necessary. Again, it adheres rigidly to the principle that it will not finance projects for which private capital is available on reasonable terms; indeed, it has sometimes been influential in arranging for private financing of projects originally presented for Bank financing. And through its technical assistance and advisory services, the Bank has often had occasion to point out the role which private investment, foreign as well as domestic, can perform in strengthening the economy of the country concerned and the conditions which appear necessary to attract private capital from abroad.

Some improvement in the investment climate is clearly discernible. It is significant that nearly two-thirds of the publicly held external debt of member countries which was in default at the end of 1946 has now been settled or is in negotiation. With respect to publicly held foreign bonds of member countries and their political subdivisions issued in the United States almost one-third were in default at the end of 1945, while by the end of 1952 less than 6% were in default. And an increasing number of countries are removing or reducing discriminatory restrictions and taking other measures to attract an increased flow of foreign private capital.

International Finance Corporation Proposal

In March 1951, the United States International Development Advisory Board published a report entitled *Partners in Progress*. This report, prepared after consultation with the management of the Bank, proposed, among other things, that an International Finance Corporation be created as an affiliate of the Bank which would be authorized to make loans to private enterprise without governmental guarantee and to make equity investments in participation with private investors.

This proposal was prompted by a recognition that the ability of the Bank itself to finance the establishment or expansion of private undertakings is limited. For the reasons already pointed out in Chapter 5 (see page 57), the guarantee requirement is a serious obstacle to Bank loans to private enterprises. And the fact that the Bank does not engage in equity financing has meant that the Bank has sometimes had to abandon consideration of promising private projects because they required more equity capital than the entrepreneur was able to obtain.

The Bank has attempted to overcome these limitations in some cases by extending credits to private undertakings through a local development bank. This type of lending has been useful and the Bank hopes to do more of it. Intermediary institutions of this kind, however, cannot entirely escape the necessity of governmental sanction; and the extent to which borrowed funds can be used for equity investment is obviously limited. Moreover, these institutions are not well placed to attract the interest and

113

participation of foreign firms and investors in the projects they finance.

Accordingly, the management of the Bank felt that the proposal for an International Finance Corporation deserved careful study by the staff. The results of this study were embodied in a report on the proposal made public in May 1952. The report envisages that the capital of the Corporation would be subscribed by member governments since it was not believed that the Corporation would be able to raise substantial funds by the sale of securities in private markets and, even apart from legal considerations, the provision of funds by the Bank was considered inappropriate. The purpose of the Corporation would be to promote economic development through the stimulation of private investment, "by bringing together investment opportunities, capital (both domestic and foreign) and experienced management, and by helping to finance private productive undertakings through equity investment and loans without government guarantee." The Corporation would not accept responsibility for managing an enterprise in which it invested, and would not hold a controlling equity interest in it. No special immunity or status would attach to any enterprise solely by reason of the Corporation's participation. The Corporation would attempt to revolve its funds as rapidly as possible by selling securities in its portfolio whenever possible at a fair price.

The Corporation is presented in the report as an experiment in stimulating international private investment. In the words of the report, "Although the extent to which the Corporation could generate such flow of capital can be determined only by experience, there are good reasons for concluding that over a period of years the Corporation would be able to give a substantial stimulus to the growth of private enterprise and thus contribute significantly to the further development of the Bank's member countries."

The President of the Bank sent a copy of this report, through the Secretary-General of the United Nations, to the Economic and Social Council as had been requested by it. In transmitting the report, he called attention to the fact that the Executive Directors of the Bank, in authorizing its transmittal, did not express any opinion on the merits of the proposal or any opinion on behalf of the governments they represented. In June 1952 the Economic and Social Council considered the report and adopted a resolution requesting the Bank to continue its study in consultation with member governments and interested business and financial groups, and to inform the Council of the results of its study and of any action it might take on the proposal.

Subsequent exploration of the matter by the Bank with its member governments indicated that while the less developed countries, almost without exception, supported the proposal, most of the more highly developed countries, on which the proposed Corporation would necessarily have to depend for the greater part of its funds, although expressing sympathetic interest in the proposal, were not ready to commit themselves to subscribe to its capital. Some of these countries based their inability to commit themselves on their present economic circumstances. Others indicated doubts about particular aspects of the project. Reaction to the proposal in business and financial communities was also very mixed. The Bank set forth these facts in a second report, published in May 1953, in which the Bank's management expressed its belief that, unless and until there appeared to be a reasonable prospect that sufficient financial participation for the Corporation would be forthcoming, no point would be served by greater formalization of the project. The management expressed its intention, however, to continue its explorations with member countries.

This second report was considered by the Economic and Social Council during the summer of 1953 and by the General Assembly during the fall of that year. Those bodies have requested the Bank to analyze in detail the questions raised and views expressed about the Corporation by governments and non-governmental institutions, to continue its consultations with its members in a more intensive manner, and to report on these matters to the Economic and Social Council at its 1954 summer session.

The Bank is continuing its study of the project with a view to presenting concrete proposals to its member governments for their consideration if and when enough capital for the Corporation appears likely to be made available.

PART III

Country-by-Country Summary of Bank Activities

Bank Activities

THIS SECTION CONTAINS a country-by-country description of the Bank's activities. Representatives of the Bank have visited nearly all of the 55 member countries; the great majority of the members have had discussions with the Bank looking forward to possible financing, or have sought technical advice from the Bank on development problems or projects. In the interests of brevity, this account is confined to countries in which loans actually have been made or where substantial technical assistance activities have been carried out.

Preceding the account of operations in each country is a list of the loans made in that country. Unless otherwise indicated, loans have been made to member governments; loans to other borrowers have the guarantee of the member governments concerned. The interest rates shown include the 1% commission allocated to the special reserve. Additional details, such as maturity dates of loans, amounts disbursed and repayments of principal, are shown in Appendix F.

ASIA AND THE MIDDLE EAST

Indus River System

In March 1952 the Governments of India and Pakistan accepted an invitation from the President of the Bank to send engineers to the Bank to study, together with Bank engineers, possible technical measures to increase the supplies of water available from the Indus system of rivers for purposes of economic development. The working party, since its first meeting in May 1952, has been collecting data and making technical studies regarding the characteristics of the river system, the historic manner of its use and the facilities required to permit additional uses. The function of the working party is to work out a plan by which the supplies of water effectively available to each country can be increased substantially.

ASIA

Ceylon

In the latter part of 1951 the Bank organized a general survey mission to study Ceylon's economic potentialities and to make recommendations to assist the Government in drawing up a long-range development program. The mission consisted of 12 experts, including a specialist provided by the Food and Agriculture Organization of the United Nations and one nominated by the World Health Organization. The mission's report was presented to the Government in July 1952.

For some generations past Ceylon's productivity has maintained a lead in the race with population. Today, the odds in the race are shifting. Anti-malarial measures taken during and since the war have sharply reduced the death rate and, as a result, Ceylon has one of the highest rates of population increase in the world—2.8% a year. Hitherto, Ceylon's national income has depended largely on tea, rubber and coconut products; but the mission

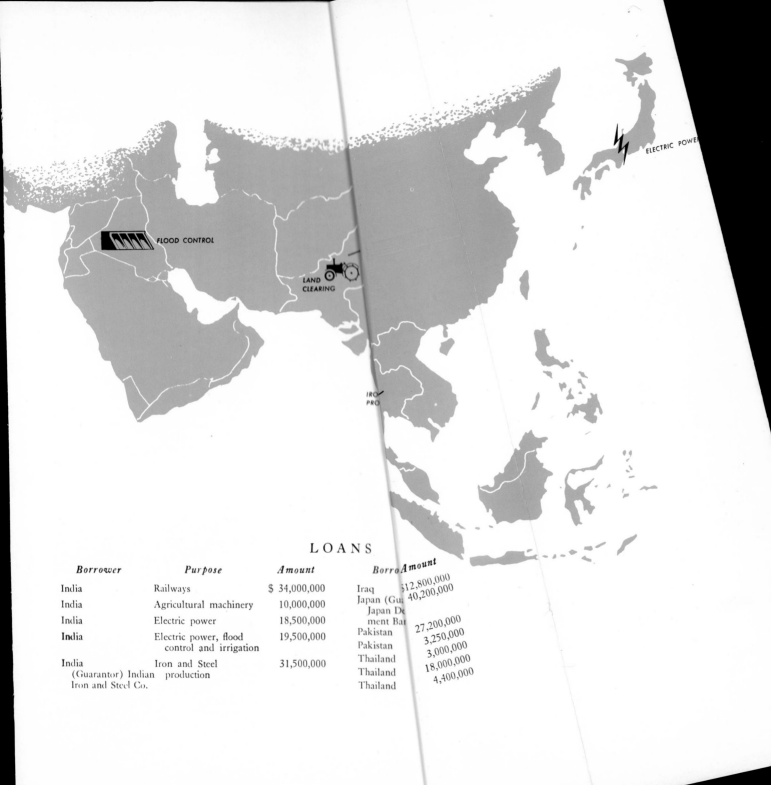

ELECTRIC POWER

FLOOD CONTROL

LAND
CLEARING

IRO
PRO

LOANS

Borrower	Purpose	Amount
India	Railways	$ 34,000,000
India	Agricultural machinery	10,000,000
India	Electric power	18,500,000
India	Electric power, flood control and irrigation	19,500,000
India (Guarantor) Indian Iron and Steel Co.	Iron and Steel production	31,500,000

Borro	Amount
Iraq	$12,800,000
Japan (Gua Japan De ment Ba	40,200,000
Pakistan	27,200,000
Pakistan	3,250,000
Thailand	3,000,000
Thailand	18,000,000
Thailand	4,400,000

pointed out that to maintain and raise the standard of living of its people Ceylon would have to expand and diversify the use of its productive resources.

The mission's report expressed the belief that Ceylon's resources in land, materials and money would be sufficient, if wisely managed, to meet the needs of the growing population, to improve the standard of living and to strengthen the economy. The report recommended a six-year program of development, designed largely to increase agricultural production. The report emphasized the need for improvement of agricultural techniques and for putting new lands under cultivation through irrigation, jungle clearance and settlement. It pointed out that the substantial investments proposed for electric power, industry and transport should also lead to higher output from the land. It stressed the need for surveys in many sectors—in particular water and irrigation, electric power, land use, soils and forests—and urged that, until these studies were completed, new large-scale schemes be deferred in favor of a greater number of smaller projects.

The mission suggested that a healthy industrial development could not be achieved without investment in education and research; that, in general, government management of factories should be avoided; and that, at first, encouragement should be given to small industries rather than to large projects which would make heavy demands on the limited financial, technical and managerial resources available. The mission recommended that the Government, in order to draw up and efficiently carry out development plans, should establish an economic committee of the Cabinet which would be served by a separate secretariat divorced from the regular departments of government and without departmental responsibilities.

The Government has given careful consideration to the mission's recommendations. The scale of investment has been set at about the level proposed by the mission; a planning secretariat has been established; work on some government industrial projects has been postponed and the Government is studying the possibilities of disposing of some of its factories to private interests; plans are being formulated for the establishment of a technical research institute which the Bank and the United Nations Technical Assistance Administration have offered to help organize; and consideration is being given to the creation of a development bank.

India

Fiscal 1950:	$34 million 15-year 4% loan of August 18, 1949 for railway rehabilitation; reduced at request of borrower on May 16, 1950 to $32.8 million, which had been disbursed by March 1951.
	$10 million 7-year 3½% loan of September 29, 1949 for importation of agricultural machinery; reduced to $8.5 million on July 27, 1951 and to $7.5 million on August 25, 1952 at request of borrower.
	$18.5 million 20-year 4% loan of April 18, 1950 for power development project.
Fiscal 1953:	$31.5 million 15-year 4¾% loan of December 18, 1952 to Indian Iron and Steel Company, Limited, for expansion of iron and steel production facilities.
	$19.5 million 25-year 4⅞% loan of January 23, 1953 for electric power development, flood control and irrigation.

The Bank's five loans in India have been for projects which have had high priority in the Government's plans for promoting the development of agriculture and industry. Before the Government drafted its Five Year Plan in 1950, the Bank had lent funds for the improvement of the national railways, for the reclamation of large tracts of land in central India, and for a thermal power project which was a first step in a larger scheme for developing the Damodar Valley of eastern India. Since work began on the Five Year Plan in 1951, the Bank has lent for projects within the Plan: for a second phase of Damodar Valley development and for the expansion of pig iron and steel production.

Railways

The Bank's first loan to India was made in August 1949 to aid the Government in completing a program to increase the carrying capacity of the railways. The railways are the most important means of transport in India and their efficiency is essential to the economy. During the war they deteriorated badly because of lack of maintenance and heavy military use. The Bank loan was to help remedy this situation by financing part of the cost of importing 418 locomotives, 16 spare boilers and miscellaneous spare parts. This equipment supplemented much larger purchases made by the Indian Government out of its own resources.

By 1950 delays in the movement of essential freight had been considerably reduced. Improved service also lessened a handicap to the expansion of India's mining and industrial capacity; it permitted such important commodities as manganese, iron, coal, coke and pig iron to move more freely in the country's internal and export trade. In addition to physical improvements, administrative and operational measures undertaken by the Indian Railway authorities contributed largely to improved efficiency.

Agriculture

The purpose of the second loan, for $10 million, was to purchase part of the heavy equipment needed to clear about one and a half million acres of land infested with kans grass, a deep-rooted weed, and for a pilot project to clear several thousand acres of jungle land. The restoration to cultivation of land infested by kans grass is expected at the end of seven years to add about 500,000 tons annually to India's production of food grains. The work is being carried out in central India by the Government's Central Tractor Organization. It is believed to be the largest land reclamation project in the world.

The Bank's loan financed the purchase of 240 tractors with equipment and spare parts for the kans grass project and 30 tractors and spare parts for the jungle-clearance operation. Organi-

123

zational and managerial difficulties were experienced in the earlier stages of the kans project but these have now been largely overcome and the rate of progress, although not up to original expectations, has improved. By the end of 1953, nearly three-quarters of a million acres had been cleared of kans and were being put under cultivation. Jungle-clearance operations in the Himalayan foothills have resulted in the reclamation and plowing of nearly 18,000 acres and have demonstrated that the clearance of jungle in India can be successfully carried out with mechanical equipment.

Damodar Valley Development

Two loans have been made for the development of the Damodar River Valley: $18.5 million in April 1950 and $19.5 million in January 1953. The Damodar Valley, extending northwest from Calcutta about 200 miles, lies in the richest mineral and the most highly developed industrial region in India. The region accounts for over three-quarters of India's total known coal deposits and practically all of its present coal production. In and near this area are India's rich iron ores, large deposits of bauxite, and high quality mica. In 1948 the Government established the Damodar Valley Corporation to carry out a unified scheme of development. The scheme includes flood control; the provision of 300,000 kilowatts of firm power for mining, industrial and domestic use; supplies of water for industrial and domestic use; an 80-mile navigation canal; and a system of canals to irrigate a million acres of land.

The Bank's loan of $18.5 million is being used for the construction of a thermal power plant at Bokaro with a capacity of 150,000 kilowatts, a dam at Konar to provide water for Bokaro and for future power installations, and a transmission system. The Bokaro plant is the largest thermal power plant in India and the first to use pulverized coal. By October 1953 all three of the 50,000 kilowatt generating units had been installed. It is expected that the transmission system will be finished early in 1954. The Konar dam is nearly completed.

The Bank's loan of $19.5 million is being used for a second group of projects within the Damodar Valley program. These are two multi-purpose dams, each with a hydroelectric plant, and an extensive irrigation system, including a diversion dam on the Damodar River. Apart from savings from the prevention of flood damage, the elimination of the danger of floods will remove an obstacle to industrial and agricultural investment. The power plants will have an installed capacity of 100,000 kilowatts and will complement the power being generated by the Bokaro steam plant. The irrigation system will include 1,550 miles of irrigation and drainage canals serving an area of one million acres in West Bengal. When fully developed the system should make possible the production of an additional 400,000 tons of foodgrains, mostly rice. The main irrigation canal will be 80 miles long and constructed to carry barge traffic; it is designed to relieve the over-burdened railways and provide a cheap means of transporting coal and other goods between the Valley and Calcutta.

Iron and Steel

The $31.5 million lent to the Indian Iron and Steel Company (IISCO) was the first Bank loan made directly to a private manufacturer. It resulted from recommendations made by a Bank mission to India which examined means of increasing iron and steel production to facilitate execution of the Five Year Plan. Iron is needed primarily for farm equipment and steel for the construction of irrigation and flood control works, hydroelectric plants, the extension of railroads and roads, and new housing. Demands for steel are now considerably larger than can be met by Indian producers and substantial amounts of foreign exchange are spent each year for steel imports.

The Bank's loan will be used to finance imported equipment

125

and services for a five-year project to increase IISCO's annual capacity from 350,000 tons to 700,000 tons of finished steel, and from 160,000 tons to 400,000 tons of pig iron for sale to foundries. When this project is completed, finished steel capacity in India will be about one-third higher than in 1952, and foundry iron capacity will be doubled.

Japan

> Fiscal $21.5 million 20-year 5% loan of October 15, 1953 to Japan
> 1954: Development Bank to be re-lent to Kansai Electric Power Company, Inc. for power development.
>
> $11.2 million 20-year 5% loan of October 15, 1953 to Japan Development Bank to be re-lent to Kyushu Electric Power Company, Inc. for power development.
>
> $7.5 million 20-year 5% loan of October 15, 1953 to Japan Development Bank to be re-lent to Chubu Electric Power Company, Inc. for power development.

The Bank's three loans will help to finance the construction of three high-efficiency thermal power stations being built by private companies in central and south Japan. The new power will help to meet the demands of industrial plants manufacturing metals, machinery, textiles and chemicals, and of coal mines and shipyards. These industries are expected to expand substantially over the next five years and are of key importance in Japan's efforts to improve its international balance of payments by increasing exports.

Although power production has increased markedly since the war, supply is still running behind demand and shortage of power is seriously limiting the growth of industrial production. To help meet the demands for power, Japan's public utility companies are planning to add 2.9 million kilowatts to their generating capacity by 1957. The projects being assisted by the Bank will make up about one-tenth of this total.

The borrower, the Japan Development Bank, will re-lend the

proceeds of the Bank's loans as follows: $21.5 million to the Kansai Electric Power Company, Inc.; $11.2 million to the Kyushu Electric Power Company, Inc.; and $7.5 million to the Chubu Electric Power Company, Inc. The three companies serve approximately 30% of the total area of Japan containing about 40% of the population. In 1951 they generated nearly two-fifths of all the electric power produced in Japan.

The new Kansai plant will be situated in central Japan at Tanagawa on Osaka Bay. It will have two steam units of 75,000 kilowatts each, designed to operate at high temperatures and pressures. It will serve the highly industrialized cities of Osaka, Kobe, Sakai and Amagasaki. The Kyushu plant will have a capacity of 75,000 kilowatts and will be situated at Karita in southern Japan. This area accounts for more than half of Japan's coal production, and is also important for its production of basic metals and chemicals. The Chubu plant will have a capacity of 66,000 kilowatts, and will be located at Mie on Ise Bay, in central Japan. The area to be served includes the cities of Nagoya and Yokkaichi and contains many key export industries.

All three of the new thermal plants are scheduled to begin operations during 1956. The need for additional thermal capacity is particularly acute both because of wide seasonal fluctuations in the availability of hydroelectric power and because of the obsolescence of much existing thermal capacity. The new plants will add about 10% to the nominal thermal plant capacity (considerably more if effective capacity is taken as a base). Furthermore, the unit fuel requirements of the three new thermal plants will be half or less those of existing older installations and only about 60% of those in more modern Japanese generating plants.

Westinghouse Electric International Company and International General Electric Company are prime contractors for the supply of equipment and services being financed by the International Bank. The two companies have entered into arrangements with the Bank to participate in the loans to the extent of approximately

$6.1 million, and will be repaid from the early maturities of the loans.

Malaya

Late in 1953 the Bank completed the organization of a general survey mission to the Federation of Malaya and the Crown Colony of Singapore, and the mission was preparing to leave Washington to undertake its studies in the field. The mission has 13 members, of whom four were nominated by the Food and Agriculture Organization.

Thailand

Fiscal 1951:
$3 million 15-year 3¾% loan of October 27, 1950 for railway rehabilitation.

$18 million 20-year 4% loan of October 27, 1950 for irrigation project.

$4.4 million 15-year 3¾% loan of October 27, 1950 for port development.

The Bank's $3 million loan is financing a part of the Government's program for the rehabilitation of the railway system. At the end of the war, Thailand's railway system was left with half of its rolling stock unserviceable, and a large number of bridges, stations and workshops destroyed. Damage to workshops prevented repairs and proper maintenance of rolling stock and equipment both during and after the war, and the renewal of rails continued to be neglected.

The railway rehabilitation program of the Government includes the replacement of rails, rolling stock, bridges, stations and workshop equipment, and the improvement and increase in capacity of railway services. The Bank loan is being used to finance the foreign exchange cost of redesigning and reequipping the main railway workshops at Makkasan near Bangkok and the purchase of signaling equipment and of some spare parts. The improvement of the Makkasan Workshops will permit maintenance and repairs of rolling stock and locomotives. The signaling equipment will facilitate the safe movement of trains and thus increase the capacity of the railways.

Work at Makkasan is progressing satisfactorily. Several service buildings have been constructed and others are under construction, and the equipment is now in process of delivery. The workshops should be completed in the second half of 1954. Delivery of the signaling equipment is under way and some has been installed.

In June 1951, as part of its effort to improve the efficiency of the railway system, the Government created the State Railway of Thailand as an autonomous agency to be responsible for the management, operation and development of the railway system. In 1952 the Railway chose a general adviser, from several persons suggested by the Bank, to assist it in improving its operations.

The Bank's $18 million loan is financing the cost of imported equipment, materials and services required for a project to improve and extend irrigation in an important rice-producing area on Thailand's central plain. As rice is the staple food of Thailand's population and its principal source of foreign exchange earnings, the Chao Phya project takes an important place in its development plans. The additional annual rice surplus of the area should amount to about 475,000 tons, after allowing for increased local consumption, and the additional annual surplus of soya beans is estimated at about 75,000 tons.

The project consists of the construction of a reinforced concrete barrage near Chainat on the Chao Phya River, about 100 miles north of Bangkok, and of a complete system of canals and regulating structures in the area commanded by the barrage. The barrage will assure a water supply, properly controlled and distributed, for the irrigation of some 2,260,000 acres. It will also make it possible to maintain a sufficient depth of water for all-year navigation of river craft in the Noi and Suphan effluents of the Chao Phya River and in a canal to be constructed east of that

129

river. The barrage will also permit the eventual installation of hydroelectric power units.

Proceeds from the Bank loan are also being used to cover the foreign exchange costs of equipment for the new Central Workshops of the Royal Irrigation Department in Bangkok.

Excavation of the barrage and the building of a navigation lock at the site are under way. Construction on the headworks for the distribution system is progressing satisfactorily. Some buildings of the Central Workshops in Bangkok have been erected and others have reached an advanced state; the shop equipment is being delivered. It is expected that the entire project will be completed on time, at the end of 1958.

The Bank's $4.4 million loan is being used mainly to meet the foreign exchange costs of services and equipment required to deepen the channel through the sand bar at the mouth of the Chao Phya River. This sand bar blocks the approach to the Port of Bangkok, which handles the bulk of Thailand's import and export trade. Fully laden vessels over 5,000 deadweight tons must anchor in the lee of an island some 20 miles from the river mouth and transfer their cargo to smaller vessels or barges. Extra lighterage and transshipment charges are thus incurred and the movement of vessels to and from the port is retarded. Completion of the channel will permit vessels of up to 10,000 tons to enter the river. Work on the channel has been delayed, but is expected to be finished at the beginning of 1954.

The Bank's loan is also financing the import of cargo-handling equipment, a tugboat and navigational aids. The cargo-handling equipment is being installed at Klong Toi, 10 miles downstream from Bangkok. This new port, begun in 1938, will be able to handle the larger vessels that can pass the bar at the mouth of the river. The Port of Bangkok, which handled some 500,000 tons of freight in 1949, should be able to handle one million tons when the project is finished.

In the interests of efficiently operating and developing the port and navigational facilities in the Bangkok area, the Government created the autonomous Port Authority of Thailand in May 1951. In 1953 the Bank helped the Government to obtain the services of a qualified expert to give advice on improving the organization and administration of the port.

THE MIDDLE EAST

Regional Representative

In October 1953 the Bank stationed a staff member at Beirut, Lebanon, accredited to Egypt, Iraq, Jordan, Lebanon and Syria. He has the responsibility for creating a better understanding of the Bank by explaining and interpreting its objectives, policies and activities; he advises prospective borrowers on the preparation and presentation of projects for the Bank's consideration; and he develops and maintains contacts with governments, business communities, regional organizations and international organizations in the area.

Iran

A Bank mission visited Iran in 1950 to study the economic situation and to discuss a possible basis for Bank financing of development projects. Shortly thereafter, the oil industry was nationalized. Conditions became so uncertain that discussions about possible Bank loans were suspended.

After expressions of interest by Iran and the United Kingdom the Bank offered in November 1951 to try to work out interim arrangements for the restoration of oil operations in Iran. A proposal was put forward which it was hoped would be acceptable to the two parties to the dispute, and several weeks were spent by officials of the Bank in discussions in London and Teheran. An attempt to arrive at an agreement in Teheran was unsuccessful. and in March 1952 it was decided to discontinue the talks.

Iraq

Fiscal $12.8 million 15-year 3¾% loan of June 15, 1950 for flood
1950:   control.

The Bank's loan is helping to finance a project to protect
Baghdad and the surrounding agricultural area from flooding by
the Tigris River which has periodically caused heavy damage to
crops and urban property. The project includes the construction
of a dam across the Tigris at a point about 50 miles above
Baghdad and the building of an embankment to divert flood water
into the Wadi Tharthar, a large uninhabited depression northwest
of Baghdad.

Funds from the Bank's loan have been used principally to
import construction equipment. Work on the embankment began
late in 1951 and has since proceeded steadily. Construction of
the dam was begun in August 1953. When completed, the project
will prevent flood damage and enable the Government to save
substantial sums now spent on levee maintenance and flood relief
measures.

A general survey mission composed of 14 experts was organized
by the Bank in 1951. The agricultural experts were provided by
the Food and Agriculture Organization and the specialists in
health and education were nominated respectively by the World
Health Organization and the United Nations Educational, Scientific and Cultural Organization. While in Iraq the group worked
closely with the Iraq Development Board, an autonomous agency
established in 1950 for the planning and financing of development.
The mission's report was transmitted to the Government in
February 1952.

The mission reported that Iraq's three principal resources—
land, water and oil—can ultimately maintain a much larger population with a considerably higher standard of living. Rapidly
rising revenues from oil would make it possible for the Government to undertake a large-scale development program. The report

outlined a five-year program of development calling for expenditures equivalent to $470 million.

The mission was of the opinion that agriculture should receive major emphasis in the development of the country. The most urgent needs are flood control and irrigation to bring additional land under cultivation, drainage to improve existing crop land, and the introduction of better agricultural techniques. In the industrial field the report suggested the expansion of certain existing industries and the creation of new ones. In particular, it proposed the establishment of a chemical plant which would use natural gas from the vast Kirkuk oil field to make fertilizer and other valuable chemical products.

The mission found the transport system adequate for present needs; but for the future it recommended the standardization of railway gauges, to be carried out in conjunction with a comprehensive replacement program, and the building of an adequate network of surfaced roads. The report stressed in every field the importance of increasing the productivity of workers through better education and reduction of the incidence of debilitating diseases.

The Government has prepared a five-year investment program which, as the mission recommended, puts major emphasis on the development of water resources and the improvement of agriculture. It has also undertaken studies in the industrial field along lines suggested by the mission.

Pakistan

Fiscal 1952: $27.2 million 15-year 4⅝% loan of March 27, 1952 for railway rehabilitation.

$3.25 million 7-year 4⅛% loan of June 13, 1952 for agricultural machinery.

The Bank's railway loan is helping to finance a program for improving the railways in both East and West Pakistan. The Government undertook the program as a matter of high priority

133

in 1951, following a period during and after the war when the two systems had suffered badly from lack of maintenance of both track and rolling stock. The program provides for the introduction of diesel electric locomotives onto the main lines of both systems, the replacement of obsolete rolling stock, and the restoration of track and equipment to good condition.

The Bank's loan is financing the import of 37 diesel electric main line locomotives, 41 diesel electric shunting locomotives, 12 locomotive boilers, about 200 passenger cars and 1,200 freight cars, workshop equipment and a limited amount of ties. Orders have been placed for all of this equipment. All the diesel main line locomotives have arrived in Pakistan and 23 of them have been operating in West Pakistan for more than 18 months. Operation and maintenance of the locomotives have been satisfactory; and the introduction of diesel traction has led to reduced expenditures for fuel, with consequent savings of foreign exchange.

The Bank's agricultural loan was made to finance imports of machinery to be used in reclaiming 660,000 acres of land in the Thal, a desert area in West Pakistan. Goods to be imported under the loan consist of tractors and ancillary equipment needed to construct irrigation ditches and to clear, plow and seed the land. Completion of the project will require about five years. It will permit colonization by some 44,000 farm families and by a larger number of families who will process agricultural crops grown in the area and provide general community services. Increased crop production will consist mainly of wheat and cotton.

At the end of 1953, the loan had not been made effective since all the conditions to the loan had not yet been fulfilled. These had to do primarily with organization and staffing of the project. Most of the equipment arrived at the site in the summer of 1953, and sufficient progress has been made in the past few months to get much of this equipment into operation. By the end of 1953, most of the irrigation canals in the area to be reclaimed had been constructed, irrigation ditches were being dug, and settlers were being brought onto the land.

In November 1953 the Bank stationed a special representative in Pakistan to assist in carrying forward Bank-financed projects.

Syria

At the end of 1953 the Bank was organizing a general survey mission to Syria; the mission was scheduled to leave Washington in February to undertake its studies in the field. The mission will have 10 members, two of whom have been nominated by the Food and Agriculture Organization. The Ford Foundation will provide the services of an agricultural economist, and the International Monetary Fund, the services of a public finance adviser.

EUROPE, AFRICA AND AUSTRALASIA

AFRICA

Belgian Congo

Fiscal 1952: $40 million 25-year 4½% loan of September 13, 1951 to the Belgian Congo for development plan. Guaranteed by Belgium. Made simultaneously with loan of $30 million to Belgium.

The $40 million loan was the first made by the Bank to an overseas territory of a member country. The purpose of the loan, and of a $30 million loan made simultaneously to Belgium (see page 147), is to help carry out the Ten Year Development Plan for the Congo.

This Plan was put into effect in 1950. Over the 10-year period, it calls for public investment of up to $800 million equivalent in transport, communications, electric power, water supply, housing, health, education and research. Private investment on a similar scale is expected in mining and manufacturing, large-scale agriculture, commerce and electric power. As a result of expansion

135

in both the public and private sectors of the economy, exports are expected to rise by 30% to 50% during the life of the Plan.

The high rate of expenditures has increased the demand for imports of consumer goods as well as of capital equipment. The Bank's $40 million loan to the Congo is helping to pay for part of the imports from countries other than Belgium during the period 1951-1954. At the same time, the franc equivalent of the Bank's $30 million loan to Belgium is being made available to the Congo to pay for imports from Belgium.

Because of the wide variety of goods being imported, it was impracticable to base disbursements from the Bank's loan on purchases of specified goods. Disbursements, therefore, are geared to the rate of public investment under the Plan.

Although the pace of investment has not been so rapid as was originally expected, good progress is being made under the Plan. The value of investment goods imported in 1952 accounted for nearly half the Congo's total imports and was 50% higher than in the preceding year.

Ethiopia

Fiscal 1951:

$5 million 20-year 4% loan of September 13, 1950 for rehabilitation of roads.

$2 million 20-year 4% loan of September 13, 1950 for Development Bank.

$1.5 million 20-year 4% loan of February 19, 1951 for rehabilitation and development of telecommunications.

The $5 million loan is paying the foreign exchange cost of a three-year program begun in 1951 to repair and maintain the national highway system. Reconstruction of main roads and an improved feeder system are essential to the economic growth of Ethiopia. A large part of the country's exports and imports are carried by truck to and from the main stations on the railway which links the capital city of Addis Ababa to the port of Djibouti,

LOANS

Borrower	Purpose	Amount
Belgium (Guarantor) Belgian Congo	Development of the Belgian Congo	$40,000,000
Ethiopia	Road program	5,000,000
Ethiopia	Development Bank	2,000,000
Ethiopia	Telecommunications	1,500,000
Union of South Africa	Expansion of transport facilities	50,000,000
Union of South Africa (Guarantor) Electricity Supply Commission	Electric power	60,000,000
United Kingdom (Guarantor) Northern Rhodesia	Railway development	14,000,000
United Kingdom (Guarantor) Southern Rhodesia	Electric power	28,000,000

RAILWAY DEVELOPMENT

ELECTRIC POWER

ELECTRIC POWER

ELECTRIC POWER

TRANSPORT

Africa

in French Somaliland. Much trade also moves by truck to and from other ports on the Red Sea.

For want of maintenance during and after the war, the highways deteriorated seriously. Travel became extremely slow and transportation costs high; and the development of the country was adversely affected. To rehabilitate the roads, the Government established an Imperial Highway Authority in 1951 and, after consultation with the Bank, contracted with the United States Bureau of Public Roads to provide management for the Authority. The Bureau's original contract was for a period of three years; the contract has recently been extended for a fourth year, to February 1955.

At the close of 1953, the rehabilitation work on the 2,500 miles of primary roads had made substantial progress. As a result, movement of motor vehicles over some of the roads is faster and safer, and freight rates have been reduced.

The $2 million loan of September 1950 was made to help establish a new credit institution which would make medium-and long-term loans for agricultural and industrial investment projects. The Government established this institution, the Development Bank of Ethiopia, in 1951, merged with it the state-owned Agricultural and Commercial Bank which had pioneered in agricultural credit, and selected a general manager for it in consultation with the International Bank.

The International Bank loan provided foreign exchange for the Development Bank. The Government is providing the domestic currency; it has subscribed to all of the Development Bank's capital stock of Eth. $11 million (equivalent to U. S. $4.4 million), of which Eth. $5 million (U. S. $2 million) is being purchased with the counterpart of the International Bank loan. The Bank started operations in May 1951; at the end of 1953 outstanding agricultural and industrial loans amounted to about Eth. $5 million. Foreign exchange from the International Bank's loan has been applied to industrial projects, mostly for the processing of agricultural products. Agricultural loans have been mainly in Ethiopian dollars.

A loan contract for $1.5 million was signed in February 1950 for financing the import of equipment to expand and improve three different communications systems: the local telephone service at Addis Ababa; an inter-urban system; and an international radio-telephone and radio-telegraph service. At the end of 1953, the loan was not yet in effect; work had been slow in getting under way because of delays in organizing the Imperial Board of Tele-communications, an agency established by the Government to carry out the project. The charter of the Board had been promulgated and a general manager appointed late in 1952, but other steps remained to be taken by the Board to make the loan effective.

Nigeria

A general survey mission organized by the Bank visited Nigeria for 11 weeks beginning in September 1953, and at the end of the year had begun work on a report designed to assist the Government in drawing up a program for economic development. The mission consisted of 16 members, including one from the staff of the International Monetary Fund, one from the World Health Organization, and two from the Food and Agriculture Organization.

Northern Rhodesia

Fiscal $14 million 19-year 4¾% loan of March 11, 1953 to the
1953:   Territory of Northern Rhodesia for railway development.
          Guaranteed by the United Kingdom.

The loan is being used to purchase equipment for the Rhodesia Railways which serve Northern Rhodesia, Southern Rhodesia and Bechuanaland.

Owing to the exceptionally rapid development of the areas which they serve, the Railways have been heavily overburdened since the war. In 1952 the tonnage carried was more than 70% greater than in 1946. The difficulties which have been encountered in handling this increase have, among other things, led to the accumulation of large stockpiles of chrome ore at railway sidings awaiting transport to ports for shipment overseas and to delays in the distribution of coal.

In addition to locomotives and rolling stock, the loan is financing equipment which will be used in the improvement of permanent way, the enlargement of yards and sidings, and the extension of repair shops. Bank funds are also being applied to the construction of a new line from Bannockburn in Southern Rhodesia to the border of Portuguese East Africa. This new line will relieve the pressure on the East African port of Beira, which has hitherto been the chief outlet of the landlocked territories served by the Railways. It will connect with a line being built by the Portuguese Government to the port of Lourenco Marques with the help of a credit from the Export-Import Bank of Washington.

The Railways' program of expansion and improvement is expected to cost the equivalent of $79 million during the three years ending March 1955. Although most of the goods purchased with Bank financing will come from the United Kingdom, the loan is in dollars. This and the loan to Southern Rhodesia which has been handled similarly, will help to offset part of the drain on the United Kingdom's foreign exchange reserves resulting from the capital contributed by the United Kingdom to the development of both Rhodesias.

Although the loan was made to Northern Rhodesia, the responsibility for the execution of the program is shared also by Southern Rhodesia and both governments have undertaken to see that it is carried out.

Southern Rhodesia

Fiscal 1952: $28 million 25-year 4¾% loan of February 27, 1952 to the Colony of Southern Rhodesia for power development. Guaranteed by the United Kingdom.

This loan is helping to finance electric power expansion under a plan of general economic development covering a four-year period which ends March 31, 1955. It contemplates governmental investment equivalent to about $280 million, mostly in basic services like transportation, electric power generation and distribution, and water supply. Private investment in industry and agriculture is expected to equal this amount.

The Bank's loan is helping to finance imported equipment and materials required for power expansion during the last three years of the program. The expansion consists of the installation of about 230,000 kilowatts of new thermal generating capacity, the erection of some 2,000 miles of transmission lines, and the installation of distribution equipment. Most of the equipment is being bought in the United Kingdom, although some will come from the Union of South Africa and a small amount from the United States. The projects being financed are progressing about on schedule.

A large part of the capital for the development of Southern Rhodesia is coming from the United Kingdom. To help offset this drain on the United Kingdom's foreign exchange reserves, the Bank's loan is providing dollars to finance purchases in the United Kingdom.

Union of South Africa

Fiscal 1951: $30 million 20-year 4% loan of January 23, 1951 to Electricity Supply Commission for power development. Fully disbursed by October 1953.

$20 million 15-year 3¾% loan of January 23, 1951 for expansion of transportation facilities. Fully disbursed by March 1953.

Fiscal $30 million 10-year 4¾% loan of August 28, 1953 to Elec-
1954:   tricity Supply Commission for power development.

   $30 million 10-year 4¾% loan of August 28, 1953 for
   expansion of transportation facilities.

The purpose of the Bank's lending has been to provide additions to electric power and transportation service made necessary by the rapid expansion of the economy. The fast growth of light industry and the expansion of gold mining operations in the Orange Free State during the post-war period put a heavy and continuing strain on public services, and especially on the railway system and power supply. The tonnage carried by the South African railways increased by one-third between 1947 and 1953; and there was an even greater increase in power requirements.

Transportation

Two loans totaling $50 million have been made to the Union Government to finance imports of equipment and goods needed by the South African Railways and Harbours Administration in a continuing program to improve transportation. The larger part of the proceeds of the first loan, of $20 million, has been applied to imports needed for the railways, mainly locomotives and rolling stock, workshop machinery and structural materials. An amount of $2 million has been used for road vehicles and $1 million for harbor craft.

This loan was completely disbursed by mid-1953; the second transport loan of $30 million was made to help finance imports needed from that time to mid-1956. Two-thirds of the new loan is being applied to the purchase of steam and electric locomotives and rolling stock. Most of the remainder will pay for other railway equipment and materials; an amount of $2 million has been set aside for road transport and a smaller amount for harbor craft. Equipment financed by the two loans should help the railways to meet the increase of nine million tons of traffic expected during the next two years.

Simultaneously with the Bank's first railway loan, eight commercial banks in the United States extended a credit of $10 million, maturing in 1954 and 1955, to the Union Government. An amount equivalent to this credit was lent by the Union Government to the Railways and Harbours Administration for purposes complementary to those of the loan from the International Bank.

Electric Power

The two power loans, amounting to $60 million, were made to the Electricity Supply Commission (ESCOM), an autonomous state corporation. ESCOM supplies about three-quarters of the electricity consumed in the Union of South Africa. Despite the rapid expansion of power facilities since the war, ESCOM has been unable to keep pace with demand. Shortages are particularly acute on the Rand, which includes gold fields and the industrial complex of the Transvaal. Here and elsewhere, the supply of power has been inadequate to meet demands for new or increased services and in some cases ESCOM has had to ration or reduce supplies to existing customers.

ESCOM is engaged in a construction program which by 1958 is intended to add 1.4 million kilowatts of generating capacity to the existing capacity of 1.6 million. Additions are to be made to six existing stations, and eight new stations are to be built at points throughout the Union. New substations and 900 miles of major transmission lines are also to be constructed.

The $30 million loan of January 1951 financed imports needed during a two-year period of the expansion program. The loan of $30 million made in August 1953 will help to finance imports needed for the continuation of this program. It is being applied particularly to the purchase of turbo-generators, boilers, structural materials and electrical supplies.

AUSTRALASIA

Australia

Fiscal 1951: $100 million 25-year 4¼% loan of August 22, 1950 for development program. Fully disbursed by December 1953.

Fiscal 1953: $50 million 20-year 4¾% loan of July 8, 1952 for development program.

These two loans were made to finance imports of dollar equipment and goods needed for projects being undertaken by Commonwealth and State authorities and by private businesses and individuals during a period of rapid economic development. Projects being carried out in the private sector have included farm mechanization and improvement, modernization of coal mining and minerals extraction, expansion of iron, steel and non-ferrous metals production, and equipment of miscellaneous industries. Projects in the public sector have included water conservation, expansion of electric power supply, extension and improvement of road and rail transport, increase of irrigation and development of land resources.

Australia has been able to buy most of the imports for these projects with sterling, but to finance all the dollar purchases necessary would have required extraordinary calls on the dollar reserves of the sterling area. The Government therefore sought dollar loans from the International Bank. The loans, however, have not been used as the basis for new internal credit; they have enabled public and private investors to purchase dollars (and with these, dollar goods) with their own Australian pounds.

The first loan, of $100 million, was made to cover dollar imports for a period of approximately two years; the second, of $50 million, was to cover imports during an additional year.

Agriculture

Although Australia's industrial growth has been rapid, her exports have consisted very largely of agricultural products, especially wool, meat and wheat. To meet the requirements of her growing population and at the same time maintain or improve export earnings, Australia must produce more food and wool.

A total of some $45 million was allocated to the purchase of agricultural machinery—tractors, hay balers and the like—of which the greater part has already been imported and retailed by commercial distributors to individual farmers and ranchers. Australian agricultural development has also greatly benefited under the first loan from the importation of about $19 million worth of heavy earth moving equipment, a large part of which has been used in public works for irrigation and land development —for instance, the Big Eildon project of the Victoria Government, providing irrigation for an additional 350,000 acres in the Goulburn Valley area and an increase in hydroelectric power. The remainder of the heavy earth moving equipment included machinery for road construction, electric power projects, among others the Snowy Mountains hydroelectric scheme, and general industrial construction.

A Bank mission which visited Australia early in 1953 to study agricultural production found that many deficiencies in materials and equipment that had limited the expansion of agriculture were being overcome, and that the output of cereals, milk and meat would benefit considerably from the use of Bank-financed equipment.

Transportation

Rapid economic development in Australia has put increasing burdens on transport facilities of all kinds, and the problem of moving goods has been accentuated by the long distances between the urban centers which contain the great majority of the continent's population. Nearly $14 million of the first loan was used for railway locomotives and railway equipment. The second loan puts greater stress on transport with an allocation of $21 million.

Together the two loans allocate $16 million for railway improvement. Most of it has been used to purchase locomotives and locomotive components, one objective being to substitute diesel for steam tractive power on long stretches of railway poorly supplied with water. The loans have helped bring into service 11 new diesel electric locomotives for the Commonwealth Railways, 20 for the New South Wales Railways, 17 for the Victoria Railways, 10 for the Queensland Railways, and 20 steam locomotives for the New South Wales Railways. In the second loan $13 million is earmarked for road transport; of this amount the greater part is financing the importation of trucks and the remainder road construction machinery. For aircraft, spare engines and other spare parts, $6 million has been allocated from the second loan.

Electric Power

The bulk of the Bank's investment in the development of electric power—about $28 million—was accomplished with the first loan. The important part of this expenditure was for thermal plants with a total generating capacity of 150,000 kw, all of which are presently in or coming into operation. They are supplying electricity to important coal and steel producing areas and population centers.

Mining and Manufacturing

Although minerals are an important export, and domestically mined coal is basic to the economy, mineral and coal production in the six years after the war did not keep pace with the growth of the economy; and Australia, despite ample domestic reserves, actually had to import coal to meet rising demands for this fuel.

About $6 million of the two loans was allocated to increase mineral, metallurgical and coal production. Equipment has been provided, for instance, for the mining and refining of copper, lead and zinc, and for strip and shaft mining of coal. Mineral and metal exports have been rising; and domestic coal production has been on a level with demand since 1952.

About $16 million from the two loans has been applied to the purchase of manufacturing equipment. In the steel industry loan funds are helping to supply machinery for a hot and cold strip mill and tin plate plant, a skelp mill and a cold reversible sheet mill. Equipment is being provided for the installation of modern mechanical foundry capacity; for the expansion of automotive production; and for food-processing, textile and other industries.

EUROPE

Belgium

Fiscal $16 million 20-year 4¼% loan of March 1, 1949 for steel
1949:   plants and electric power.

Fiscal $30 million 25-year 4½% loan of September 13, 1951 for
1952:   development of the Belgian Congo. Made simultaneously
           with loan of $40 million to the Belgian Congo.

The Bank's first loan to Belgium, for $16 million, was made to help modernize steel manufacture and the generation of electric power. In March 1949 the Bank sold the entire loan, with its guarantee, to a number of institutional investors.

Part of the loan was used for imports needed by the Union des Centrales Electriques de Liege-Namur-Luxembourg (Linalux) to construct a new thermal electric power plant at Awirs. The new plant was completed in January 1952, and replaced obsolete generating facilities. The plant has a generating capacity of 100,000 kilowatts and supplies power to heavy industries in the Liege basin.

The major part of the loan was allocated to three steel projects. One was the installation of a slabbing and blooming mill by S. A. d'Ougree-Marihaye, one of the largest steel companies in Belgium. The mill has been in operation since 1950 and has an annual capacity of 900,000 tons of slabs and billets. A second steel project was a cold rolling and tin plating mill installed at Tilleur by the Compagnie des Fers Blancs et Tôles à Froid (Ferblatil). The cold rolling plant began operating in June 1950. The tin plating plant started operations in March 1951. It has an annual capacity of approximately 60,000 tons of tin plate and 24,000 tons of steel sheets. The plant produces high-quality tin plate and is the only mill in continental Europe using the electrolytic process for this purpose.

In February 1953, at the request of the borrower, the Bank approved the use for a third steel project of undisbursed funds originally allocated to Linalux and Ferblatil. These funds are being used by S. A. d'Ougree-Marihaye to finance part of the cost of a hot strip finishing mill purchased in the United States. Shipment of this equipment began late in 1953 and the mill is expected to be completed in 1954.

The $30 million loan of September 1951 was the first made to a member country to assist it in developing an overseas territory. The specific purpose of the loan was to aid in carrying out the Ten Year Development Plan for the Belgian Congo (see page 135). Belgium is the leading supplier of manufactured goods to the Congo and is providing most of the capital equipment needed for the Plan. The demand for goods for the Congo stimulates economic activity in Belgium—raising employment and income, increasing imports of raw materials and foodstuffs, and increasing the expenditure of foreign exchange. The loan was intended to reduce the resulting pressure on Belgium's foreign exchange reserves during the two years ending in September 1953. Because of delays in carrying out the program, however, the disbursement of the loan will extend into 1954. Withdrawals under the loan are not related to specific imports but are geared to the rate of public investment in the Congo Development Plan as a whole.

Denmark

Fiscal 1948: $40 million 25-year 4¼% loan of August 22, 1947 for reconstruction. Fully disbursed by March 1949.

The loan of $40 million was made in 1947 to aid Denmark's recovery in the immediate postwar period by financing the import of essential capital goods and raw materials.

War damage, deterioration of farm and industrial machinery, and the loss of 40% of the prewar merchant fleet had greatly impaired the efficiency and competitive power of the Danish economy by the end of World War II. At the time of the Bank loan, energetic measures already had been taken to promote recovery: the budget was balanced, production was increasing and price and wage levels were under control. The loan was used to pay for the import of agricultural and textile machinery, machine tools, trucks, steel, textile fibres, non-ferrous metals and chemicals. It corresponded to about 9% of the net capital expenditures made during 1947 and 1948.

Finland

Fiscal 1950: $12.5 million 15-year 4% loan of August 1, 1949 to Bank of Finland for development of power, wood-products industries and limestone powder production. Fully disbursed by December 1953.

$2.3 million 2-year 3% loan of October 17, 1949 for equipment for timber production; reduced at request of borrower on September 30, 1951 to $2.1 million. This loan has been completely repaid.

Fiscal 1952: $20 million 18-year 4¾% loan of April 30, 1952 to Bank of Finland for development of power and wood-products industries and for agricultural improvement.

Fiscal 1953: Swedish kronor 18 million ($3,479,464) 18-year 4¾% loan of November 13, 1952 to Bank of Finland for wood-products industries.

Most of the Bank's lending in Finland has been for the

modernization and expansion of the wood-products industries and for the development of electric power. The wood-products industries account for nearly a third of national income and nearly the whole of export earnings; they also consume more than half of electric power production.

Wood Products and Timber

Bank funds made available for the manufacture of wood products amount to the equivalent of more than $23 million: $10.5 million from the loan of August 1949, $9.5 million from the loan of April 1952, and all of the 18 million Swedish kronor (about $3.48 million) lent in November 1952. In each case the Bank of Finland, which was the borrower, made the funds available to well-established firms in the industry for the purchase of equipment.

The first loan enabled the industry to modernize and expand its plants, so as to reduce costs and increase output in chemical and mechanical pulp mills and in board and paper mills. Funds from the other two loans are helping to increase plant capacity for the manufacture of chemical pulp, paper, newsprint, and other products. It is estimated that by 1956 the production of chemical pulp will be increased by 20%, newsprint by 30% and kraft paper by 70%. Virtually all the additional output will be for export.

A loan of $2.3 million was made in October 1949 to increase exports of timber; it was made simultaneously with a loan of $2.7 million to Yugoslavia for the same purpose. The loans were the outcome of proposals by the United Nations Economic Commission for Europe and the Food and Agriculture Organization to increase the supplies of sawn timber needed in European reconstruction. The loan enabled Finland to purchase timber-producing equipment in the United States. Finland entered into an agreement whereby it exported timber to the United Kingdom, Belgium and Denmark and these countries paid dollars directly to the

Bank for a sufficient part of the timber to cover the Bank's loan. Repayment of the loan was completed in 1951.

Electric Power and Agriculture

The Bank has lent $11.2 million for electric power development: $1.7 million from the loan of August 1949, and $9.5 million from the loan of April 1952. In 1948 Finland began a power development program which by 1951 had nearly doubled the output of electricity; the $1.7 million was applied to equipment for this phase of the program. The $9.5 million has been applied to projects for increasing generating capacity by another third; it is financing equipment for four hydroelectric plants in northern and eastern Finland and one steam plant in western Finland.

Small additional portions of the two loans have been used for agricultural development. About $300,000 from the first was used to buy equipment for producing limestone powder which is particularly needed in Finnish agriculture to correct the excessive acidity of the soil. The sum of $1 million from the second of the two loans is being used to buy tractors and earth moving equipment for clearing land and building forest roads. This will aid a Government program begun in 1940 to increase farm and forestry production, and to resettle farmers from Karelia.

France

| Fiscal 1947: | $250 million 30-year 4¼% loan of May 9, 1947 to Credit National for reconstruction. Fully disbursed by January 1948. |

This loan was the first made by the Bank, and remains the largest single loan to any borrower. It came at a critical time for France, for its dollar resources were almost exhausted, it had fully utilized the credits it had received from the U. S. Government and the European Recovery Program had not yet been formulated.

The loan helped to sustain the flow of essential imports and to avoid a serious setback in French recovery during 1947.

Bank funds financed the purchase of a wide variety of goods and equipment necessary to France's economic rehabilitation. The transportation system was improved through the purchase of equipment and materials for rail, ship and air transport. The loan financed a portion of the cost of 113 diesel locomotives, and of parts needed to repair damaged railroad cars and to construct new ones. It also financed a part of the cost of 18 tankers totaling 302,000 tons, 36 dry cargo vessels totaling 193,000 tons, and some 180 smaller craft such as trawlers, tugs and barges. The loan also helped to finance nine Constellations.

Coal and oil, essential to industry and transport, figured largely among the purchases made out of the proceeds of the loan, as did industrial raw materials, including semi-finished steel products, copper, zinc, lead and cotton. The coal purchased amounted to 6,919,000 tons, or two-thirds of coal imports from the United States during the first 11 months of 1947 and more than a tenth of all the coal available in France during that period. The coal was delivered to users in metropolitan France and French North Africa for railway, gas, steel, coking and other industrial uses. The loan also paid for 1,218,000 metric tons of petroleum products, for 165,000 bales of cotton; and for more than 250,000 tons of steel products which were used for public works, reconstruction, public utilities and transportation, reconversion of armament factories, and the repair and building of the merchant marine.

In addition, Bank funds helped finance two steel mill projects: a continuous cold rolling mill at Montataire with an annual capacity of 300,000 tons of high-grade steel sheets, and a continuous hot rolling mill at Denain with an annual capacity of 800,000 tons of hot strip. The two plants are among the most modern steel installations in Europe and are producing rolled steel products of a type basic to Western Europe's industrial economy.

Iceland

Fiscal 1951:   £875,000 ($2,450,000) 22-year 4⅜% loan of June 20, 1951 for power development.

Fiscal 1952:   £360,000 ($1,008,000) 22-year 4½% loan of November 1, 1951 for agricultural development. Fully disbursed by March 1953.

Fiscal 1953: $854,000 equivalent in European currencies 17-year 4¾% loan of August 26, 1952 for a fertilizer plant.

Fiscal 1954: $1,350,000 equivalent in European currencies 22-year 5% loan of September 4, 1953 to Iceland Bank of Development for agricultural development.

£90,000 ($252,000) equivalent in European currencies 12-year 4¾% loan of September 4, 1953 to Iceland Bank of Development for building to house radio transmitter equipment.

All of these loans have consisted entirely of European currencies, mainly pounds sterling and French francs. They have been so constituted because Iceland can service debt with less difficulty in European currencies than in dollars. The Bank's loans for power development and a fertilizer plant were complementary to funds made available from the U. S. Economic Cooperation Administration; Bank funds financed imports from Europe, while the ECA financed equipment needed from the United States and provided counterpart funds for the financing of local expenditures.

Power

The loan of £875,000 ($2.45 million) financed the purchase of equipment for two hydroelectric projects on the Sog and Laxa Rivers. These projects are of high priority in Iceland's investment program. Additional power will make possible the establishment of new industries as well as the expansion of fish-processing industries. It will also improve the general standard of living by making power available for agricultural and household uses.

The Sog project, completed in December 1953, will supply electricity to Iceland's capital, Reykjavik, and to the surrounding area, in which are concentrated 50% of Iceland's population and over 80% of its industries. It should meet all demands for electric power in the area until about 1957. The Laxa project will increase the supply of electricity to an area which includes Akureyri, the second largest city in Iceland, and should meet its growing power requirements until about 1960. This project was completed in November 1953.

Agriculture

The Bank has made two loans in support of Iceland's agricultural development program, begun in 1951. The purpose of this program is to restore agriculture to its former place of importance in Iceland's economy and to lessen the country's dependence on the fishing industry. The cultivated area will be extended to permit further mechanization of hay making and to increase sheep and cattle flocks. This calls for the drainage, ploughing, reseeding and fencing of natural grasslands, and the construction of farm buildings to store winter feed, to shelter animals, and to provide better dwellings for farmers and their families.

Both loans were made to finance the purchase in Europe of building materials required for the construction of farm houses and other farm buildings and of equipment and materials needed to reseed and fence grasslands. Amounts of Icelandic kronur equivalent to the loans are being deposited in a special account in the Iceland Agricultural Bank to assist farmers with loans toward buildings and other improvements.

The loan of $854,000 for the construction of a nitrogen fertilizer plant is closely related to the agricultural and power loans. An increase in Iceland's agricultural production depends upon a plentiful supply of nitrogen fertilizer, which is now imported at a considerable cost in foreign exchange. The new plant will produce enough fertilizer to meet the country's increasing needs for some years to come. The plant will use power produced by the Sog hydroelectric project and will be so operated as to make the fullest use of electricity at times of day when other demands for power are low. The Bank's loan is providing funds for the purchase in Europe of rectifier equipment, cement, reinforcing steel, lumber, building materials and window glass for the plant.

Radio Transmitter Building

The loan of £90,000 is helping to finance the construction of a building to house some of the radio equipment operated by the Icelandic Post and Telegraph Administration for civilian aircraft flying over the North Atlantic. The equipment is at present sheltered in an inadequate temporary structure and a new building is needed to assure adequate and reliable service.

Maintenance of the radio service will help Iceland continue to earn foreign exchange from international aviation and will benefit the airlines of the participating countries. Under an arrangement administered by the International Civil Aviation Organization (ICAO), the cost of the radio service is paid from contributions by 11 countries, including Iceland, whose airlines operate over the North Atlantic. ICAO has arranged for increased contributions from these countries to assure sufficient revenue to service the Bank's loan.

The borrower in the case of the second agricultural loan and the radio transmitter building loan was the Iceland Bank of Development. This institution was established in February 1953 along the general lines recommended by a Bank representative who visited the country in 1952 to discuss means of channelling investment into productive channels.

Italy

Fiscal 1952: $10 million 25-year 4½% loan of October 10, 1951 to Cassa per Opere Straordinarie di Pubblico Interesse nell' Italia Meridionale (Cassa per il Mezzogiorno) for development of southern Italy. Fully disbursed by September 1953.

Fiscal $10 million 25-year 5% loan of October 6, 1953 to Cassa
1954:   per Opere Straordinarie di Pubblico Interesse nell' Italia
             Meridionale (Cassa per il Mezzogiorno) for development
             of southern Italy.

Both loans have been made in support of the Government's plan for the development of southern Italy, including the Islands of Sicily and Sardinia. The plan is the first comprehensive attempt to remedy the unemployment and low standard of living from which southern Italy has suffered for decades. The Government adopted the program, and established the Cassa per il Mezzogiorno to administer it, in 1950.

The plan covers a 12-year period ending in 1962, and contemplates expenditures of about 100 billion lire ($160 million) a year. More than half the expenditures contemplated are for developing agriculture through projects for land reclamation, irrigation, flood control and soil conservation. The reclamation program covers an area of about eight million acres. Of this, about 900,000 acres will be irrigated, or 10 times as many as before; the rest will be drained, leveled and cleared. About a quarter of the Cassa's funds will be spent on roads, water works and tourist facilities. Completion of 44 aqueducts will provide drinking water for about 1,000 communities. The construction of some 1,300 miles of new roads and the repair of 6,400 miles of existing roads are to be carried out by the end of 1954.

The Bank loans were not intended to finance equipment, for this can be obtained in Italy. They were made primarily to enable Italy's dollar position to withstand the increased demand for dollar goods that will be caused by rising employment under the plan.

Disbursement of the loans is geared to investment under the plan at the rate of $1 of disbursement per 10,000 lire of expenditure. The lira counterpart of the Bank's first loan is being used to assist industrial development in southern Italy. The Cassa is lending the counterpart to private enterprises for projects related

155

to, but not part of, the plan. Projects so far selected by the Cassa and approved by the Bank for financing include a superphosphate plant, a welded tube plant, two cement factories and a woolen mill. The use of the counterpart of the second loan is still to be agreed between the Bank and Italy.

Luxembourg

Fiscal 1948: $12 million 25-year 4¼% loan of August 28, 1947 for equipment for steel mill and railroads; reduced at request of borrower on December 19, 1949 to $11.8 million, which was disbursed by the end of that month.

The loan financed the import of equipment for the steel industry and of rolling stock for the railways.

Iron and steel account for 80% of the value of Luxembourg's industrial production and about 60% of industrial employment. Since the industry produces almost entirely for export, the economy of Luxembourg is highly sensitive to foreign demand for steel. After the war, the industry needed modernization to adapt its products to postwar market requirements. Of the Bank's loan, $7.5 million was used to pay for imported equipment needed in the construction of two steel mills at Dudelange using the most modern productive techniques: a hot rolling mill with an annual capacity of 400,000 tons, and a cold rolling mill with an annual capacity of 180,000 tons. The mills have been in operation since January 1951 and are at present processing the entire ingot production of the Dudelange steel works.

The railways of Luxembourg are important both as adjuncts to the country's heavy industry and as international carriers linking the Ruhr, the Saar, Lorraine, Switzerland and other inland areas and the Low Country ports. At the time of the Bank's loan the railways were suffering from a shortage of rolling stock. About $4.3 million of the loan was spent on locomotives, autorails and freight cars. This equipment enabled the Luxembourg railways to replace a quantity of obsolete rolling stock which would have been uneconomical to repair, and to return a number of locomotives leased from France.

The Netherlands

Fiscal 1948:	$195 million 25-year 4¼% loan of August 7, 1947 for reconstruction. Fully disbursed by June 1948.
Fiscal 1949:	$12 million 10-year 3⁹⁄₁₆% loans of July 15, 1948 to N. V. Stoomvaart Maatschappij "Nederland" (two loans of $2 million each), N. V. Vereenigde Nederlandsche Scheepvaartmaatschappij (one loan of $2 million), N. V. Nederlandsche-Amerikaansche Stoomvaart-Maatschappij "Holland-Amerika Lijn" (one loan of $2 million), and N. V. Rotterdamsche Lloyd (two loans of $2 million each), for purchase of ships. Fully disbursed by August 1948.
Fiscal 1950:	$15 million 15-year 4% loan of July 26, 1949 to Maatschappij tot Financiering van het National Herstel N. V. (Herstelbank) for industrial re-equipment projects; reduced at request of borrower to $7.5 million, which amount had been disbursed by December 1953.
Fiscal 1952:	$7 million 6-year 4⅛% loan of March 20, 1952 to Koninklijke Luchtvaart Maatschappij N. V. (KLM) for purchase of aircraft. Fully disbursed by August 1953.

The Bank's lending operations in the Netherlands have been designed to assist and maintain postwar recovery, to increase foreign exchange receipts from transport services and to expand production of industrial products for export. In addition, at the request of the Netherlands and Surinam Governments, the Bank sent a general survey mission to Surinam (formerly Dutch Guiana) in 1951; the mission's report was transmitted to the Governments in 1952 (see pages 200–201).

Reconstruction

The loan of $195 million was used to pay for essential imports needed for Netherlands reconstruction in the period prior to the formulation of the European Recovery Program. Roughly one-third of the loan was spent on machinery and equipment; about one-fifth was used in the acquisition of surplus U. S. merchant vessels, chiefly Liberty ships; rolling mill products accounted for one-seventh, and fodder, feed grains and oil cake also accounted for about that proportion. Imports financed under the loan were estimated at 12% of total Dutch imports during the disbursement period and corresponded to 15% of net investment in 1947 and 1948.

Shipping

In July 1948 loans were made to four private Netherlands shipping companies: Royal Rotterdam Lloyd, Nederland Line, Holland-America Line and United Netherlands Navigation Company. The loans financed the purchase in the United States of six " baby flat-tops " which had been converted for merchant use. They were acquired for $2 million each, a price below current cost of construction at a time when delivery of new ships of similar type could not be guaranteed in less than 18 months. They are operating profitably in the companies' intercontinental cargo services.

The loans were secured by mortgages on ships and were evidenced by 2½% serial mortgage notes guaranteed by the Government of the Netherlands. In 1948 and 1949, the Bank sold all four shipping loans, with its guarantee, to a group of institutional investors. Half the notes were paid when due; and in mid-1953 the 1954-58 maturities were purchased and canceled by the shipping companies, completing repayment of the loans five years before final maturity.

Manufacturing

The loan to the Finance Corporation of National Reconstruction (Herstelbank) in July 1949 originally amounted to $15 million; it was for imports of United States, Swiss, Belgian and German equipment to modernize Netherlands manufacturing industries.

158

In 1950 many enterprises changed their investment plans because of currency devaluations, greater availability of European equipment and new payments arrangements with Belgium and Germany. The loan was accordingly reduced to about $7.5 million and has been used to finance purchases in the United States and Switzerland only. The textile industry absorbed about one-half of the proceeds, and the chemical industry about one-third; the rest was divided among firms in the metal, electrical, glass and paper industries. Of the 35 industrial re-equipment projects assisted by the loan, all but three were completed by the end of 1953.

Air Transport

The $7 million loan to KLM Royal Dutch Airlines financed about one-fifth of the cost of a program being carried out by KLM to modernize and re-equip its airfleet. The program included the purchase in the United States of 23 aircraft, including 17 for intercontinental flights and six for use on European routes. At the end of 1953, almost all aircraft had been delivered and put into service.

The Chase National Bank of the City of New York made available to the International Bank, for disbursement to KLM, $3.5 million for which the Chase received notes of KLM representing the early maturities under the loan. This was the first time a private bank participated directly in an International Bank loan.

Turkey

Fiscal $12.5 million 25-year 4¼% loan of July 7, 1950 for develop-
1951:   ment of ports.

$3.9 million 18-year 3⅞% loan of July 7, 1950 for grain storage facilities.

$9 million 15-year 3¾% loan of October 19, 1950 to Industrial Development Bank of Turkey for development of private industry.

Fiscal $25.2 million 25-year 4¾% loan of June 18, 1952 for
1952:   multipurpose dam and power facilities on the Seyhan River.

159

Fiscal $9 million 15-year 4⅞% loan of September 10, 1953 to
1954:   Industrial Development Bank of Turkey for development
of private industry.

The Bank's loans in Turkey total nearly $60 million; they have been made for projects important for the continuation of the advances made in agricultural and industrial production during the last five years. A general survey mission organized by the Bank visited Turkey in 1950, and in 1951 its recommendations for a long-range development program were transmitted to the Government.

Port Development

The first loan, of $12.5 million, was made in July 1950 to finance the foreign exchange costs of a series of port improvement and construction projects. This program provides for the expansion of Salipazar and Haydarpasa on the Bosphorus, Alsancak (the port of Izmir) on the Aegean Sea, and Iskenderun on the Mediterranean Sea; it is also providing for additional permanent equipment at several smaller ports. At Haydarpasa, Alsancak and Iskenderun the improvements will also service new grain elevators being built with the help of another Bank loan. The program also includes construction of a new port at Samsun on the Black Sea, where Turkey has no natural harbor; this port will give access to a potentially rich hinterland.

The work at Salipazar, Haydarpasa and Iskenderun should be completed during 1955. Samsun and Alsancak will take longer and will be the last of the port projects to be finished.

Grain Storage Facilities

In July 1950 the Bank lent the Government $3.9 million to finance the import of materials and equipment for the construction and mechanization of grain storage facilities throughout Turkey. The individual projects include three new reinforced concrete silos at the ports of Haydarpasa, Izmir and Iskenderun;

eight new silos and the expansion of an existing one at nine inland points; 29 new steel storage sheds at 21 other inland points; and the mechanization of six existing warehouses. The loan also provides for the purchase of 2,000 tarpaulins for use where warehouse space is not available. Completion of the project will add 165,000 tons to Turkey's storage capacity and will result in significant savings by preventing losses from spoilage and from infestation by rats and other pests. The project is of particular importance because of Turkey's new position as a large exporter of breadgrains.

The steel sheds for grain storage have been completed and most of them were available for storing the 1953 harvest. Three of the nine inland silos have been completed and were in operation at the end of 1953; construction on the others is progressing. Work on the port silos at Iskenderun and Haydarpasa is under way and contracts for the construction at Izmir will be awarded early in January 1954. The tarpaulins have been purchased and are in use throughout the country.

Seyhan Multipurpose Project

The loan of $25.2 million was made to help finance a multi-purpose dam, a power-generating plant and transmission system. The new dam will help control floods on the Seyhan River and will provide water for irrigation and power in the Adana Plain, a productive agricultural and industrial area in south-central Turkey. The economic development of this area has been restricted by ruinous floods, an inadequate and irregular supply of water for cultivation, and a shortage of electric power. The new dam is the key to a comprehensive plan being carried out by the Government for the control and use of the waters of the Seyhan River.

The power plant will be designed for three 18,000 kilowatt generators, two of which will be installed at once and the third when needed. The plant will make possible the growth of existing industries (chiefly textiles and processing of vegetable oils), the establishment of new ones, and additional public use of electricity. Construction of the dam is already under way and orders have been placed for the electrical equipment for the power plant. When completed, the power-generating and transmission facilities will be turned over to a new corporation, the Cukurova Utility Power Company, in which a majority of the stock is privately held.

Industrial Development Bank

The Bank has made two loans, each for $9 million, to the Industrial Development Bank of Turkey. This bank was established in June 1950 with the assistance of the Government and of the International Bank, to stimulate the growth of private industrial enterprise in Turkey. The initial equity capital of the Industrial Development Bank, amounting to 12,500,000 Turkish liras ($4.5 million), was entirely subscribed by private interests; an additional T.L. 12,500,000 was borrowed from the Central Bank of Turkey.

The International Bank's loans furnish the Development Bank with foreign exchange which it re-lends to private entrepreneurs for projects requiring imports of equipment from abroad. These projects are submitted to the International Bank for approval before loans are made.

Since it began operations early in 1951 the Development Bank has made an important contribution to an increase of private investment in Turkish industry. By the end of October 1953, the Bank had made 178 loans, totaling the equivalent of almost $30 million, for a wide variety of industrial projects, principally manufacturing, food processing and the fabrication of building materials. It had also helped to establish a variety of smaller industries, including machine repair shops.

Most of the loans have been made in Turkish liras from the Development Bank's local currency resources, which include counterpart funds made available under agreement between the

Turkish Government and the United States Foreign Operations Administration. In addition, private industrialists are investing larger amounts in projects financed by the Development Bank. The International Bank's first loan, made in October 1950, has provided foreign exchange for 25 of the projects.

To meet the continuing demands of Turkish industry for new investment, the Development Bank is increasing its resources. The second loan from the International Bank, made in September 1953, will replenish the Development Bank's foreign exchange resources. To increase local currency resources, the Development Bank in late 1953 sold new stock amounting to T.L. 12,500,000, and is now arranging for a loan of additional Turkish currency from domestic sources.

General Survey Mission

A general survey mission organized by the Bank went to Turkey in 1950. Its report was transmitted to the Government in May 1951. Three basic principles underlie the program proposed by the mission: the development of agriculture as the essential foundation for further industrialization; better use of Turkey's human and physical resources, in particular the training of technical, administrative and managerial personnel; and coordination of economic policy and activity by the Government to ensure that the resources available for development will be applied to the areas of greatest economic need. To achieve these objectives, the report made recommendations on policy and administration and suggested the broad outlines of an investment program.

Since August 1952 a special representative of the Bank has been resident in Turkey. He is available for consultation by the Government on financial and economic questions relating to Turkey's economic development.

Yugoslavia

Fiscal 1950: $2.7 million 2-year 3% loan of October 17, 1949 for equipment for timber production. Fully disbursed by December 1950, and now completely repaid.

Fiscal 1952: $28 million equivalent 25-year 4½% loan of October 11, 1951 for power, mining, industrial and other projects.

Fiscal 1953: $30 million equivalent 25-year 4⅞% loan of February 11, 1953 for power, mining, industrial and other projects.

The first of the Bank's three loans was to increase Yugoslavia's timber exports to Western Europe; it was negotiated apart from consideration of the country's plans for economic development. For the most part, the second and third loans were made to finance equipment needed to complete key projects in which Yugoslavia had already made large investments of domestic currency and foreign exchange. The projects were chosen for financing because they were expected to promptly increase production which would substantially improve Yugoslavia's international balance of payments. The two loans will be repaid in 11 different European currencies; they do not include dollars, since Yugoslavia can service debt in European currencies with less difficulty than dollar debt.

The $2.7 million timber loan of 1949 was made simultaneously with a similar loan of $2.3 million to Finland. It had its origins in findings by the United Nations Economic Commission for Europe and by the Food and Agriculture Organization that Finland and Yugoslavia could materially increase exports of sawn timber if they could obtain timbering and sawmill equipment in Europe and the United States. The Bank's loan provided Yugoslavia with dollars for equipment purchases in the United States. Under arrangements made in connection with the loan, Yugoslavia exported timber to the United Kingdom, the Netherlands, France and Italy; these countries paid dollars directly to the Bank for a sufficient part of the timber to service the Bank's loan. Repayment of the loan was completed in 1951.

The second loan, of European currencies equivalent to $28 million, was made in October 1951. It was concluded after more than two years of consultation between the Bank and Yugoslavia about financing the development of Yugloslavia's economy.

The loan is financing the import of equipment in seven basic fields of the economy. The projects include: (1) extension of electric power facilities; (2) modernization and expansion of coal mines; (3) installation of additional equipment at the Bor copper mine, and the erection of a new zinc electrolysis plant at Sabac; (4) erection of new ceramic plants, opening of a new salt mine and expansion of three metal-working plants, a ceramic plant, a soda ash plant and eight cement plants; (5) erection of new plants for the manufacture of plywood, pulp and kraft paper; (6) acquisition of farm machinery and of equipment for the fishing industry; and (7) importation of equipment for railways and ports.

A Bank mission visited Yugoslavia in the middle of 1952 and found that progress on projects supported by the loan had been satisfactory. It also noted improvement in the availability of goods. This improvement had been facilitated by grant aid from the United States, the United Kingdom and France, and by changes in economic organization aimed at decentralization of management and the encouragement of initiative.

The mission's studies and recommendations resulted in February 1953 in another loan of European currencies equivalent to $30 million. This loan was similar in purpose to the second. The projects include (1) extension of electric power facilities; (2) modernization and expansion of coal mining; (3) the completion of the first phase in the construction of the Strnisce aluminum plant; (4) the expansion of iron and steel production; (5) the erection of a newsprint plant, and other measures to utilize forest resources; (6) the erection of a copper cable and wire plant, the completion of a starch plant and the addition of modern equipment in a chemical fertilizer plant and a glass factory; and (7) the importation of equipment for railways, harbors and airports.

WESTERN HEMISPHERE

Brazil

Fiscal 1949:
$75 million 25-year 4½% loan of January 27, 1949 to Brazilian Traction, Light and Power Company, Limited, for power and telephone development. Fully disbursed by December 1953.

Fiscal 1950:
$15 million 25-year 4¼% loan of May 26, 1950 to Companhia Hidro Eletrica do Sao Francisco for power development.

Fiscal 1951:
$15 million 25-year 4¼% loan of January 18, 1951 to Brazilian Traction, Light and Power Company, Limited, for power development. Fully disbursed by December 1953.

Fiscal 1952:
$25 million 25-year 4¾% loan of June 27, 1952 to Comissao Estadual de Energia Eletrica of Rio Grande do Sul for power development.

$12.5 million 14-year 4⅝% loan of June 27, 1952 for improvement of railways.

Fiscal 1953:
$3 million 5-year 4¼% loan of April 30, 1953 for highway improvements.

Fiscal 1954:
$7.3 million 20-year 5% loan of July 17, 1953 to Centrais Eletricas de Minas Gerais and Companhia de Eletricidade do Alto Rio Grande for power development.

$12.5 million 15-year 4⅞% loan of December 18, 1953 for improvement of railways.

$10 million 20-year 5% loan of December 18, 1953 to Usinas Eletricas do Paranapanema, S. A. for power development.

The purpose of Bank lending in Brazil has been to overcome major obstacles to development which are presented by deficiencies in electric power supply and transportation. Power projects being financed with the help of Bank loans will add more than a million kilowatts to generating capacity in Brazil.

The Bank maintained close contact with the Joint Brazil-United States Economic Development Commission, which worked during the years 1951-53 to develop an investment program for Brazil, to establish priorities within the program, and to assist in the technical preparation of projects. Bank loans made in Brazil in and after June 1952 were for projects approved by the Commission; other projects prepared with the help of the Commission were under study in the Bank at the end of 1953.

Electric Power

The first Brazilian loan was made in January 1949 to the Brazilian Traction, Light & Power Company, Ltd.; it was for $75 million, and was increased two years later by $15 million. Brazilian Traction, a Canadian corporation, is the largest private enterprise in Brazil. It supplies about 65% of the electric energy produced in Brazil and serves the areas of Rio de Janeiro and Sao Paulo, which produce 75% of Brazil's industrial output. In addition to the principal industries, the company's customers include four of the most important railways and the National Steel Mill at Volta Redonda.

The company began a five-year program in 1949 to expand both its power and telephone services. The Bank's loan is paying for the major part of the imported equipment and materials needed for this program. Most of the projects have already been completed and have increased the supplies of power substantially. Four hydroelectric generating units have been installed: three units of a total capacity of 195,000-kilowatts at Cubatao in the Sao Paulo area, and one 52,000-kilowatt unit at Ilha dos Pombos in the Rio area. In addition, a floating power plant, the " Piraqua," with a capacity of 25,000 kilowatts, has been bought and is in use at Rio; it will eventually be used at Santos to augment the Sao Paulo system. Construction and pump installations have been completed for diverting water from the Paraiba to the Pirai River for generating power at the old Fontes and new Forçacava plants in the Rio area. Of the six generator units being installed at Forçacava, three with a total capacity of 135,000 kilowatts are expected to begin operating early in 1954.

The telephone project has been nearly completed. It includes the installation of equipment to serve 125,000 additional telephone subscribers and to increase toll traffic capacity between Rio and Sao Paulo by about half. Approximately 24,000 miles of toll circuits and 1,800 miles of toll lines are being added to the areas served. The entire program is expected to be completed by the end of 1954.

In May 1950, the Bank made a loan of $15 million to the Companhia Hidro Eletrica do Sao Francisco for a project to increase electric power supplies in northeastern Brazil. The company is building a hydroelectric plant at Paulo Afonso Falls, about 150 miles from the mouth of the Sao Francisco River. It is designed for three 60,000-kilowatt generating units, of which two will be installed initially. The plant will supply power to Recife (the most important port of northern Brazil and the center of the sugar industry), to Salvador (another port city and the center of the tobacco and cocoa industries), and to a large number of smaller towns. Power from the plant will replace higher-cost thermal power and save foreign exchange now being spent on imported fuels. By making ample power available in the northeastern part of Brazil, the project is expected to have a generally stimulating effect on both agriculture and industry in this relatively undeveloped region.

The Bank's third power loan, amounting to $25 million, was for the expansion of facilities in the State of Rio Grande do Sul, in the southern part of the country. Because of its favorable climate and fertile land, the State is an important agricultural and cattle-raising area. Light industries, such as food processing, shoe manufacturing and textile production, have already been established. The State contains Brazil's largest known deposits of coal, and prospects are good for further development of industry as well as agriculture.

Demands for electric power for industrial, commercial and residential purposes in the State have been steadily increasing and shortages have necessitated power rationing. The State has undertaken an electrification program to meet these needs and to provide for future requirements. The first stage of the program is nearly completed, and will add 40,000 kilowatts to generating capacity. The second stage, which is to be completed in 1960, will add another 185,000 kilowatts to the system and more than double present capacity. This portion of the program includes the construction of four hydroelectric power stations, two steam turbine plants and some small diesel plants. The Bank's loan was made in June 1952 to the Comissao Estadual de Energia Eletrica and is being applied to the second stage. It will pay for imported equipment and materials for projects to be completed in or before 1957.

A loan of $7.3 million is helping to build an electric power project in the State of Minas Gerais, in central Brazil. The project includes a dam at Itutinga Falls on the Rio Grande, a power station with 24,000 kilowatts of generating capacity, and transmission lines and substations. Itutinga lies within the industrial complex of Rio de Janeiro, Belo Horizonte and Volta Redonda. The area contains important deposits of iron ore, manganese and tin-bearing ores. Industry will take about 80% of the power to be generated at the new plant and the remainder will be taken by public utilities serving three small towns. The plant is expected to start operations in January 1955 and to be in full operation by the end of 1956.

The Bank's fifth power loan was made in December 1953 to the Usinas Eletricas do Paranapanema S. A., a corporation owned almost entirely by the State of Sao Paulo. The loan amounts to $10 million. It will finance the foreign exchange costs of a hydroelectric project consisting of a dam across the Paranapanema

River at Salto Grande, a hydroelectric plant with a generating capacity of 60,000 kilowatts, and associated transmission and distribution facilities in the States of Sao Paulo and Parana. The power will serve rapidly expanding agricultural and urban centers in this coffee-growing region, and will help electrify the Sorocabana Railroad, one of the important railways in Sao Paulo.

Transportation

The Bank has made two loans totaling $25 million for an emergency program to improve the services of the Central do Brasil Railroad. The Central connects Brazil's major industrial centers, and is a large carrier of iron ores, steel, fuel and food products, as well as of passengers. The first loan was made in June 1952 and amounted to $12.5 million. It was made to finance the equipment most immediately needed to improve the Central's freight service. At the same time, the Bank indicated that it would be prepared to consider an additional loan, for the suburban service of the Central in the Rio district, as soon as effective steps were taken to improve administration and operating conditions on the suburban lines. This loan, also of $12.5 million, was made in December 1953.

The first loan is being applied to a project which includes an increase of rolling stock, the rehabilitation of track, the equipping of a diesel shop, the construction of a marshaling yard and the strengthening of bridges. Most of the loan has been allocated to the import of components of freight cars to be assembled in Brazil; the remainder will be used to buy equipment for track maintenance, stone-quarrying (for track ballast) and repair shops.

The loan for the suburban services of the Central will help to finance the import of 100 electric motor cars, 100 trailer cars, parts for another 100 trailer cars to be assembled in Brazil, and spare parts. Some of the funds will also be used for the rehabilitation of suburban track and the improvement of repair and maintenance facilities. The Central's suburban service is an important means of transport for industrial, commercial and government workers living in suburbs of Rio de Janeiro and the areas adjoining the Federal District. Properly equipped and operated, the service will be the best and cheapest form of mass suburban transport in the Rio area.

In April 1953 the Bank made a loan of $3 million to finance equipment needed by the Highway Department of the State of Rio de Janeiro, principally for road maintenance but also for some new highway construction and paving. The State road network serves large and important industrial and agricultural areas adjacent to the city of Rio de Janeiro. Trucks haul a heavy volume of freight, including food products, steel, metal and chemical products. Since 1939, 2,200 miles of roads, part of a projected 3,100-mile road program, have been built by the State to cope with this traffic but they include only 20 miles of paved road. A further 700 miles of roads will be constructed or improved during the next five years.

British Guiana

A general survey mission visited British Guiana in February and March 1953 to prepare recommendations to the Government for a long-term investment program. Three members of the eight-man group were nominated by the Food and Agriculture Organization, which also shared their expenses. The Bank transmitted the mission's report to the Governor of British Guiana in August 1953.

The report pointed out that one of British Guiana's chief problems is its rapidly growing population. Since 1945 the annual rate of growth has risen from 1.5% to 2.8%. In the face of this trend, the investment program recommended by the mission aimed to increase national income by 20% and per capita income by 6% over the next five years. The program would require government expenditure of 66 million British West Indies dollars (equivalent to U. S. $38.5 million) over the five years from 1954

171

through 1958. Most of this amount, in the opinion of the mission, could be financed from the internal and external resources normally available to the Government.

Agriculture is the chief economic activity in British Guiana and the largest investment was recommended in this field. The report endorsed drainage and irrigation projects which would increase by about 25% (67,000 acres) the land now under cultivation. The mission emphasized the importance of stepping up the production of food crops and recommended, among other things, the expansion of agricultural research and extension services as aids to the small-scale farming which is becoming more prevalent in British Guiana.

Improvements in transportation and communications, especially in the road system, were regarded by the mission as likewise deserving priority in the public investment program. The report also contained proposals for expanding industries based on timber and agricultural resources, and for improvements in education and housing.

The mission urged that the groundwork be laid now for projects to be undertaken after 1958, the last year of its proposed program. It emphasized particularly the desirability of studies looking toward new land reclamation projects and toward exploring possibilities in the interior of the Colony for the development of hydroelectric power, timber production, cattle raising and mining.

Chile

Fiscal 1948: $13.5 million 20-year 4½% loan of March 25, 1948 to Corporacion de Fomento de la Produccion (Fomento) and Empresa Nacional de Electricidad, S. A. (Endesa) for power development.

$2.5 million 6½-year 3¾% loan of March 25, 1948 to Corporacion de Fomento de la Produccion for agricultural machinery. Fully disbursed by December 1949.

Fiscal $1.3 million 10-year 4⅜% loan of October 10, 1951 to
1952:   Corporacion de Fomento de la Produccion for exploration
and use of water resources of the Rio Elqui Valley.

Fiscal $20 million 17-year 5% loan of September 10, 1953 to
1954:   Corporacion de Fomento de la Produccion and Cia.
Manufacturera de Papeles y Cartones S. A. for construction of paper and pulp mills.

Chile was the first country to receive development loans from the Bank. They have been made to support power development, to finance the private manufacture of paper pulp and newsprint, and to promote food production. In addition the Bank, in cooperation with the Food and Agriculture Organization, organized a mission which carried out an intensive study of Chile's agricultural problems and prepared an agricultural development program. The report and recommendations of the mission were transmitted to the Government in 1952.

Power Development

Despite the excellent hydroelectric power potential offered by many rivers falling from the Andes to the Pacific, electric generating capacity in Chile has long been inadequate for the country's power requirements. Development of cheap hydroelectric power is basic to the expansion of industry and the improvement of agriculture. The Government, acting through the Corporacion de Fomento and Fomento's subsidiary, the Empresa Nacional de Electricidad (Endesa), has therefore given power expansion a high priority.

Endesa is carrying forward an electrification program drawn up by Fomento in 1942, designed to more than double generating capacity by 1955. The Bank's loan of $13.5 million is being used for a number of power projects within the program. These projects will increase generating capacity by 86,000 kilowatts and inter-connect two important power networks. The largest project is a hydroelectric plant at Los Cipreses which will serve the city of Santiago, in central Chile; here the Bank is financing 58,900 kilowatts of capacity out of a total of some 88,000. Other Bank-financed units in northern and southern Chile have already gone into operation.

A loan of $20 million was made in September 1953 to the privately owned Cia. Manufacturera de Papeles y Cartones S. A., with Fomento as joint borrower, to help finance the construction of a chemical pulp mill and a newsprint paper mill. Papeles y Cartones is Chile's only pulp and paper manufacturer. Despite a steady growth in production, the company has not been able to meet domestic demands for paper and paper products. In 1950 Chilean imports of newsprint and cellulose pulp were valued at the equivalent of over $5 million.

The newsprint paper mill, to be located at Concepcion, will make 44,000 tons of newsprint and 6,600 tons of boxboard a year from mechanical pulp, chemical pulp and scrap paper. The chemical pulp mill, to be built about 40 miles southeast of Concepcion, will make about 50,000 tons of chemical pulp and 10,000 tons of kraft paper annually. The plants will be constructed so that with added equipment they could manufacture rayon pulp.

The establishment of the new mills will be an important step toward the fuller use of Chile's extensive forest resources. The Bank-FAO mission had stressed the importance of forestry, pointing out that timber resources could become an important source of foreign exchange earnings and a valuable means of diversifying Chilean exports. An afforestation program undertaken some 30 years ago and later intensified following the recommendations of a United States Forestry Mission, is now yielding large quantities of insignis pine. This tree grows with extraordinary rapidity in central Chile. Papeles y Cartones has been using it since 1938 for making mechanical pulp and extensive tests have shown that the wood is also well suited to the making of chemical pulp.

Agriculture

Agricultural production has failed to keep pace with the growth of population and imports of food have risen sharply since the end of the war. Fomento, accordingly, has undertaken a program to mechanize farming and increase production; and the Bank's $2.5 million loan was made to import equipment for this program. About $1 million of it was spent on tractors, another $1 million on threshers and harvesters, and the remainder on plows and miscellaneous equipment. All the equipment was sold by Fomento to individual farmers; Fomento has used the proceeds to import still more equipment and to help defray the cost of irrigation studies.

Agricultural production in the northern valleys of Chile is at present small and large areas are uncultivated. The supply of surface water is extremely uncertain. If underground sources could provide an assured and adequate water supply, agricultural productivity could be increased and some new land could be brought under cultivation.

In 1951 the Bank made a loan to Fomento for drills and equipment needed to measure the underground water resources of the Rio Elqui Valley in north central Chile. The $1.3 million loan included funds to be spent, if sufficient water were found, on pumps and electric power units to pump the water for irrigation. The exploratory phase of the project was nearing completion at the end of 1953. The data collected had been submitted to the United States Bureau of Reclamation for analysis and the final report was expected to be ready early in 1954. Present indications are that only a limited amount of underground water is available. The equipment bought with the Bank's loan will be used for similar explorations in other parts of Chile.

In 1951 the Bank joined with the Food and Agriculture Organization in organizing an agricultural mission to study Chile's agricultural problems and draw up recommendations for an agricultural development program. The mission spent four months in Chile and its report was presented to the Government at the end of 1952. The report recommended steps to increase agricultural output over eight years to a level some 40% above that for the period 1945-49. The mission emphasized the need for the Government to pursue long-term financial and agricultural policies which would give farmers an incentive to increase production. It also suggested measures to bring about (1) an increase in the area under cultivation by means of irrigation and land reclamation, and (2) improvement of farming methods by more mechanization, an increase in mixed farming (i. e. growing of both livestock and crops), disease control, improvement of seeds, and the like. The mission felt that if its recommendations were effectively carried out, Chile would be able to meet its basic food requirements from its own soil. The Government is now preparing a number of projects based on the mission's recommendations.

Colombia

Fiscal 1950: $5 million 7-year 3½% loan of August 19, 1949 to Caja de Credito Agrario, Industrial y Minero for agricultural machinery; reduced at request of borrower on April 2, 1951 to $4.9 million, which had been disbursed by February 1951.

Fiscal 1951: $3.53 million 20-year 4% loan of November 2, 1950 to Central Hidroelectrica del Rio Anchicaya, Limitada, for power development.

$2.6 million 20-year 4% loan of December 28, 1950 to Central Hidroelectrica de Caldas, Limitada, for power development. Fully disbursed by July 1953.

$16.5 million 10-year 3⅞% loan of April 10, 1951 for highway construction and rehabilitation.

Fiscal 1952: $2.4 million 20-year 4½% loan of November 13, 1951 to Central Hidroelectrica del Rio Lebrija, Limitada, for power development.

Fiscal $25 million 25-year 4¾% loan of August 26, 1952 for
1953: construction of the Magdalena Valley Railroad and
central repair shops.

Fiscal $14.35 million 10-year 4¾% loan of September 10, 1953
1954: for highway rehabilitation and maintenance.

Over a four-year period, the Bank has lent nearly $70 million
for basic development projects in Colombia. The first general
survey mission organized by the Bank went to Colombia in 1949,
and the Government since that time has frequently consulted the
Bank on a wide range of development problems.

General Survey Mission and Other Technical Assistance

The report of the general survey mission was transmitted to
the Government in July 1950. Thereupon the Government established a non-partisan Economic Development Committee to consider the report and to assist it in drawing up a development
program based on the mission's recommendations. Several members of the staff of the Bank assisted the Committee. Before the
Committee completed its work in September 1951, the Government had already taken a number of actions based on its recommendations. Inflation was checked, foreign exchange controls
were relaxed, and a comprehensive highway rehabilitation program
was adopted. The Government reorganized the Banco de la
Republica and liberalized its policy regarding the importation and
export of capital.

In April 1952 the Government established a central planning
office to coordinate development policies and projects. The Bank
has given leave of absence to one of its staff members to serve
as Planning Advisor to this office, and has nominated several
specialists to serve it in various capacities.

In addition to helping the Government in its overall planning
for development, the Bank has provided assistance in working out
specific measures to achieve development objectives in particular
fields. In 1951 the Government and the Bank jointly sponsored

a visit by a financial expert to advise on measures to increase the flow of capital into productive private industry and to develop the market for government securities. The Bank also joined the Government in engaging an engineering firm to study a proposed reorganization of the railroads and of civil aviation ground facilities. The same firm was subsequently retained to coordinate and supervise the execution of the railway program. Bank representatives have from time to time been stationed in Bogota to assist the Government on special problems.

Agriculture

Expansion of industry in Colombia in recent years has drawn labor away from rural districts and at the same time increased the demand for agricultural commodities. The mechanization of agriculture is the chief means by which more land can be brought under cultivation and production can be increased. Even in those areas where labor is still relatively abundant, traditional hand methods make farming operations unduly costly.

The Bank's first loan in Colombia, made in August 1949, was designed to promote an increase in mechanized farming. This loan of $5 million was made to the Caja de Credito Agrario, Industrial y Minero, a government credit institution, for the import of agricultural machinery, spare parts and equipment for repair and maintenance centers. For its agricultural activities, the Caja maintains about 100 branches throughout the country which sell agricultural implements and supplies and which provide credit and banking facilities to the rural community.

By early 1951 the loan had been completely disbursed. About $4 million was spent on tractors and the remainder on equipment for repair shops, hand tools and animal-drawn equipment. Most of the machinery is being used in four areas particularly suited to mechanized agriculture: in the Sinu River area to expand cotton production; in the Department of Tolima for increased production of rice and sesame; in the Cauca Valley for the production of sugar cane, rice, beans and maize; and on the plain of Bogota for the cultivation of potatoes, wheat and vegetables.

The equipment acquired with the loan has been sold to farmers, some of whom have received credit from the Caja for this purpose. Repayments to the Caja have been deposited in a revolving fund; and the Caja has used these funds for additional purchases of machinery. By the end of June 1953, purchases from the revolving fund amounted to about $8 million.

Electric Power

The Bank has made loans for three hydroelectric power projects in Colombia, each serving an important urban area. In November 1950 the Bank lent $3.53 million to the Central Hidroelectrica del Rio Anchicaya, Limitada, to cover part of the foreign exchange costs of a 24,000-kilowatt hydroelectric plant on the Anchicaya River, together with the necessary transmission lines and substations. The plant will supply power to Cali in western Colombia, one of the country's four major industrial centers, and will assist in the development of the Cauca Valley, a rich agricultural region which also has a large industrial potential. Cali's industry is growing rapidly, due to its favorable geographical location, natural resources and good communications with the rest of the country, and it requires an ample supply of power. This power project was started in 1945, but progress was slow because of lack of capital and adequate equipment. Construction was finally stopped because of technical difficulties that required the project to be redesigned. Work was resumed after the Bank loan was made and should be completed in late 1954.

In December 1950 the Bank lent $2.6 million to the Central Hidroelectrica de Caldas, Limitada, to cover most of the foreign exchange costs of a 15,000-kilowatt hydroelectric plant on the Chinchina River, transmission lines to Manizales and neighboring municipalities, and the rehabilitation and expansion of the distribution systems in this area. Manizales, a fast-growing city of considerable commercial and industrial importance, is in the center of Colombia's main coffee-producing area. Work on the power project began in 1944 but encountered many difficulties, both technical and financial, and progress was slow. These problems had been resolved when the Bank's loan was made and since then work has proceeded steadily. The plant began supplying power to Manizales at the end of 1951; the expansion of the distribution system will soon be completed.

The Bank's third power loan, of $2.4 million, was made in November 1951 to the Central Hidroelectrica del Rio Lebrija, Limitada. This project will quadruple the supply of power to Bucaramanga, the center of the rapidly expanding tobacco-processing industry. The project includes the construction of a power plant on the Lebrija River, transmission lines and the enlargement of Bucaramanga's distribution system. Initially the plant will have an installed capacity of 7,500 kilowatts but it is designed for an eventual capacity of about 15,000 kilowatts. The plant is scheduled to be in operation early in 1954.

Highways

The Bank has made two loans to the Government for highway improvement: the first of $16.5 million in April 1951 and a second of $14.35 million in September 1953. The loans were made to help finance an emergency program for the rehabilitation of over 1,800 miles of trunk roads (82½% of these roads are to be paved), the construction of 96 miles of new connecting-link highways, and a comprehensive maintenance program for the entire national highway system. The Bank loans cover the import of construction equipment and materials, repair-shop machinery and supplies, such engineering fees as must be paid in foreign exchange, and the salaries of foreign personnel to assist in the initial stages of the maintenance program.

Colombia's Economic Development Committee recommended this program as a necessary first stage of a long-range program of highway construction and expansion. Because of its mountainous terrain, Colombia is particularly dependent on its highway system, which since 1945 has had to cope with a sharply increasing volume of traffic. The usefulness of the existing system is severely curtailed by gaps in the network, by faulty alignment and outmoded bridges, and by extensive deterioration resulting from inadequate maintenance. The emergency program will remedy the more critical of these deficiencies and should reduce transport costs substantially.

The Colombian Ministry of Public Works has determined that road conservation will hereafter take precedence over new construction; funds will be allocated to other highway operations only after adequate funds to meet all maintenance requirements are assured. The Ministry is also engaged in reorganizing its maintenance administration. For an initial period of at least two years, the Ministry will retain the services of a provisional staff of consultants from abroad who will assist and train the permanent Colombian staff in modern methods of road maintenance.

The Bank has had a highway engineering consultant stationed in Colombia since 1951 to assist the Ministry of Public Works and the contractors and to keep the Bank informed of the progress of the work.

Railroads

The railroad project being financed with the help of a $25 million Bank loan is also an outgrowth of recommendations made by the general survey mission. The project is part of an extensive program for the improvement of the national railroad system. It consists of the construction of a railroad in the Magdalena River Valley and of the construction and equipment of railroad repair shops in Bogota. The new line, 235 miles long, will connect the country's eastern and western rail networks and provide rail transportation between the Pacific port of Buenaventura and important centers in the interior. It will also assure reliable communication between the Caribbean coast and central Colombia by offering an alternative to river transportation which is often seriously delayed during dry seasons. The new repair shops will provide facilities for reconditioning and maintaining rolling stock of which large quantities have had to stand idle for long periods while awaiting repair. This reconditioned equipment should reduce the need for additional rolling stock.

The project is scheduled for completion by March 1956, but some sections of the line will be opened to traffic earlier. The Government and the Bank have agreed that, to be effective, the program for the physical rehabilitation and expansion of railroad facilities should be accompanied by an extensive administrative, operational and financial reorganization. Under the proposed reorganization, which is now under study, the railways will be administered by an autonomous body, with a manager and board of directors independent of political control.

Cuba

A general survey mission consisting of 17 members went to Cuba in 1950 to make a comprehensive survey of the economy and to make specific proposals for future development. The report of the mission was presented to the Government in August 1951. It expressed the mission's belief that Cuba has ample resources, both human and material, with which to increase the nation's output, broaden its economic base, and create a better standard of living for its people. The report recommended that an intensive effort be made to diversify the Cuban economy. It expressed the view that Cuba should seek (1) to reduce its dependence on sugar, not by curtailing sugar production but by promoting new enterprises; (2) to promote industries using sugar by-products or using sugar as a raw material; (3) to promote the export of non-sugar products, such as minerals and foodstuffs; and (4) to produce in Cuba, for domestic consumption, a wide range of foodstuffs, raw materials and consumer goods which are now imported.

The mission urged Cubans to work out for themselves a long-term program of development to accomplish those objectives. To this end, the report outlined specific action that should be taken in applied research, education, labor-management relations, and in government administration and policy. It also recommended ways to increase agricultural and industrial production and to improve railroad transportation.

El Salvador

> Fiscal $12.545 million 25-year 4¼% loan of December 14, 1949
> 1950:   to Comision Ejecutiva Hidroelectrica del Rio Lempa
> for power development.

The loan is financing the foreign exchange costs of a hydro-electric project at Chorrera del Guayabo on the Lempa River, 36 miles from San Salvador, the capital. The project includes the building of a concrete dam, an underground powerhouse, a substation at the dam, two transmission lines and a 16-mile access road to connect the dam with the Pan American Highway. The initial generating capacity being installed is 30,000 kilowatts, which will more than double the supply of electricity in El Salvador. Power from the plant will be transmitted to San Salvador and to the industrial center of San Miguel. As the market expands, the Rio Lempa Commission plans to increase the generating capacity to 75,000 kilowatts.

At the end of 1953 the dam had been built and the installation of the generating units was under way. The project is expected to be complete about the middle of 1954.

For many years there has been a shortage of power in El Salvador. Even in San Salvador power has had to be rationed and shutdowns have been frequent. More power will facilitate irrigation and encourage the production of such crops as sugar cane, cotton, corn, beans and oilseeds. It will enable water to be pumped at less cost to villages and towns which have hitherto been inadequately supplied even when water has been within easy reach. It will make possible considerable expansion of such established industries as coffee milling, textile production, food processing and gold mining, and will encourage the establishment of new light industries. Since the loan was made in December 1949, private interests have already built a fertilizer plant and a cement plant, and a second cement plant is under construction. The availability of hydroelectric power will also permit the progressive retirement of high-cost diesel and steam-generating units and thereby reduce both expenditures for imported petroleum and consumption of scarce wood fuel.

The method of financing the local currency costs of the project was of special interest, being the first operation of its kind ever undertaken in El Salvador. The Bank proposed and the Government agreed that the local currency funds required for the project should be raised by the sale of bonds issued by the Rio Lempa Commission and guaranteed by the Government. To assist in designing and floating the issue, the Bank lent the services of its Director of Marketing for four months. The issue, amounting to 13.1 million colones ($5.2 million), was fully subscribed within one week of the date of offering, and was purchased by private investors and corporations as well as by government institutions.

Guatemala

In 1950 a general survey mission spent three months in Guatemala. The six full-time members of the mission were assisted in the field by several agricultural specialists from the Inter-American Institute of Agricultural Sciences in Costa Rica. The report of the mission was submitted to the Government in July 1951.

The report recommended that Guatemala should place primary emphasis on the improvement of agriculture, particularly in coffee and low-cost food crops, and on the expansion of transportation facilities, especially highways. Improvements in these two sectors, according to the report, would lay the foundation for the gradual diversification of the economy and the expansion of manufacturing industries.

In the opinion of the mission, the opening up of the Pacific coastal plains to mechanized agriculture offered the greatest possibilities for achieving a rapid and substantial increase in food-stuffs. Before further development of this area could take place, however, a vigorous effort to eliminate the malarial mosquito would be necessary. The mission stressed the importance of improvements in marketing, storage and credit facilities. It urged an all-out effort to increase the production of coffee, Guatemala's most important export and the potential source of most of the funds for financing future development needs.

The mission found that the inadequacy of the transportation system was probably the greatest single barrier to Guatemala's economic development. As a first step toward relieving this situation, it recommended the adoption of a basic national plan for highway development and maintenance. Other steps suggested were the expansion of domestic airlines to serve isolated areas, and the establishment of a non-political public utilities commission to regulate rates and services for all forms of transport.

The report also included recommendations relating to industry, mining, telecommunications and power, and economic and financial policy. It outlined three alternative programs of public invest-ment, depending on the size of the financial resources available.

The Government established a Citizen's Committee to study the report and to recommend action based on its findings. At the Government's request, the Bank assigned a staff member to assist the Committee and to advise the Government on the fiscal aspects of the development program proposed in the report. The Com-mittee submitted its findings to the National Economic Council in December 1951. Subsequently, the Government adopted a development program which differed substantially from the mission's recommendations.

Jamaica

A general survey mission, organized by the Bank, made a two-month visit to Jamaica early in 1952. The group consisted of seven members; the Food and Agriculture Organization nominated an agricultural specialist and shared his expenses. The report of the mission was transmitted to the Government in December 1952. After considering it for several months, the Government issued a statement of policy which accepted the recommendations in the report as the framework within which government action for economic development would be planned and carried out in the coming decade.

Jamaica's chief problems are chronic unemployment and widespread poverty. The mission proposed a 10-year program to increase production and reduce unemployment, largely through the development of agriculture. Chief among the recommendations in this field were programs of soil conservation, irrigation, reclamation of swamp land, and pasture improvement. The mission also urged land surveys for proper planning of land use, and changes in the system of land taxation. Other recommendations concerned measures to increase industrial productivity, to develop the tourist industry and to expand mining, electric power and transportation facilities. In the field of social services, the mission stressed the improvement of technical education as a means of bringing about an increase in the country's productive capacity.

Mexico

Fiscal 1949: $24.1 million 25-year 4½% loan of January 6, 1949 to Comision Federal de Electricidad and Nacional Financiera for power development.

$10 million 1-year 4½% loan of January 6, 1949 to Comision

Federal de Electricidad and Nacional Financiera for power development. (Refunded)

Fiscal 1950: $26 million 25-year 4½% loan of April 28, 1950 to Mexican Light and Power Company, Limited, for power development.

Fiscal 1951: $10 million (maturity dates 1952-1957) 3½% line of credit of October 18, 1950 to a consortium of eight Mexican banks and Nacional Financiera for financial assistance to small enterprises. Expired on June 30, 1952 with $532,000 of loans outstanding. Of this amount $4,000 was canceled on July 1, 1953. The balance of $528,000 has been disbursed.

Fiscal 1952: $29.7 million 25-year 4½% loan of January 11, 1952 to Comision Federal de Electricidad and Nacional Financiera for power development.

Nearly all Bank lending in Mexico has been for electric power development. With its rapidly growing population, Mexico urgently needs a greater supply of power to make possible the continued expansion of industry and to increase agricultural production through modern methods of irrigation. When the projects being financed with the help of three Bank loans are completed in 1955, they will have added 700,000 kilowatts to Mexico's generating capacity, and total capacity will have risen to 1,850,000 kilowatts, almost double the amount in existence when the Bank's first loan was made in 1949. Despite this growth, power production will be sufficient to cover only the most essential requirements. The Bank has agreed to cooperate with the Mexican authorities in the preparation of a comprehensive study of future power development in Mexico.

Electric Power

The Bank has made two loans, one of $24.1 million in 1949 and one of $29.7 million in 1952, to the Comision Federal de Electricidad, a government agency, with Nacional Financiera, an official financing institution of the Government, as joint borrower. The projects included under the loan of $24.1 million total 326,000 kilowatts of generating capacity, together with the necessary transmission and distribution facilities. The capacity of the Miguel Aleman hydroelectric system, serving the Mexico City area, is being increased by 185,000 kilowatts; and miscellaneous thermal and hydroelectric plants have been installed in other parts of Mexico. Nearly all the projects under the first loan are in operation, but there has been some delay in completing the installation of a 45,000-kilowatt unit in the Miguel Aleman system because of the elaborate civil engineering works involved.

The second loan is helping to finance two hydroelectric plants, four thermal plants and increased distribution facilities in widely separated parts of the country. One of the two hydroelectric plants, an extension of the Miguel Aleman system at Tingambato in the State of Mexico, will generate 150,000 kilowatts and will be the largest power plant in Mexico. The other, at El Cobano in the State of Michoacan, will generate 55,000 kilowatts and will make use of hydraulic works already constructed for irrigation. One of the steam plants (30,000 kilowatts) will be built in Monterrey, Mexico's second most important industrial city. In the State of Sonora new distribution facilities will permit fuller use of the generating stations constructed at Ciudad Obregon and Guaymas with the aid of the Bank's first loan to the Comision.

A loan of $26 million was made to the Mexican Light and Power Co., Ltd. (Mexlight) in April 1950. In connection with this loan, Mexlight's capital structure was reorganized to permit the Bank to rank equally with other bondholders and to provide Mexlight with better prospects of access to the private capital market in the future. Pending this reorganization, the Bank in January 1949 lent the Comision and Nacional Financiera $10 million for relending to Mexlight; this credit was refunded out of the $26 million loan.

The loan is enabling Mexlight to continue with its share of a long-range program, coordinated with that of the Comision,

188

to increase the supply of electric power to Mexico City and the surrounding districts. Under the program, Mexlight will add 155,000 kilowatts to its previously installed generating capacity of 279,000 kilowatts, and will increase the transmission and distribution facilities by which it distributes the power generated in the Comision's Miguel Aleman system as well as its own.

Of Mexlight's new capacity, 110,000 kilowatts were in operation at the end of 1953. Work on a 45,000-kilowatt hydroelectric plant at Patla, and on a transmission line from Patla to Mexico City, should be completed by mid-1954.

Line of Credit to Consortium of Mexican Banks

A $10 million line of credit was extended to a consortium of eight Mexican private commercial banks, together with Nacional Financiera, in October 1950. It was to be used to make small loans for the foreign exchange costs of private industrial projects in Mexico. When the line of credit expired on June 30, 1952, only six loans totaling $595,050 had been granted, and one of these had been canceled by the borrower. The projects financed were expansions of textile and other light manufacturing concerns.

The disappointing results of this experiment in making Bank credit available through private commercial banks to small borrowers may be traced to several factors. First, the line of credit became effective at a time when foreign exchange holdings in Mexico were increasing rapidly and private capital from abroad was becoming more readily available. The Bank's line of credit therefore became less attractive. Second, the strict and complex requirements of Mexican law regarding commercial bank loans for industrial expansion made the practical operation of the line of credit difficult. Third, potential borrowers under the line of credit were reluctant to assume any part of the foreign exchange risk involved.

Study of the Mexican Economy

In April 1951, at the suggestion of the Mexican Government, a working party consisting of an economist from the Nacional Financiera, one from the Banco de Mexico and two economists from the Bank's staff, began a study of the long-term trends in the Mexican economy, with special reference to Mexico's capacity to absorb additional foreign investment. The group spent more than a year on this work, and presented its report to the Government and the Bank in October 1952.

The report pointed out that Mexico's remarkable development between 1939 and 1950 was made possible by an unusually high rate of savings resulting from credit expansion and restrictions on consumption and by confining investment largely to fields which offered quick and substantial returns. These returns were possible as long as existing public facilities, such as railways, roads and power stations, could be made to carry additional burdens and as long as existing oil fields and mines continued to give rich yields. The report stated that a stage had now been reached when heavy capital investment was needed for the improvement of public facilities and for the development and conservation of natural resources, and that an increasing proportion of investment would have to be devoted to the maintenance of existing undertakings.

The report expressed the view that it will be difficult to raise domestic savings above the present high level. Accordingly, it concluded that if the pace of development is to be maintained, Mexico will have to rely more on external capital in the future than it did in the past and appropriate financial policies will have to be adopted to prevent increased external borrowing from disturbing the balance of payments. The report stressed the importance of a greater degree of central coordination of both private and public development projects.

The Government has given serious consideration to the report and has formulated a preliminary investment program for the years 1953-58 which marks an important step toward a coordinated development policy.

Nicaragua

Fiscal 1951: $3.5 million 10-year 4⅛% loan of June 7, 1951 for highway construction.

$1.2 million 7-year 4% loan of June 7, 1951 to the Banco Nacional de Nicaragua for agricultural machinery.

Fiscal 1952: $550,000 10-year 4⅜% loan of October 29, 1951 for grain storage facilities. $3,006 canceled in December 1953. Net amount disbursed by December 1953.

Fiscal 1954: $3.5 million 10-year 4¾% loan of September 4, 1953 for highway construction.

$450,000 10-year 4¾% loan of September 4, 1953 for power development.

The Bank's lending in Nicaragua has been chiefly directed to projects for the development of the country's considerable agricultural potential. In addition, the Bank has provided Nicaragua with technical advice on many problems, largely through special representatives it has maintained in the country since July 1951. The first special representative, assisted by other experts, drew up recommendations for a long-range development program and worked closely with the Government in the early steps taken to put the program into effect. His successor has continued to work closely with the Government in the further elaboration and execution of the program.

Agriculture

A loan of $1.2 million was made in June 1951 to the Banco Nacional de Nicaragua for the importation of agricultural machinery.

Although Nicaragua is a predominantly agricultural country, its agricultural resources are at present far from being fully

191

exploited. Large areas of fertile land have never been opened up and the shortage of farm labor is causing the limited acreage under cultivation to shrink still further. Moreover, methods of farming are inefficient and costly.

Machinery financed by the loan included: 265 units consisting of a tractor, plow and harrow; limited numbers of planters, cultivators and dusters; and maintenance equipment. In the first two years about 15,000 acres, much of it new land, were plowed with the new tractor units and put into cultivation.

The machinery was imported by regular dealers and sold to farmers on credit from the Banco Nacional. These loans were made with the cordobas received by the Banco Nacional from the sale to machinery importers of the foreign exchange proceeds of the International Bank loan. Improvement of Nicaragua's economic position enabled $245,000 of the Bank loan to be repaid ahead of schedule in April 1953.

The loan of $550,000 was made for the construction in Managua of a grain storage elevator equipped to dry, fumigate and store grain. The elevator has a static capacity of 6,100 tons, but since Nicaragua produces two crops a year, the total annual capacity of the plant will be about 12,000 tons. The plant was constructed in the record time of 230 days and is now in its first year of operation.

Like many tropical countries, Nicaragua loses a substantial portion of its grain through spoilage due to mold and insects. Farmers, lacking facilities for drying and storing, have been forced to sell their crops as soon as they are gathered for whatever price they will bring. By providing drying and storage facilities, the new plant will help to stabilize the supply and price and to improve the quality of grain and grain foods for both local consumption and export. It is anticipated that successful operation of the new plant will encourage construction of similar plants in other parts of the country.

Highways

Two loans of $3.5 million each have been made for highway construction: one in June 1951 and the other in September 1953. Both were to aid the Government in its long-range program to develop an adequate road system.

Inadequate transportation is one of the chief obstacles to the development of Nicaragua's rich agricultural land. Under the highway program, a system of all-weather highways is being constructed to link Managua, the provincial capitals and seaports, and a network of farm-to-market roads will be built to the main highways and around the principal cities. The first loan is being used for the main highway system and is helping to construct eight sections of road totaling 162 miles in length, all asphalt-paved to permit heavy year-round traffic. The second loan is helping to finance the farm-to-market network and two roads in the main highway system.

The roads in the main highway system fall into three regional groups: the western, linking Managua (the capital) with Leon (the second largest city), not previously connected by road; the east-west; and the northern. The new roads will complement the two main trunk highways of the country: the Inter-American Highway, running north-south, and the Rama Road, running east-west and ultimately terminating at Rama, a Caribbean port.

The principal roads, Managua to Leon in the west and Matagalpa to Jinotega in the northern group, are expected to be finished in the first half of 1954. Preliminary work has been started on the remaining sections and all are expected to be completed in 1955.

The second phase of the highway program, being financed with the help of the Bank's second $3.5 million loan, is expected to take about five years to complete. It includes the construction of 412 miles of all-weather feeder and access roads and two paved roads totaling 24 miles. When the secondary roads are completed, trucks should be able to provide transportation at one-fifth to one-tenth of present costs; commerce of all kinds should be greatly stimulated; and farm production can be expected to increase by about 30%.

The effect of the highway and the farm machinery projects on agricultural production is already becoming apparent. The acreage devoted to the principal cash crops (cotton, sesame, rice and beans) increased in 1951-52 by 67% over the previous year. Much of this increase has taken place on land opened up by new roads and it has been greatly facilitated by imports of tractors and farm machinery.

Electric Power

The loan of $450,000 was made for the installation of a new diesel electric unit to ease a serious power shortage in the Managua area.

The Government is planning ultimately to meet the country's power needs by a program of hydroelectric power development, but this program will have to await the completion of preliminary surveys. In the meantime, with the assistance of private consultants, the Government is studying interim means of meeting the growing industrial, commercial and domestic needs of Managua and other major centers of population.

The 3,000-kilowatt unit financed by the Bank's loan will help bridge the gap until steam, and possibly hydroelectric, generating equipment can be installed, and will thereafter provide a useful reserve to cover peak loads or to provide standby capacity. It is of the same type as the unit financed by the Export-Import Bank of Washington in 1951 and brought into operation early in 1953. The new unit should be in operation early in 1954.

Bank's Resident Mission in Nicaragua

In 1951 the Government asked the Bank to assist it in the formulation of a development program. In response to that request, the Bank in July 1951 established in Nicaragua a resident mission consisting of an economist and an engineer; other technical experts were called in as required to assist the mission. These experts included a representative of the Corporacion de Fomento de la Produccion of Chile; an official of the Federal Reserve Bank of New York; a specialist from the Food and Agriculture Organization; and a transportation and communications specialist from the Bank's own staff. In addition to advising the Government on day-to-day problems, the mission, in consultation with the National Economic Council, drew up a development program.

The mission's report recommended a five-year program of investment designed to help the country move forward simultaneously in agriculture, transportation, power, industry, education and health. It also recommended certain administrative and fiscal reforms which the mission felt were required for effective execution of the proposed investment program. The report was formally presented to the President in September 1952 and the proposed development program was thereafter adopted by the Government. At the Government's request, the Bank has continued to maintain a representative in Nicaragua to advise and assist in the execution of the program.

The Government has been effectively carrying out the program of administrative and fiscal reforms recommended by the mission. It organized the National Economic Council to coordinate economic activities while the mission was in Nicaragua, and the Bank gave leave of absence to a Nicaraguan member of its staff in December 1951 so that he could serve as Executive Secretary of the Council. Legislation has been enacted establishing a National Development Institute to promote the growth of industry and agriculture; a Budget Bureau has been organized and budgets prepared providing for a marked increase in development expenditures; an income tax law has been passed; customs duties and the general tax structure are being studied and revised; the mining laws and power development policy have been revised;

and a consultant nominated by the Bank has been employed by the Government to assist in improving operation of the railroad. The highway program being undertaken with Bank financing also closely follows the mission's recommendations.

Panama

Fiscal $1.2 million 7-year 4⅝% loan of September 25, 1953 to
1954:   Instituto de Fomento Economico for agricultural development.

$290,000 8-year 4⅝% loan of September 25, 1953 to Instituto de Fomento Economico for grain storage facilities.

Late in 1951 the Bank sent a small staff mission to Panama to make a preliminary survey of the economy to determine how the Bank might most effectively help in Panama's further development. The report of this mission was transmitted to the Government in August 1952.

The report recommended that, as a first step in a concerted development effort, the Government should initiate a program of administrative and fiscal reforms. This recommendation was accepted and the Bank was asked for help in starting the program. The Bank then arranged for the necessary advisers: experts were made available by the United States Technical Cooperation Administration to advise on public administration, by the United Nations Technical Assistance Administration on tax administration, and by the National Bank of Costa Rica on the organization of a government agency to help finance agricultural and other development.

The Government adopted a series of measures recommended by these experts. An Instituto de Fomento Economico (IFE) was created by special legislation in January 1953 to make loans for private enterprises and to plan public developmental investment, especially in agriculture. Other measures taken to strengthen the financial position of Panama included action to fund and liquidate the internal floating debt, to improve the structure and administration of the tax system, and to establish sound budgetary practices.

These steps made it possible for the Bank to give active consideration to financing development projects in Panama, and in September 1953 two loans totaling $1.49 million were made to IFE for agricultural development. Panama has much good soil but has done little in the past to develop agriculture. The Government is now making intensive efforts in this field, and is carrying out a program to improve farm techniques through extension services and technical advice. The imports to be financed by the Bank's loans will begin to meet the most urgent requirements of the farming community for better equipment and improved storage facilities.

The Bank's loan of $1.2 million will pay for farm machinery and implements. Nearly half of it will be used to buy tractors and other equipment for agricultural machinery pools. IFE will operate the pools and will perform services for farmers on a contract basis. The pools will be located at three key points throughout the country and the machinery will be used for land clearance as well as for cultivation and harvesting. The loan also provides funds which will be used to import machinery and equipment for sale to farmers who will obtain credits from IFE for its purchase.

The $290,000 loan will be used for imported materials and services needed by IFE to build a 4,000-ton capacity plant at Panama City for drying and storing corn and beans. For lack of modern storage facilities, in most years 20% to 30% of these crops spoil before they can be used. The new plant will enable local production to provide a year-round supply of corn and beans of good quality. This should reduce fluctuations in price and raise the income of producers. It should also improve Panama's trade position by reducing imports of grain and beans that now amount to about $2 million a year.

At the request of the Government, the Bank in October 1953

stationed a special representative in Panama to assist the Government in drawing up and carrying out a comprehensive development program.

Paraguay

Fiscal 1952: $5 million 9-year 4⅜% loan of December 7, 1951 for agricultural machinery and supplies and road-building equipment.

The loan was made for two purposes: to increase farm production and to improve road communications between farm areas and urban markets. The goods being purchased with Bank funds include tractors and other agricultural machinery, tools and farm supplies, trucks, and road-building and maintenance equipment. It was agreed in September 1952 that for the time being only $1.9 million of the loan would be disbursed. To assist the Government in working out the procedures for purchasing and distributing the goods being financed, the Bank stationed a special representative in Paraguay from December 1952 to July 1953.

The loan is being administered in four parts: (1) Farm tools, wire and other supplies are being sold to farmers and farm colonies for cash or on credits extended by the Banco del Paraguay and by a government agricultural credit agency, the Credito Agricola de Habilitacion. (2) Tractors and other farm machinery are being used by the Ministry of Agriculture and Livestock to establish a farm machinery pool. The pool will be operated to clear and cultivate land, to spray, dust, harvest, and dry crops and in general to provide farmers, on a fee basis, with the benefits of equipment which they could not afford to own individually. (3) The Ministry of Public Works and Telecommunications is using the road-building equipment to construct and maintain roads connecting the most important agricultural areas with marketing centers. (4) The Banco del Paraguay is operating a truck service to collect crops and deliver farm supplies.

In November and December 1953 a Bank mission visited

Paraguay to examine the general economic situation, to observe the progress being made in the agricultural and transportation projects financed by the loan, and to discuss with Paraguayan authorities plans for the use of the remaining $3.1 million of the loan.

Peru

Fiscal $2.5 million 15-year 4½% loan of January 23, 1952 for
1952:   port improvements.

Fiscal $1.3 million 7-year 4⅛% loan of July 8, 1952 for agricultural
1953:   ·   machinery.

The loan of $2.5 million was made to improve the port of Callao, Peru's main harbor, by modernizing its facilities for handling general cargo and for unloading and storing bulk grain. To operate the port, the Government agreed to establish an autonomous authority and to obtain an experienced administrator to serve as its technical director.

About one-third of Peru's foreign trade passes through the port of Callao. Nevertheless, at the time of the Bank's loan, methods of handling cargo were slow and wasteful and they caused serious delays in unloading ships at the port. As a consequence the European, South Pacific and Magellan Shipping Conference had imposed a 25% surcharge on freight rates for goods moving between European ports and Callao.

One million dollars of the Bank's loan has been spent on equipment for handling general cargo. The principal items imported were forklift trucks, tractors and trailers, pallets and truck-mounted cranes, together with tools and spare parts for maintenance. All of this equipment had arrived and been put in use by the middle of 1953. As a result of the reorganization of the port and the utilization of the new equipment, the turn-around time of ships calling at Callao was greatly reduced; in June 1953 the 25% freight surcharge was removed.

The remaining $1.5 million of the loan is being spent on

equipment able to unload bulk grain from ships at the rate of about 400 tons per hour and on grain elevators with a storage capacity of about 20,000 tons. Work on the elevator foundations is making good progress.

The $1.3 million loan was to finance the import of tractors and other equipment for the agricultural machinery pools of the Servicio Cooperativo Inter-Americano de Produccion de Alimentos (SCIPA). SCIPA is an agency of the Ministry of Agriculture, established in 1943 by the Government of Peru and the U. S. Institute of Inter-American Affairs to develop a program which would increase food production during the war and lay the foundations for long-range improvements in agriculture. Since its establishment, SCIPA has developed an effective extension program and its farm machinery pools operate widely throughout Peru.

On a fee basis, the pools cultivate land and harvest crops for medium and small landowners, and improve land through clearing, draining, leveling and ditching for irrigation. The equipment financed by the Bank loan, according to SCIPA estimates, will enable the pools to service about 50,000 additional acres of land already under cultivation and to reclaim about 12,500 acres annually of once-productive coastal land which is not now being cultivated. Virtually all the equipment had been purchased and was at work by the end of 1953 and SCIPA's monthly reports indicate that the acreage targets will be reached.

Surinam

At the request of the Netherlands and Surinam Governments, a general survey mission from the Bank visited Surinam (Dutch Guiana) in November 1951. The six-man group included two experts nominated by the Food and Agriculture Organization. The mission's report was transmitted to the two Governments in May 1952.

The mission recommended a 10-year public investment program

(1952-1962) of 100 million Surinam guilders (equivalent to about U. S. $50 million) on the assumption that financing from the Netherlands would be available to the extent of 4 million Surinam guilders a year and that other external credits could be obtained. A supplementary program of 30 million guilders was outlined to be undertaken to the extent that additional resources, technical as well as financial, proved to be available. The report stated that if the recommended program were carried out, the volume of gross production in 1962 should be about 50% above the 1950 level. This increase would enable Surinam to achieve financial independence and at the same time maintain and perhaps gradually raise its standard of living.

Major emphasis in the report was placed on the development of Surinam's three principal productive resources—agricultural land, tropical forests and mineral deposits, primarily bauxite. Recommendations were made for increasing the productivity of agricultural workers, largely through the improvement of small farms. Other recommendations related to extension and improvement of forestry operations, development of the fisheries industry, improvement and expansion of transport, new housing, additional health and educational facilities and town improvements. The mission suggested that the program be administered by a development board to be created jointly by the Governments of the Netherlands and of Surinam.

Uruguay

Fiscal $33 million 24-year 4¼% loan of August 25, 1950 to Adminis-
1951: tracion General de las Usinas Electricas y los Telefonos del Estado (UTE) for power and telephone development program.

Approximately four-fifths of the Bank's loan is being applied to a program for increasing supplies of electric power and the remainder to the improvement and extension of the telephone system. The borrower, the Administracion General de las Usinas

Electricas y los Telefonos del Estado (UTE), is an autonomous government agency charged with providing electric power and telephone service.

Over the past decade demands for power and communications services have outgrown UTE's capacity to meet them and in 1950, therefore, UTE undertook a four to five-year program to expand both its power and telephone systems. New supplies of electric power will allow for the growth and modernization of industry, reduce production costs and make possible further rural electrification. Better and more widely distributed telephone service will reduce the heavy overloading of present equipment and greatly increase the efficiency of the communications system.

The electric power program includes an increase of 50,000 kilowatts in the effective thermal generating capacity in Montevideo, the capital; the installation of approximately 18,000 kilowatts of additional diesel-generating capacity in the rural areas of the interior; the conversion of a number of plants in the interior from direct to alternating current; the construction of 538 miles of main transmission lines; and the expansion of the distribution networks both in Montevideo and in the interior. The steam plant in Montevideo and most of the transmission systems will be completed by the end of 1954 and the remainder of the program will be finished by mid-1955.

The telephone program provides for an increase of telephone exchanges, cables, telephone sets and accessory apparatus, and for the construction of new toll lines cross-connecting and supplementing the existing network in the interior. About 28,000 new telephones, representing an increase of about two-fifths, are being installed. The program is expected to be completed in 1955.

At the request of the Government, a technical mission sponsored jointly by the Bank and the Food and Agriculture Organization visited Uruguay in late 1950 to survey the country's agriculture and to make recommendations for increasing and improving production. Agricultural development is particularly important as a source of foreign exchange; Uruguay is one of the world's four or five leading exporters of wool and meat products. The mission consisted of 10 members, including specialists in production, marketing, animal husbandry, pasture and forage, dairying, soils and fertilizers, forestry, extension services and agricultural engineering. The mission's report was transmitted to the Government in July 1951.

The report recommended measures to increase and improve agricultural and livestock production, to reduce costs and to improve marketing methods. It stressed the need for expanding research to develop and test new methods for increasing production. The report recommended a program of increased afforestation to protect agricultural and grazing land and to increase domestic fuel and lumber supplies. In the opinion of the mission there were numerous opportunities for improvements in the transportation, storage and marketing of agricultural products.

The report also suggested changes in the organization of public agencies concerned with agriculture, to assure the services needed for the successful execution of the recommended production and marketing program.

Along lines suggested by the mission, the Government is sponsoring a project to extend improved methods of pasture and livestock management; the measures for the implementation of this project were prepared with the help of a member of the Bank staff and a consultant who visited Uruguay early in 1953. In agreement with the Government, a Bank consultant is now in Uruguay to collaborate in working out the organization of the project.

Appendices

A

Balance Sheet

December 31, 1953
Expressed in United States Currency
See Note A of Notes to Financial Statements

ASSETS

DUE FROM BANKS AND OTHER DEPOSI-
TORIES (*See Appendix C*)
Member currencies, including $7,573,-
969 United States Dollars

Unrestricted	$ 8,022,650		
Subject to restrictions—*Note B*	103,066,502	$ 111,089,152	
Non-member currency		14,061,837	$ 125,150,989

INVESTMENT SECURITIES
United States Government obligations
($379,727,000 face amount; at
cost less amortized premium) $379,727,496
Canadian   Government   obligations
(Can $2,200,000 face amount; at
cost plus accumulated discount)   1,976,151
United Kingdom Government obliga-
tions (£1,485,000 face amount;
at cost)   4,136,279
Swiss Government obligations (Sw fr
2,000,000 face amount; at cost)   463,060 $ 386,302,986
Accrued interest   3,115,863   389,418,849

RECEIVABLE ON ACCOUNT OF SUB-
SCRIBED CAPITAL (*See Appendix D*)
Receivable in United States currency
Calls on subscription to capital
stock—*Note C* $ 3,495,000
Receivable in other member currencies
—*Note B*
Non-negotiable, non-interest-bear-
ing, demand notes   886,469,042   889,964,042

EFFECTIVE LOANS HELD BY BANK (*See
Appendix F*)—*Note D* (Including
undisbursed balance of $392,849,-
263)   1,535,114,213

ACCRUED INTEREST, COMMITMENT AND
SERVICE CHARGES ON LOANS—
Note D   9,148,274

207

RECEIVABLE ON ACCOUNT OF LOANS
SOLD OR AGREED TO BE SOLD   6,142,879

OTHER RECEIVABLES AND OTHER ASSETS   734,147

SPECIAL RESERVE FUND ASSETS—*Note E*
Due from Banks—member currency—
    United States $ 3,880
Investment securities—United States
    Government obligations ($40,-
    159,000 face amount; at cost)   40,159,000
Accrued loan commissions—*Note D*   2,637,190   42,800,070

STAFF RETIREMENT PLAN ASSETS
(Segregated and held in trust)   2,640,521

             TOTAL ASSETS $3,001,113,984

LIABILITIES, RESERVES AND CAPITAL

LIABILITIES

Accounts payable and accrued expenses, including
    $6,164,238 bond interest $ 6,850,399
Collections on loans in advance of due date   476,805
Undisbursed balance of loans (*See Appendix F*)
    On loans held by Bank $ 392,849,263
    On loans sold or agreed to be sold   7,680,889   400,530,152
Funded debt (*See Appendix E*)
    (Of this amount $12,326,934 is due within one
    year)   653,479,877
    Bonds called for redemption not presented $ 2,020
    Less funds on deposit with Fiscal Agent therefor   2,020   —

RESERVES FOR LOSSES
Special reserve—*Note E* $ 42,800,070
Supplemental reserve against losses on loans and
    guarantees—*Note F*   86,636,160   129,436,230

STAFF RETIREMENT PLAN RESERVE   2,640,521

CAPITAL (*See Appendix D*)
Capital stock
    Authorized 100,000 shares of $100,000 par value
    each
    Subscribed 90,385 shares $9,038,500,000
    Less—Uncalled portion of subscriptions—
    Note G   7,230,800,000   1,807,700,000

CONTINGENT LIABILITY—Loans Sold Under Guarantee
    —*Note H*—$27,579,933

        TOTAL LIABILITIES, RESERVES AND CAPITAL $3,001,113,984

B

Comparative Statement of Income and Expenses

For the Fiscal Years Ended June 30, 1952 and June 30, 1953 and
For the Six Months Ended December 31, 1952 and December 31, 1953

Expressed in United States Currency

See Note A of Notes to Financial Statements

	July 1-June 30		July 1-December 31	
	1951-1952	1952-1953	1952	1953
INCOME				
Interest earned on investments	$ 8,500,740	$ 9,245,538	$ 4,725,170	$ 4,526,843
Income from loans:				
Interest	23,669,009	29,983,062	14,179,246	17,804,121
Commitment charges	2,838,343	3,366,376	1,669,712	1,399,792
Commissions	7,558,906	9,551,822	4,536,682	5,563,593
Service charges	80,203	99,879	49,523	49,124
Other income	100,449	144,352	73,064	151,055
GROSS INCOME	$42,747,650	$52,391,029	$25,233,397	$29,494,528
Deduct—Amount equivalent to commissions appropriated to Special Reserve—*Note E*	7,558,906	9,551,822	4,536,682	5,563,593
GROSS INCOME LESS RESERVE DEDUCTION	$35,188,744	$42,839,207	$20,696,715	$23,930,935
EXPENSES				
Administrative expenses:				
Personal services	$ 3,137,202	$ 3,374,507	$ 1,684,699	$ 1,781,806
Fees and compensation	318,832	317,772	188,519	123,456
Representation	56,092	61,178	34,477	38,633
Travel	538,211	843,360	452,338	419,982
Supplies and material	42,574	33,636	17,649	22,478
Rents and utility services	397,770	432,430	234,428	210,812
Communication services	114,332	111,476	54,491	67,697
Furniture and equipment	38,493	31,887	12,895	15,129
Books and library services	69,463	71,720	34,865	33,730
Printing	67,765	67,946	30,143	35,532
Contributions to staff benefits	336,559	344,394	167,956	171,154
Insurance	16,704	31,864	5,655	5,751
Handling and storage of gold	2,080	—	—	—
Other expenses	1,281	2,100	1,742	729
Total Administrative Expenses	$ 5,137,358	$ 5,724,270	$ 2,919,857	$ 2,926,889
Interest on bonds	11,793,631	16,208,117	7,766,225	9,158,640
Bond issuance and other financial expenses—*Note I*	2,346,692	2,421,409	2,370,890	1,722,757
Exchange adjustments	38,180	—	—	—
GROSS EXPENSES	$19,315,861	$24,353,796	$13,056,972	$13,808,286
NET INCOME—Appropriated to Supplemental Reserve Against Losses on Loans and Guarantees—*Note F*	$15,872,883	$18,485,411	$ 7,639,743	$10,122,649

209

C

Statement of Currencies Held by the Bank

December 31, 1953
See Note A of Notes to Financial Statements

	Unit of Currency	Amount Expressed In Member Currency (Restricted)		Rate of Exchange	Total Expressed In United States Dollars
Member Currencies					
Australia	Pound	154,399	$ =	0.4464	$ 345,853
Austria	Schilling	1,749,608	$ =	26.00	67,293
Belgium	Franc	35,576,707	$ =	50.00	711,534
Bolivia	Boliviano	2,249,308	$ =	190.00	11,838
Brazil	Cruzeiro	348,279,796	$ =	18.50	18,825,935
Burma	Kyat	104,151	$ =	4.7619	21,872
Canada	Dollar	1,366,826	$ =	1.10	1,242,569
Ceylon	Rupee	111,993	$ =	4.7619	23,519
Chile	Peso	688,751,417	$ =	110.00	6,261,376
China	Gold Yuan	21,550,341	$ =	20.00	1,077,517
Colombia	Peso	12,186,465	$ =	1.949981	6,249,530
Costa Rica	Colon	1,996,515	$ =	5.615	355,568
Cuba	Peso	55,604	$ =	1.00	55,604
Czechoslovakia	Koruna	1,581,169	$ =	7.20	219,607
Denmark	Krone	2,312,449	$ =	6.90714	334,791
Dominican Republic	Peso	982	$ =	1.00	982
Ecuador	Sucre	8,432,641	$ =	15.00	562,176
Egypt	Pound	19,352	$ =	0.3482	55,570
El Salvador	Colon	428,917	$ =	2.50	171,567
Ethiopia	Dollar	1,283,126	$ =	2.4845	516,458
Finland	Markka	1,571,958,713	$ =	230.00	6,834,603
France	Franc	2,786,229,608	$ =	349.60	7,969,764
Germany	Mark	2,540,022	$ =	4.20	604,767
Greece	Drachma	22,480,000,000	$ =	5,000.00	4,496,000
Guatemala	Quetzal	349,750	$ =	1.00	349,750
Honduras	Lempira	355,400	$ =	2.00	177,700
Iceland	Krona	2,861,354	$ =	16.2857	175,697
India	Rupee	3,047,428	$ =	4.7619	639,960
Iran	Rial	993,839	$ =	32.25	30,817
Iraq	Dinar	2,507	$ =	0.3571	7,020
Italy	Lira	198,069,669	$ =	350.00	565,913
Japan	Yen	157,631,293	$ =	360.00	437,865
Jordan	Dinar	1,296	$ =	0.3571	3,628
Haiti	Gourde	18,000	$ =	5.00	3,600
Lebanon	Pound	1,707,686	$ =	2.19148	779,239
Luxembourg	Franc	615,223	$ =	50.00	12,304
Mexico	Peso	100,259,537	$ =	8.65	11,590,698
Netherlands	Guilder	572,011	$ =	3.80	150,529
Nicaragua	Cordoba	664,665	$ =	5.00	132,933
Norway	Krone	1,814,382	$ =	7.14286	254,013
Pakistan	Rupee	458,495	$ =	3.30852	138,580

	Unit of Currency	Amount Expressed In Member Currency (Restricted)		Rate of Exchange	Total Expressed In United States Dollars
Member Currencies					
Panama	Balboa	28,070	$ =	1.00	28,070
Paraguay	Guarani	1,256,787	$ =	6.00	209,465
Peru	Sol	122,329	$ =	6.50	18,820
Philippine Republic	Peso	2,376,584	$ =	2.00	1,188,292
Sweden	Krona	88,358,408	$ =	5.17321	17,079,996
Syria	Pound	39,696	$ =	2.19148	18,114
Thailand	Baht	24,497	$ =	12.50	1,960
Turkey	Lira	102,816	$ =	2.80	36,720
Union of South Africa	Pound	358,721	$ =	0.3571	1,004,420
United Kingdom	Pound	169,735	$ =	0.3571	475,259
United States	Dollar	141,299	$ =		141,299
Uruguay	Peso	2,814,611	$ =	1.519	1,852,876
Venezuela	Bolivar	4,561,828	$ =	3.35	1,361,740
Yugoslavia	Dinar	2,154,879,315	$ =	300.00	7,182,932

Restricted Currency (*Note B*) $103,066,502

Unrestricted Currency (Belgium,
  Canada, Denmark, Sweden,
  Union of South Africa, United
  Kingdom and United States)   8,022,650

                                                                      $111,089,152
Non-Member Currency (Switzerland)   14,061,837

                                   TOTAL $125,150,989

D

Statement of Subscriptions
to Capital Stock and Voting Power

	Member	Shares	Subscriptions Amount (Note J)	In United States Dollars	Amounts Paid in In Currency of Member Other Than United States Dollars (Note B)
1	Australia................	2,000	$ 200,000,000	$ 4,000,000	$ 360,368
2	Austria.................	500	50,000,000	1,000,000	299,018
3	Belgium................	2,250	225,000,000	4,500,000	4,844,422
4	Bolivia.................	70	7,000,000	140,000	12,600
5	Brazil..................	1,050	105,000,000	2,100,000	18,900,000
6	Burma..................	150	15,000,000	300,000	27,000
7	Canada.................	3,250	325,000,000	6,500,000	31,598,636
8	Ceylon.................	150	15,000,000	300,000	32,997
9	Chile...................	350	35,000,000	700,000	6,300,000
10	China..................	6,000	600,000,000	9,130,000	1,080,000
11	Colombia...............	350	35,000,000	700,000	6,300,000
12	Costa Rica..............	20	2,000,000	40,000	360,000
13	Cuba...................	350	35,000,000	700,000	63,000
14	Czechoslovakia..........	1,250	125,000,000	1,875,000	225,000
15	Denmark................	680	68,000,000	1,360,000	1,425,400
16	Dominican Republic......	20	2,000,000	40,000	3,600
17	Ecuador................	32	3,200,000	64,000	576,000
18	Egypt..................	533	53,300,000	1,066,000	95,940
19	El Salvador.............	10	1,000,000	20,000	180,000
20	Ethiopia................	30	3,000,000	60,000	540,000
21	Finland................	380	38,000,000	760,000	6,840,000
22	France.................	5,250	525,000,000	10,500,000	22,932,494
23	Germany...............	3,300	330,000,000	6,600,000	614,286
24	Greece.................	250	25,000,000	500,000	4,500,000
25	Guatemala..............	20	2,000,000	40,000	360,000
26	Haiti...................	20	2,000,000	40,000	3,600
27	Honduras...............	10	1,000,000	20,000	180,000
28	Iceland.................	10	1,000,000	20,000	180,000
29	India...................	4,000	400,000,000	8,000,000	721,800
30	Iran....................	336	33,600,000	672,000	60,480
31	Iraq....................	60	6,000,000	120,000	20,880
32	Italy...................	1,800	180,000,000	3,600,000	3,685,714
33	Japan..................	2,500	250,000,000	5,000,000	450,000
34	Jordan.................	30	3,000,000	60,000	5,400
35	Lebanon................	45	4,500,000	90,000	810,000
36	Luxembourg............	100	10,000,000	200,000	18,000
37	Mexico.................	650	65,000,000	1,300,000	11,700,000
38	Netherlands.............	2,750	275,000,000	5,500,000	815,789
39	Nicaragua..............	8	800,000	16,000	144,000
40	Norway................	500	50,000,000	1,000,000	370,000
41	Pakistan................	1,000	100,000,000	2,000,000	180,008
42	Panama................	2	200,000	4,000	36,000
43	Paraguay...............	14	1,400,000	28,000	252,000
44	Peru...................	175	17,500,000	350,000	62,269
45	Philippines.............	150	15,000,000	300,000	1,200,000
46	Sweden................	1,000	100,000,000	2,000,000	18,000,000
47	Syria...................	65	6,500,000	130,000	43,642
48	Thailand...............	125	12,500,000	250,000	32,500
49	Turkey.................	430	43,000,000	860,000	113,115
50	Union of South Africa....	1,000	100,000,000	2,000,000	3,120,000
51	United Kingdom........	13,000	1,300,000,000	26,000,000	7,830,000
52	United States............	31,750	3,175,000,000	635,000,000	....
53	Uruguay...............	105	10,500,000	210,000	1,890,000
54	Venezuela..............	105	10,500,000	210,000	1,365,000
55	Yugoslavia.............	400	40,000,000	800,000	7,200,000
		90,385	$9,038,500,000	$748,775,000	$168,960,958

In Non-Interest-Bearing, Non-Negotiable Demand Notes (Note B)	Amounts Due (Note C)	Subject to Call to Meet Obligations of Bank (Note G)	Number of Votes	
$ 35,639,632	$	$ 160,000,000	2,250	1
8,700,982	....	40,000,000	750	2
35,655,578	....	180,000,000	2,500	3
1,247,400	....	5,600,000	320	4
....	....	84,000,000	1,300	5
2,673,000	....	12,000,000	400	6
26,901,364	....	260,000,000	3,500	7
2,667,003	....	12,000,000	400	8
....	....	28,000,000	600	9
106,920,000	2,870,000	480,000,000	6,250	10
....	....	28,000,000	600	11
....	....	1,600,000	270	12
6,237,000	....	28,000,000	600	13
22,275,000	625,000	100,000,000	1,500	14
10,814,600	....	54,400,000	930	15
356,400	....	1,600,000	270	16
....	....	2,560,000	282	17
9,498,060	....	42,640,000	783	18
....	....	800,000	260	19
....	....	2,400,000	280	20
....	....	30,400,000	630	21
71,567,506	....	420,000,000	5,500	22
58,785,714	....	264,000,000	3,550	23
....	....	20,000,00	500	24
....	....	1,600,000	270	25
356,400	....	1,600,000	270	26
....	....	800,000	260	27
....	....	800,000	260	28
71,278,200	....	320,000,000	4,250	29
5,987,520	....	26,880,000	586	30
1,059,120	....	4,800,000	310	31
28,714,286	....	144,000,000	2,050	32
44,550,000	....	200,000,000	2,750	33
534,600	....	2,400,000	280	34
....	....	3,600,000	295	35
1,782,000	....	8,000,000	350	36
....	....	52,000,000	900	37
48,684,211	....	220,000,000	3,000	38
....	....	640,000	258	39
8,630,000	....	40,000,000	750	40
17,819,992	....	80,000,000	1,250	41
....	....	160,000	252	42
....	....	1,120,000	264	43
3,087,731	....	14,000,000	425	44
1,500,000	....	12,000,000	400	45
....	....	80,000,000	1,250	46
1,126,358	....	5,200,000	315	47
2,217,500	....	10,000,000	375	48
7,626,885	....	34,400,000	680	49
14,880,000	....	80,000,000	1,250	50
226,170,000	....	1,040,000,000	13,250	51
....	....	2,540,000,000	32,000	52
....	....	8,400,000	355	53
525,000	....	8,400,000	355	54
....	....	32,000,000	650	55
$886,469,042	$3,495,000	$7,230,800,000	104,135	

213

E

Funded Debt of the Bank

December 31, 1953
Expressed in United States Currency
See Note A of Notes to Financial Statements

Issue and Maturity	Principal Outstanding	Annual Sinking Fund Requirement	
PAYABLE IN UNITED STATES DOLLARS			
2% Serial Bonds of 1950, due 1954-62	$ 90,000,000		None
3% Three Year Bonds of 1953, due 1956	75,000,000		None
3½% Nineteen Year Bonds of 1952, due 1971	60,000,000	1957-66	$2,000,000
		1967-70	$2,500,000
3% Twenty-Five Year Bonds of 1947, due 1972	150,000,000	1958-62	$3,000,000
		1963-67	$4,500,000
		1968-72	$7,500,000
3⅜% Twenty-Three Year Bonds of 1952, due 1975	50,000,000	1958	$1,000,000
		1959-74	$1,500,000
3% Twenty-Five Year Bonds of 1951, due 1976	50,000,000	1963	$1,000,000
		1964-75	$2,000,000
3¼% Thirty-Year Bonds of 1951, due 1981	100,000,000	1966-67	$2,000,000
		1968-73	$3,000,000
		1974-80	$4,000,000
SUB-TOTAL	$575,000,000		
PAYABLE IN CANADIAN DOLLARS			
4% Ten-Year Bonds of 1952, due 1962 (Can$15,000,000)	$ 13,636,364	1955-60	Can$700,000
		1961	Can$800,000
PAYABLE IN POUNDS STERLING			
3½% Twenty-Year Stock of 1951, due 1971 (£5,000,000)	$ 14,000,000	1957-71	£166,700
PAYABLE IN SWISS FRANCS			
2½% Serial Bonds of 1950, due 1954-56 (Sw fr 18,500,000)	$ 4,304,829		None
3½% Ten-Year Bonds of 1952, due 1962 (Sw fr 50,000,000)	11,634,671		None
3½% Twelve-Year Bonds of 1951, due 1963 (Sw fr 50,000,000)	11,634,671		None
3½% Fifteen-Year Bonds of 1953, due 1968 (Sw fr 50,000,000)	11,634,671		None
3½% Fifteen-Year Bonds of 1953 (Nov. Issue), due 1968 (Sw fr 50,000,000)	11,634,671		None
SUB-TOTAL	$ 50,843,513		
GROSS TOTAL	$653,479,877		

Each issue, except the 2% Serial Bonds of 1950, is subject to redemption prior to maturity at the option of the Bank at varying prices and upon the conditions stated in the respective bonds. The amounts shown as annual sinking fund requirements are the principal amounts of bonds to be purchased or redeemed to meet each year's requirement, except that in the case of the 3½% Twenty-Year Stock of 1951 the amount shown is the amount of funds to be provided annually for purchase or redemption.

The following table shows the aggregate principal amount of the maturities and sinking fund requirements each year for the five years following the date of this statement:

Period	Amount
January 1, 1954 to December 31, 1954	$ 12,326,934
January 1, 1955 to December 31, 1955	12,032,525
January 1, 1956 to December 31, 1956	86,218,097
January 1, 1957 to December 31, 1957	13,103,124
January 1, 1958 to December 31, 1958	17,103,124
	$140,783,804

F

Statement of Loans

Loan Number		*Borrower and Guarantor*	*Program or Project*	*Date of Loan Agreement*	*Maturities*	*Interest Rate (Including Commission)*
29	AU	AUSTRALIA	Equipment and materials for development	Aug. 22, 1950	1955–1975	4¼%
66	AU		Equipment and materials for development	July 8, 1952	1957–1972	4¾%
14	BE	BELGIUM	Equipment for steel and power industries	Mar. 1, 1949	1953–1969	4¼%
48	BE		Equipment and materials for 10-year Development Plan of the Belgian Congo	Sept. 13, 1951	1957–1976	4½%
47	BE	BELGIUM (Guarantor) Belgian Congo	Equipment and materials for 10-year Development Plan of the Belgian Congo	Sept. 13, 1951	1957–1976	4½%
65	BR	BRAZIL	Railway rehabilitation	June 27, 1952	1955–1967	4⅜%
75	BR		Highway maintenance and improvement	April 30, 1953	1954–1959	4¼%
*92	BR		Railway rehabilitation	Dec. 18, 1953	1959–1969	4⅞%
		BRAZIL (Guarantor)				
11	BR	Brazilian Traction (First Installment)	Electric power development and telephone equipment	Jan. 27, 1949	1953–1974	4½%
11	BR-S	Brazilian Traction (Second Installment)	Electric power development	Jan. 18, 1951	1955–1976	4¼%
25	BR	Sao Francisco Hidro Elec. Co.	Electric power development	May 26, 1950	1954–1975	4¼%
64	BR	Comissao Estadual de Energia Eletrica	Electric power development	June 27, 1952	1957–1977	4¾%
76	BR	CEARG & CEMIG	Electric power development	July 17, 1953	1957–1973	5%
*93	BR	Usinas Eletricas do Paranapanema	Electric power development	Dec. 18, 1953	1958–1974	5%
		CHILE (Guarantor)				
5	CH	Fomento and Endesa	Electric power development	Mar. 25, 1948	1953–1968	4½%
6	CH	Fomento	Agricultural development	Mar. 25, 1948	1950–1955	3¾%
49	CH	Fomento	Exploration and use for irrigation of underground water resources	Oct. 10, 1951	1955–1961	4⅜%
83	CH	Fomento and Cia. Manufacturera de Papeles y Cartones	Construction of paper and pulp mills	Sept. 10, 1953	1958–1970	5%
43	CO	COLOMBIA	Highway construction and rehabilitation	Apr. 10, 1951	1954–1961	3⅞%
68	CO		National railways project	Aug. 26, 1952	1957–1978	4¾%
*84	CO		Highway construction and rehabilitation	Sept. 10, 1953	1956–1963	4¾%
		COLOMBIA (Guarantor)				
18	CO	Caja de Credito	Agricultural development	Aug. 19, 1949	1952–1956	3½%
38	CO	CHIDRAL	Electric power development	Nov. 2, 1950	1954–1970	4%
39	CO	Caldas Hidro-Elec. Co.	Electric power development	Dec. 28, 1950	1952–1971	4%
54	CO	Hidroelectrica del Rio Lebrija	Electric power development	Nov. 13, 1951	1954–1972	4½%
3	DE	DENMARK	Equipment and materials for reconstruction and development	Aug. 22, 1947	1953–1972	4¼%
		EL SALVADOR (Guarantor)				
22	ES	Comision del Rio Lempa	Electric power development	Dec. 14, 1949	1954–1975	4¼%
31	ET	ETHIOPIA	Highway rehabilitation	Sept. 13, 1950	1956–1971	4%
32	ET		Foreign exchange for Development Bank	Sept. 13, 1950	1956–1971	4%
*42	ET		Rehabilitation and extension of telephone and telegraph systems	Feb. 19, 1951	1956–1971	4%
21	FI	FINLAND	Equipment for timber production	Oct. 17, 1949	1950–1951	3%

Original Principal Amount	Loans Not Yet Effective	Cancellations and Refundings	Principal Repayments to Bank	Loans Sold or Agreed to be Sold	Effective Loans Held by Bank	Principal Amount Disbursed	Undisbursed Balance of Effective Loans[1]
$100,000,000	$	$	$	$	$100,000,000	$100,000,000	$ ....
50,000,000	....	....	....	....	50,000,000	24,776,256	25,223,744
16,000,000	....	....	....	16,000,000	....	14,461,990	1,538,010
30,000,000	....	....	....	....	30,000,000	24,066,000	5,934,000
40,000,000	....	....	....	....	40,000,000	32,096,000	7,904,000
12,500,000	....	....	....	....	12,500,000	....	12,500,000
3,000,000	....	....	....	....	3,000,000	....	3,000,000
12,500,000	12,500,000	....	....	....	....	....	....
75,000,000	....	....	500,000	4,028,411	70,471,589	75,000,000	....
15,000,000	....	....	....	....	15,000,000	15,000,000	....
15,000,000	....	....	....	....	15,000,000	12,636,218	2,363,782
25,000,000	....	....	....	....	25,000,000	....	25,000,000
7,300,000	....	....	....	....	7,300,000	786,692	6,513,308
10,000,000	10,000,000	....	....	....	....	....	....
13,500,000	....	....	332,000	....	13,168,000	11,937,575	1,562,425
2,500,000	....	....	518,000	1,745,000	237,000	2,500,000	....
1,300,000	....	....	....	....	1,300,000	795,710	504,290
20,000,000	....	....	....	....	20,000,000	....	20,000,000
16,500,000	....	....	....	800,000	15,700,000	14,772,510	1,727,490
25,000,000	....	....	....	....	25,000,000	4,213,440	20,786,560
14,350,000	14,350,000	....	....	....	....	....	....
5,000,000	....	74,559	500,000	2,000,000	2,425,441	4,925,441	....
3,530,000	....	....	....	148,000	3,382,000	3,026,355	503,645
2,600,000	....	....	46,000	194,000	2,360,000	2,600,000	....
2,400,000	....	....	....	84,800	2,315,200	2,234,735	165,265
40,000,000	....	....	599,000	1,258,000	38,143,000	40,000,000	....
12,545,000	....	....	....	1,000,000	11,545,000	11,943,271	601,729
5,000,000	....	....	....	....	5,000,000	4,698,514	301,486
2,000,000	....	....	....	....	2,000,000	686,949	1,313,051
1,500,000	1,500,000	....	....	....	....	....	....
2,300,000	....	197,869	2,102,131	....	....	2,102,131	....

Continued

Loan Number		Borrower and Guarantor	Program or Project	Date of Loan Agreement	Maturities	Interest Rate (Including Commission)
		FINLAND (Guarantor)				
16	FI	Bank of Finland	Electric power development and equipment for wood products industries and limestone powder production	Aug. 1, 1949	1953–1964	4%
61	FI	Bank of Finland	Electric power, wood products industries and agricultural development	Apr. 30, 1952	1955–1970	4¾%
70	FI	Bank of Finland	Electric power, wood products industries and agricultural development (Supplemental Loan Agreement)	Nov. 13, 1952	1955–1970	4¾%
		FRANCE (Guarantor)				
1	FR	Credit National	Equipment and materials for reconstruction and development	May 9, 1947	1952–1977	4¼%
46	IC	ICELAND	Electric power development	June 20, 1951	1956–1973	4⅜%
53	IC		Agricultural development	Nov. 1, 1951	1956–1973	4½%
69	IC		Fertilizer plant	Aug. 26, 1952	1954–1969	4¾%
		ICELAND (Guarantor)				
79	IC	Iceland Bank of Development	Agricultural development	Sept. 4, 1953	1958–1975	5%
80	IC	Iceland Bank of Development	Construction of radio transmitter building	Sept. 4, 1953	1954–1966	4¾%
17	IN	INDIA	Railway rehabilitation	Aug. 18, 1949	1950–1964	4%
19	IN		Agricultural development	Sept. 29, 1949	1952–1956	3½%
23	IN		Electric power development	Apr. 18, 1950	1955–1970	4%
*72	IN		Electric power development, flood control and irrigation	Jan. 23, 1953	1956–1977	4⅞%
		INDIA (Guarantor)				
*71	IN	Indian Iron & Steel Company	Expansion of iron and steel production facilities	Dec. 18, 1952	1959–1967	4¾%
26	IRQ	IRAQ	Construction of a flood control project	June 15, 1950	1956–1965	3¾%
		ITALY (Guarantor)				
50	IT	Cassa per Il Mezzogiorno	Equipment and materials for Development Plan of Southern Italy	Oct. 10, 1951	1956–1976	4½%
*88	IT	Cassa per Il Mezzogiorno	Equipment and materials for Development Plan of Southern Italy	Oct. 6, 1953	1958–1978	5%
		JAPAN (Guarantor)				
89	JA	Japan Development Bank	Electric power development	Oct. 15, 1953	1957–1973	5%
90	JA	Japan Development Bank	Electric power development	Oct. 15, 1953	1957–1973	5%
91	JA	Japan Development Bank	Electric power development	Oct. 15, 1953	1957–1973	5%
4	LU	LUXEMBOURG	Equipment for steel mill and railroads	Aug. 28, 1947	1949–1972	4¼%
		MEXICO (Guarantor)				
12	ME	Financiera and Comision	Electric power development	Jan. 6, 1949	1953–1973	4½%
13	ME	Financiera and Comision	Electric power development	Jan. 6, 1949	July 1, 1950	4½%
24	ME	Mexican Light and Power Co. Ltd.	Electric power development	Apr. 28, 1950	1953–1975	4½%
33	ME	Consortium of Eight Mexican Banks & Nacional Financiera	Foreign exchange for small private enterprises	Oct. 18, 1950	1952–1957	3½%
56	ME	Financiera and Comision	Electric power development	Jan. 11, 1952	1955–1977	4½%

Original Principal Amount	Loans Not Yet Effective	Cancellations and Refundings	Principal Repayments to Bank	Loans Sold or Agreed to be Sold	Effective Loans Held by Bank	Principal Amount Disbursed	Undisbursed Balance of Effective Loans [1]
$12,500,000	$	$	$ 114,790	$1,559,010	$10,826,200	$ 12,500,000	$ ....
20,000,000	....	....	....	....	20,000,000	11,346,586	8,653,414
3,479,464	....	....	....	....	3,479,464	753,511	2,725,953
250,000,000	....	....	....	7,672,000	242,328,000	250,000,000	....
2,450,000	....	....	....	....	2,450,000	2,312,948	137,052
1,008,000	....	....	....	....	1,008,000	1,008,000	....
854,000	....	....	....	....	854,000	626,200	227,800
1,350,000	....	....	....	....	1,350,000	520,168	829,832
252,000	....	....	....	....	252,000	82,286	169,714
34,000,000	....	1,200,000	4,279,224	4,759,301	23,761,475	32,800,000	....
10,000,000	....	2,500,000	850,000	3,400,000	3,250,000	7,203,813	296,187
18,500,000	....	....	....	....	18,500,000	14,293,936	4,206,064
19,500,000	19,500,000	....	....	....	....	....	....
31,500,000	31,500,000	....	....	....	....	....	....
12,800,000	....	....	....	....	12,800,000	5,905,564	6,894,436
10,000,000	....	....	....	....	10,000,000	10,000,000	....
10,000,000	10,000,000	....	....	....	....	....	....
21,500,000	....	....	....	3,244,288	18,255,712	1,000	21,499,000
11,200,000	....	....	....	1,653,591	9,546,409	1,000	11,199,000
7,500,000	....	....	....	1,245,000	6,255,000	1,000	7,499,000
12,000,000	....	238,017	187,983	1,877,000	9,697,000	11,761,983	....
24,100,000	....	....	452,300	1,135,300	22,512,400	21,293,718	2,806,282
10,000,000	....	10,000,000 (Refunding)	....	....	....	....	....
26,000,000	....	....	352,000	606,000	25,042,000	25,213,897	786,103
10,000,000	....	9,472,112	156,897	....	370,991	527,888	....
29,700,000	....	....	....	200,000	29,500,000	12,383,650	17,316,350

Continued

219

Statement of Loans—Continued

Loan Number		Borrower and Guarantor	Program or Project	Date of Loan Agreement	Maturities	Interest Rate (Including) Commission
2	NE	NETHERLANDS	Equipment and materials for reconstruction and development	Aug. 7, 1947	1954–1972	4¼%
2a	NE		Equipment and materials for reconstruction and development (Supplemental Loan Agreement)	May 25, 1948	1953–1954	4¼%
		NETHERLANDS (Guarantor)				
7, 7a	NE	N. V. Stoomvaart Mij. "Nederland"	Purchase of S.S. Raki and S.S. Roebiah	July 15, 1948	1949–1958	3⁹⁄₁₆%
8	NE	N. V. Vereenigde Schvrt. Mij.	Purchase of S.S.Almkerk	July 15, 1948	1949–1958	3⁹⁄₁₆%
9	NE	N. V. Ned.-Amer. Stoomvaart-Mij. "Holland-Amerika Lijn"	Purchase of S.S. Alblasserdijk	July 15, 1948	1949–1958	3⁹⁄₁₆%
10, 10a	NE	N. V. Rotterdamsche Lloyd	Purchase of S.S. Friesland and S.S. Drente	July 15, 1948	1949–1958	3⁹⁄₁₆%
15	NE	Herstelbank	Equipment for reconstruction and modernization of particular industrial plants	July 26, 1949	1952–1964	4%
59	NE	KLM Royal Dutch Airlines	Purchase of aircraft	Mar. 20, 1952	1954–1958	4⅛%
45	NI	NICARAGUA	Highway construction	June 7, 1951	1954–1961	4⅛%
52	NI		Construction of grain storage facilities	Oct. 29, 1951	1954–1962	4⅜%
81	NI		Highway construction	Sept. 4, 1953	1957–1963	4¾%
82	NI		Electric power development	Sept. 4, 1953	1955–1963	4¾%
		NICARAGUA (Guarantor)				
44	NI	Banco Nacional de Nicaragua	Agricultural development	June 7, 1951	1954–1958	4%
60	PAK	PAKISTAN	Railway rehabilitation	Mar. 27, 1952	1954–1967	4⅝%
*62	PAK		Agricultural development	June 13, 1952	1954–1959	4⅛%
		PANAMA (Guarantor)				
*86	PAN	Instituto de Fomento Economico	Agricultural development	Sept. 25, 1953	1955–1960	4⅝%
*87	PAN	Instituto de Fomento Economico	Construction of grain storage facilities	Sept. 25, 1953	1955–1961	4⅝%
55	PA	PARAGUAY	Agricultural development	Dec. 7, 1951	1954–1960	4⅜%
57	PE	PERU	Port development	Jan. 23, 1952	1954–1967	4½%
67	PE		Agricultural development	July 8, 1952	1954–1959	4⅛%
40	SA	SOUTH AFRICA	Expansion of transport facilities	Jan. 23, 1951	1956–1965	3¾%
77	SA		Expansion of transport facilities	Aug. 28, 1953	1955–1963	4¾%
		SOUTH AFRICA (Guarantor)				
41	SA	Electricity Supply Commission	Electric power development	Jan. 23, 1951	1954–1970	4%
78	SA	Electricity Supply Commission	Electric power development	Aug. 28, 1953	1955–1963	4¾%
35	TH	THAILAND	Railway rehabilitation	Oct. 27, 1950	1954–1966	3¾%
36	TH		Irrigation	Oct. 27, 1950	1956–1971	4%
37	TH		Port construction and development	Oct. 27, 1950	1954–1966	3¾%
27	TU	TURKEY	Construction of grain storage facilities	July 7, 1950	1954–1968	3⅞%
28	TU		Port construction and development	July 7, 1950	1956–1975	4¼%
63	TU		Electric power development, irrigation and flood control	June 18, 1952	1957–1977	4¾%

Original Principal Amount	Loans Not Yet Effective	Cancellations and Refundings	Principal Repayments to Bank	Loans Sold or Agreed to be Sold	Effective Loans Held by Bank	Principal Amount Disbursed	Undisbursed Balance of Effective Loans[1]
191,044,212	....	....	....	3,879,000	187,165,212	191,044,212	....
3,955,788	....	....	....	3,955,788	....	3,955,788	....
4,000,000	....	....	....	4,000,000	....	4,000,000	....
2,000,000	....	....	....	2,000,000	....	2,000,000	....
2,000,000	....	....	....	2,000,000	....	2,000,000	....
4,000,000	....	....	....	4,000,000	....	4,000,000	....
15,000,000	....	7,548,015	775,669	1,819,139	4,857,177	7,451,985	....
7,000,000	....	....	....	3,500,000	3,500,000	7,000,000	....
3,500,000	....	....	....	29,000	3,471,000	1,656,161	1,843,839
550,000	....	3,006	....	29,000	517,994	546,994	....
3,500,000	....	....	....	....	3,500,000	....	3,500,000
450,000	....	....	....	....	450,000	....	450,000
1,200,000	....	....	245,000	29,000	926,000	1,193,121	6,879
27,200,000	....	....	....	735,600	26,464,400	10,546,656	16,653,344
3,250,000	3,250,000	....	....	(Note 2)	....	....	....
1,200,000	1,200,000	....	....	....	....	....	....
290,000	290,000	....	....	....	....	....	....
5,000,000	....	....	....	100,000	4,900,000	1,493,977	3,506,023
2,500,000	....	....	....	141,000	2,359,000	1,149,006	1,350,994
1,300,000	....	....	....	93,250	1,206,750	1,271,944	28,056
20,000,000	....	....	....	....	20,000,000	20,000,000	....
30,000,000	....	....	....	....	30,000,000	4,668,948	25,331,052
30,000,000	....	....	....	2,224,560	27,775,440	30,000,000	....
30,000,000	....	....	....	....	30,000,000	3,077,477	26,922,523
3,000,000	....	....	....	189,000	2,811,000	2,901,643	98,357
18,000,000	....	....	....	....	18,000,000	14,720,365	3,279,635
4,400,000	....	....	....	275,000	4,125,000	3,301,077	1,098,923
3,900,000	....	....	....	144,000	3,756,000	1,942,562	1,957,438
12,500,000	....	....	....	....	12,500,000	4,299,604	8,200,396
25,200,000	....	....	....	....	25,200,000	4,648,664	20,551,336

Continued

Loan Number		Borrower and Guarantor	Program or Project	Date of Loan Agreement	Maturi-ties	Interest Rate (Including Commission)
		TURKEY (Guarantor)				
34	TU	Industrial Development Bank of Turkey	Foreign exchange for development of private industry	Oct. 19, 1950	1957–1965	3¾%
*85	TU	Industrial Development Bank of Turkey	Foreign exchange for development of private industry	Sept. 10, 1953	1958–1968	4⅞%
		UNITED KINGDOM (Guarantor)				
58	SR	Southern Rhodesia	Electric power development	Feb. 27, 1952	1956–1977	4¾%
74	NR	Northern Rhodesia	Railway development	Mar. 11, 1953	1956–1972	4¾%
		URUGUAY (Guarantor)				
30	UR	U. T. E.	Electric power development and telephone equipment	Aug. 25, 1950	1955–1974	4¼%
20	YU	YUGOSLAVIA	Equipment for timber production	Oct. 17, 1949	1950–1951	3%
51	YU		Equipment for electric power, coal mining, non-ferrous metal development, industry, forest products, agriculture and fishery, and transportation projects	Oct. 11, 1951	1955–1976	4½%
73	YU		Expansion of electric power, mining, industry, forestry and transportation	Feb. 11, 1953	1956–1978	4⅞%

* Denotes Loans Not Yet Effective.

¹ Of the Undisbursed Balance of Effective Loans, the sum of $20,358,290 has been irrevocably committed by the Bank.

² Two American firms will participate in Loan Number 62 Pakistan to the extent of $498,500 each.

³ The amount of currency repayable may differ from the amount of currency disbursed as a result of the purchase of one currency with another for purpose of disbursement. The currency used to make the purchase is the currency repayable. The amount of currency disbursed does not represent total purchases in the country whose currency is indicated.

Original Principal Amount	Loans Not Yet Effective	Cancellations and Refundings	Principal Repayments to Bank	Loans Sold or Agreed to be Sold	Effective Loans Held by Bank	Principal Amount Disbursed	Undisbursed Balance of Effective Loans [1]
9,000,000	....	....	....	....	9,000,000	2,958,236	6,041,764
9,000,000	9,000,000	....	....	....	....	....	....
28,000,000	....	....	....	....	28,000,000	13,947,879	14,052,121
14,000,000	....	....	....	....	14,000,000	8,574,916	5,425,084
33,000,000	....	....	....	300,000	32,700,000	18,366,466	14,633,534
2,700,000	....	....	2,700,000	....	....	2,700,000	....
28,000,000	....	....	....	....	28,000,000	21,798,522	6,201,478
30,000,000	....	....	....	....	30,000,000	13,291,596	16,708,404
$1,781,158,464	$113,090,000	$31,233,578	$14,710,994	$84,053,038	$1,538,070,854	$1,236,304,734	$400,530,152

Less exchange adjustment   2,956,641

TOTAL LOANS GRANTED $1,535,114,213

SUMMARY BY CURRENCY
(Expressed in United States Currency)

Currency	Amount Disbursed [3]	Amount Repayable [3]	Repayments and Loans Sold or Agreed to be Sold	Effective Loans Held by Bank
Austrian Schillings	$ 226,542	$ 226,542	$	$ 226,542
Belgian Francs	31,581,184	5,007,882	533,048	4,474,834
Canadian Dollars	55,699,108	51,507,857	4,889,707	46,618,150
Danish Kroner	1,388,23⁻	1,104,190	....	1,104,190
French Francs	16,537,566	15,234,365	28,604	15,205,761
German Marks	10,988,181	....	....	....
Italian Lire	4,441,060	2,862,412	....	2,862,412
Netherlands Guilders	3,059,530	584,094	....	584,094
Norwegian Kroner	197,946	113,729	....	113,729
South African Pounds	2,115,580	2,115,580	..:	2,115,580
Swedish Kronor	4,921,004	940,115	....	940,115
Swiss Francs	21,039,773	42,532,632	8,396,174	34,136,458
United Kingdom Pounds	85,718,634	16,395,685	47,977	16,347,708
United States Dollars	998,390,394	1,097,679,651	84,868,522	1,012,811,129
	$1,236,304,734	$1,236,304,734	$98,764,032	$1,137,540,702

Plus—Undisbursed Balance of Effective Loans   400,530,152

     $1,538,070,854

Less Exchange Adjustment   2,956,641

     $1,535,114,213

G

Notes to Financial Statements

December 31, 1953

NOTE A—Amounts in currencies other than United States dollars have been translated into United States dollars:

(i) In the cases of 45 members, at the par values established under the International Monetary Fund Agreement as specified in the " Schedule of Par Values," published by the International Monetary Fund; and

(ii) In the cases of the remaining 10 members (Canada, China, Czechoslovakia, France, Greece, Haiti, Italy, Peru, Thailand and Uruguay), the par values of whose currencies are not so specified, at the rates used by such members in making capital payments. On June 1, 1953 Czechoslovakia, in consequence of a monetary reform, established a new currency with a new gold content and unilaterally converted the Bank's holdings of currency and demand notes of Czechoslovakia into the new currency at the new exchange rate. These financial statements reflect the adjustment but the Bank has not recognized Czechoslovakia's right to take such action without the Bank's approval.

(iii) In the case of non-member currency, all Swiss francs, at the rate of 4.2975 Swiss francs to 1 United States dollar.

No representation is made that any of such currencies is convertible into any other of such currencies at any rate or rates. *See also Note B.*

NOTE B—These currencies and notes are derived from the 18% of the subscriptions to the capital stock of the Bank which is payable in the currencies of the respective members. Such 18% may be loaned by the Bank, and funds received by the Bank on account of principal of loans made by the Bank out of such currencies may be exchanged for other currencies or reloaned, only with the approval in each case of the member whose currency is involved; provided, however, that, if necessary, after the Bank's subscribed capital is entirely called, such currencies may, without restriction by the members whose currencies are offered, be used or exchanged for the currencies required to meet contractual payments of interest, other charges or amortization on the Bank's own borrowings or to meet the Bank's liabilities with respect to contractual payments on loans guaranteed by it. These currencies of the several members, and the notes issued by them for any part of such currencies, as permitted under the provisions of Article V, Section 12, are held on deposit with designated depositories in the territories of the respective member.

Article II, Section 9 provides for the maintenance of value of such 18% currencies as follows:

(a) Whenever (i) the par value of a member's currency is reduced, or (ii) the foreign exchange value of a member's currency has, in the opinion of the Bank, depreciated to a significant extent within that member's territories, the member shall pay to the Bank within a reasonable time an additional amount of its own currency sufficient to maintain the value, as of the time of initial subscription, of the amount of the currency of such member which is held by the Bank and derived from currency originally paid in to the Bank by the member under Article II, Section 7 (i), from currency referred to in Article IV, Section 2 (b), or from any additional currency furnished under the provisions of the present paragraph, and which has not been repurchased by the member for gold or for the currency of any member which is acceptable to the Bank.

(b) Whenever the par value of a member's currency is increased, the Bank shall return to such member within a reasonable time an amount of that member's currency equal to the increase in the value of the amount of such currency described in (a) above.

(c) The provisions of the preceding paragraphs may be waived by the Bank when a uniform proportionate change in the par values of the currencies of all its members is made by the International Monetary Fund.

NOTE C—Under Article II, Section 8 (a) (i), any original member of the Bank whose metropolitan territories suffered from enemy occupation or hostilities during World War II had a right to postpone payment of $\frac{1}{2}$ of 1% of the amount of its subscription payable in gold or United States dollars until June 25, 1951. All members who received such a postponement have made payment in full except China and Czechoslovakia. China has made payments totaling $130,000 and has stated that it recognized its obligation to the Bank and would pay the balance of $2,870,000 as soon as it was in a position to do so. Pursuant to resolution of the Board of Governors adopted on September 12, 1953, Czechoslovakia was suspended from membership in the Bank effective on December 31, 1953, and under the Articles, Czechoslovakia will cease to be a member of the Bank on December 31, 1954, in the absence of further action.

NOTE D—The principal disbursed and outstanding on loans and the accrued charges for interest, commitment fee, service charge and loan commission are receivable in United States dollars except the following amounts for which the dollar equivalent is shown:

225

Principal Outstanding	$124,729,573
Accrued Interest, Commitment and Service Charges	908,756
Accrued Loan Commissions	233,945
TOTAL	$125,872,274

NOTE E—The amount of commissions received by the Bank on loans made or guaranteed by it is required under Article IV, Section 6, to be set aside as a special reserve to be kept available for meeting obligations of the Bank created by borrowing or by guaranteeing loans. On all loans granted to date the effective rate of commission is 1% per annum.

NOTE F—Pursuant to action of the Board of Governors and Executive Directors the net income of the Bank has been allocated to a Supplemental Reserve Against Losses on Loans and Guarantees Made by the Bank; and the future net income of the Bank will, until further action by the Executive Directors or the Board of Governors, be allocated to this reserve.

NOTE G—Subject to call by the Bank only when required to meet the obligations of the Bank created by borrowing or guaranteeing loans.

NOTE H—The Bank has sold under its guarantee $54,875,844 of loans of which amount $25,757,901 has been retired. Of the balance of $29,117,943, $1,538,010 is reflected in the balance sheet as a direct liability subject to withdrawal. The following table sets forth the maturities of the guaranteed obligations outstanding:

Period	*Amount*
Jan. 1, 1954 to June 30, 1954	$ 5,544,700
July 1, 1954 to June 30, 1955	7,903,343
July 1, 1955 to June 30, 1956	2,089,900
July 1, 1956 to June 30, 1957	1,282,000
July 1, 1957 to June 30, 1958	1,298,000
July 1, 1958 and thereafter	11,000,000
	$29,117,943

NOTE I—The Bank has written off against income all discount and premium on bonds sold or redeemed in the respective years in which sale or redemption occurred.

NOTE J—In terms of United States dollars of the weight and fineness in effect on July 1, 1944.

GENERAL

Application for membership from Indonesia, with a subscription of $110 million was approved by the Board of Governors at the Seventh Annual Meeting. Indonesia has until March 16, 1954 to accept membership.

LITIGATION

A suit has been commenced by an individual plaintiff against the Bank asking damages of approximately $625,000 for alleged interference with plaintiff's contractual relationships (Frank H. Redicker v. Warfield et al., U. S. District Court, Southern District of New York, Civil No. 61-210). The Bank has denied the substance of the charges contained in the complaint and has been advised by trial counsel that the suit is without merit. At December 31, 1953 there was no other litigation pending against the Bank.

H

Administrative Budget

For the Fiscal Year Ending June 30, 1954

There is outlined below the **Administrative Budget** for the fiscal year ending June 30, 1954, and, for purposes of comparison, the administrative expenses incurred during the fiscal years ended June 30, 1952, and 1953. Bond registration, issuance and other financial expenditures **are not included.**

	Actual Expenses		Budget 1954
	1952	1953	
BOARD OF GOVERNORS	$ 114,220	$ 214,022	$ 121,000
OFFICE OF EXECUTIVE DIRECTORS	276,360	367,506	380,000
STAFF			
Personal Services	2,759,133	3,015,174	3,185,000
Staff Benefits	320,633	329,236	356,000
Consultants	107,927	182,467	150,000
Travel	378,170	555,223	575,000
Representation	41,833	50,673	50,000
	3,607,696	4,132,773	4,316,000
OTHER ADMINISTRATIVE EXPENSES			
Fees and Compensation	47,809	51,522	69,000
Supplies and Materials	39,676	32,241	41,000
Rents and Maintenance	394,868	427,550	415,000
Communications	112,332	107,069	107,500
Furniture and Equipment	34,953	31,225	30,500
Printing	39,701	40,350	40,000
Books and Library Service	69,375	71,704	68,000
Insurance	16,704	31,864	16,000
Other	3,361	2,100	
	758,779	795,625	787,000
CONTINGENCY			175,000
TOTAL	4,757,055	5,509,926	5,779,000
SPECIAL SERVICES TO MEMBER COUNTRIES	380,303	214,344	300,000
GRAND TOTAL	$5,137,358	$5,724,270	$6,079,000

I

Voting Power and Subscriptions of Member Countries

As of December 31, 1953

Member Country	Voting Power		Total Subscription	
	Number of Votes	Percent of Total	Amount (In Millions of Dollars)	Percent of Total
Australia	2,250	2.16	200.0	2.21
Austria	750	.72	50.0	.55
Belgium	2,500	2.40	225.0	2.49
Bolivia	320	.31	7.0	.08
Brazil	1,300	1.25	105.0	1.16
Burma	400	.38	15.0	.17
Canada	3,500	3.36	325.0	3.60
Ceylon	400	.38	15.0	.17
Chile	600	.58	35.0	.39
China	6,250	6.01	600.0	6.64
Colombia	600	.58	35.0	.39
Costa Rica	270	.26	2.0	.02
Cuba	600	.58	35.0	.39
Czechoslovakia	1,500	1.44	125.0	1.38
Denmark	930	.89	68.0	.75
Dominican Republic	270	.26	2.0	.02
Ecuador	282	.27	3.2	.03
Egypt	783	.75	53.3	.59
El Salvador	260	.25	1.0	.01
Ethiopia	280	.27	3.0	.03
Finland	630	.61	38.0	.42
France	5,500	5.28	525.0	5.81
Germany	3,550	3.41	330.0	3.65
Greece	500	.48	25.0	.28
Guatemala	270	.26	2.0	.02
Haiti	270	.26	2.0	.02
Honduras	260	.25	1.0	.01
Iceland	260	.25	1.0	.01
India	4,250	4.08	400.0	4.43
Iran	586	.56	33.6	.37
Iraq	310	.30	6.0	.07
Italy	2,050	1.97	180.0	1.99
Japan	2,750	2.64	250.0	2.76

Member Countries	Voting Power		Total Subscription	
	Number of Votes	Percent of Total	Amount (In Millions of Dollars)	Percent of Total
Jordan	280	.27	3.0	.03
Lebanon	295	.28	4.5	.05
Luxembourg	350	.34	10.0	.11
Mexico	900	.86	65.0	.72
Netherlands	3,000	2.88	275.0	3.04
Nicaragua	258	.25	.8	.01
Norway	750	.72	50.0	.55
Pakistan	1,250	1.20	100.0	1.11
Panama	252	.24	.2	—[1]
Paraguay	264	.25	1.4	.01
Peru	425	.41	17.5	.19
Philippines	400	.38	15.0	.17
Sweden	1,250	1.20	100.0	1.11
Syria	315	.30	6.5	.07
Thailand	375	.36	12.5	.14
Turkey	680	.65	43.0	.48
Union of South Africa	1,250	1.20	100.0	1.11
United Kingdom	13,250	12.72	1,300.0	14.38
United States	32,000	30.73	3,175.0	35.13
Uruguay	355	.34	10.5	.12
Venezuela	355	.34	10.5	.12
Yugoslavia	650	.63	40.0	.44
TOTAL:	104,135	100.00	9,038.5	100.00

[1] Less than .005 percent.

J

Governors and Alternates of the International Bank for Reconstruction and Development

As of December 31, 1953

Member Government	Governor	Alternate
Australia	Sir Percy Spender	Roland Wilson
Austria	Reinhard Kamitz	Wilhelm Teufenstein
Belgium	Albert-Edouard Janssen	Maurice Frere
Bolivia	Augusto Cuadros Sanchez	Fernando Pou Mount
Brazil	Oswaldo Arànha	Jose Soares Maciel Filho
Burma	U Tin	U San Lin
Canada	D. C. Abbott	John Deutsch
Ceylon	Sir Oliver Goonetilleke	Sir Claude Corea
Chile	Arturo Maschke	Felipe Herrera
China	Chia Kan Yen	Peh-Yuan Hsu
Colombia	Martin del Corral	Arturo Bonnet
Costa Rica	Angel Coronas	Mario Fernandez
Cuba	Luis Machado	Joaquin E. Meyer
Czechoslovakia	Rudolf Houdek	Bohuslav Kepka
Denmark	Svend Nielsen	Hakon Jespersen
Dominican Republic	S. Salvador Ortiz	Pedro Pablo Cabral B.
Ecuador	Luis Ernesto Borja	Ramon de Ycaza
Egypt	Mohamed Amin Fikry	A. Nazmy Abdel-Hamid
El Salvador	Catalino Herrera	Luis Escalante-Arce
Ethiopia	Jack Bennett	Ato Menassie Lemma
Finland	Artturi Lehtinen	Ralf Torngren
France	Minister of Finance	Pierre Mendes-France
Germany	Ludwig Erhard	Fritz Schaeffer
Greece	Emmanuel Tsouderos	George Mantzavinos
Guatemala	Manuel Noriega Morales	Carlos Leonidas Acevedo
Haiti	Lucien Hibbert	Christian Aime
Honduras	Rafael Heliodoro Valle	Guillermo Lopez Rodezno
Iceland	Jon Arnason	Thor Thors
India	Sir Chintaman D. Deshmukh	K. G. Ambegaokar
Iran	Ali Asghar Nasser	Djalaleddin Aghili
Iraq	Ibrahim Shabandar	Saleh Haidar
Italy	Donato Menichella	Giorgio Cigliana-Piazza

Member Governments	Governor	Alternate
Japan	Sankuro Ogasawara	Hisato Ichimada
Jordan	Abdul Monem Rifai	Omar Dajany
Lebanon	Andre Tueni	Raja Himadeh
Luxembourg		Pierre Werner
Mexico	Antonio Carrillo Flores	Jose Hernandez Delgado
Netherlands	J. van de Kieft	A. M. de Jong
Nicaragua	Guillermo Sevilla-Sacasa	J. Jesus Sanchez R.
Norway	Gunnar Jahn	Ole Colbjornsen
Pakistan	Mohammad Ali	Amjad Ali
Panama	Roberto M. Heurtematte	Julio E. Heurtematte
Paraguay	Epifanio Mendez Fleitas	Julio C. Kolberg
Peru	Fernando Berckemeyer	Carlos Gibson
Philippines	Miguel Cuaderno Sr.	Emilio Abello
Sweden	N. G. Lange	A. Lundgren
Syria	Husni A. Sawwaf	Rafik Asha
Thailand	Serm Vinicchayakul	Kajit Kasemsri
Turkey	Hasan Polatkan	Munir Mostar
Union of South Africa	N. C. Havenga	M. H. de Kock
United Kingdom	Richard Austen Butler	Sir Leslie Rowan
United States	George M. Humphrey	Samuel C. Waugh
Uruguay	Nilo Berchesi	Roberto Ferber
Venezuela	Jose Joaquin Gonzalez-Gorrondona, Jr.	Felix Miralles
Yugoslavia	Vojin Guzina	Kiro Gligorov

K

Executive Directors and Alternates
and Their Voting Power

As of December 31, 1953

Directors	Alternates	Casting the Votes of	Votes by Country	Total Votes
Appointed				
Andrew N. Overby	John S. Hooker	United States	32,000	32,000
Sir Edmund Hall-Patch	M. T. Flett	United Kingdom	13,250	13,250
Kan Lee	[Vacant]	China	6,250	6,250
Roger Hoppenot	Maurice Perouse *	France	5,500	5,500
B. K. Nehru	V. G. Pendharkar	India	4,250	4,250
Elected				
Luis Machado (Cuba)	Julio E. Heurtematte (Panama)	Mexico	900	
		Cuba	600	
		Peru	425	
		Uruguay	355	
		Venezuela	355	
		Costa Rica	270	4,475
		Dominican Republic	270	
		Guatemala	270	
		El Salvador	260	
		Honduras	260	
		Nicaragua	258	
		Panama	252	
Johannes Zahn (Germany)	A. Tasic (Yugoslavia)	Germany	3,550	4,200
		Yugoslavia	650	
Mohammad Shoaib (Pakistan)	Ali Akbar Khosropur (Iran)	Pakistan	1,250	
		Egypt	783	
		Iran	586	
		Syria	315	4,099
		Iraq	310	
		Lebanon	295	
		Ethiopia	280	
		Jordan	280	
Cabir Selek (Turkey)	Felice Pick (Italy)	Italy	2,050	
		Austria	750	3,980
		Turkey	680	
		Greece	500	
Takeo Yumoto (Japan)	Ohn Khin † (Burma)	Japan	2,750	
		Burma	400	3,925
		Ceylon	400	
		Thailand	375	

* Temporary.   † Effective January 1, 1954.

233

Directors	Alternates	Casting the Votes of	Votes by Country	Total Votes
Erling Sveinbjornsson (Denmark)	Unto Varjonen (Finland)	Sweden Denmark Norway Finland Iceland	1,250 930 750 630 260	3,820
Alfonso Fernandez (Chile)	Jorge Schneider (Chile)	Brazil Chile Colombia Philippines Bolivia Ecuador Paraguay	1,300 600 600 400 320 282 264	3,766
L. H. E. Bury (Australia)	H. A. Fuller (Australia)	Australia Union of South Africa	2,250 1,250	3,500
Louis Rasminsky (Canada)	G. Neil Perry (Canada)	Canada	3,500	3,500
D. Crena de Iongh (Netherlands)	L. R. W. Soutendijk (Netherlands)	Netherlands	3,000	3,000
Thomas Basyn (Belgium)	Jean C. Godeaux (Belgium)	Belgium Luxembourg	2,500 350	2,850

NOTE: Member Country unrepresented by an Executive Director: Czechoslovakia with 1,500 votes.

In addition to the Executive Directors and Alternates shown in the foregoing list, the following also served as Executive Director or Alternate:

Director	Country	Period of Service
Hubert Ansiaux	Belgium	One meeting
Leon Baranski	Poland	May 1946—June 1950
Jose Barreda-Moller	Peru	November 1948—October 1950
J. W. Beyen	Netherlands	June 1946—October 1952
Eugene R. Black	United States	March 1947—July 1949
R. H. Brand	United Kingdom	May 1946
Costantino Bresciani-Turroni	Italy	January 1948—October 1948
		September 1949—October 1952
R. B. Bryce	Canada	May 1946—March 1947
Yueh-Lien Chang	China	January 1949—August 1953
Emilio G. Collado	United States	May 1946—March 1947
A. M. de Jong	Netherlands	November 1952—December 1952
Franz de Voghel	Belgium	November 1946—October 1948
Manuel Jose Diez	Panama	November 1950—October 1952
Donald Gordon	Canada	November 1948—November 1949
Sir James Grigg	United Kingdom	May 1946—May 1947
Camille Gutt	Belgium	May 1946
William McChesney Martin, Jr.	United States	January 1950—February 1952
S. G. McFarlane	Australia	March 1948—October 1950
Leslie Galfreid Melville	Australia	November 1950—October 1953
Pierre Mendes-France	France	May 1946—May 1947
Victor Moller	Chile	May 1946—October 1948
Sir Gordon Munro	United Kingdom	May 1947—October 1949
Mekin H. Onaran	Turkey	November 1948—October 1950
Guillermo Perez-Chiriboga	Ecuador	November 1950—October 1952
Sir Ernest Rowe-Dutton	United Kingdom	November 1949—November 1951
Yaqub Shah	Pakistan	November 1950—October 1952
Yuen-Ting Shen	China	May 1946—November 1948
N. Sundaresan	India	May 1946—October 1949
Emilio Toro	Colombia	November 1948—October 1950
Graham F. Towers	Canada	March 1947—October 1948
K. Varvaressos	Greece	May 1946—October 1948

Alternate		
Aramis Alvarez	Cuba	July 1946—April 1947
Djahangir Boushehri	Iran	January 1952—November 1952
Sir Sydney Caine	United Kingdom	July 1950—September 1951
Esteban F. Carbo	Ecuador	April 1950—October 1950
Allan Christelow	United Kingdom	September 1951—May 1953
Tsoo-Whe Chu	China	January 1951—November 1952
Ole Colbjornsen	Norway	November 1948—December 1948
Ignacio Copete-Lizarralde	Colombia	December 1948—March 1950
Guy de Carmoy	France	October 1947—February 1948
Ernest de Selliers	Belgium	June 1946—July 1946
		November 1950—October 1953
Jorge del Canto	Chile	November 1952—February 1953
Nasrollah Djahanguir	Iran	February 1951—January 1952
Alf Eriksen	Norway	April 1949—December 1949
Frank Figgures	United Kingdom	February 1948—June 1948
Oswaldo Garcia	Ecuador	April 1952—October 1952
J. M. Garland	Australia	June 1949—March 1951
Francesco Giordani	Italy	July 1948—March 1949

Alternate	Country	Period of Service
Louis Goffin	Belgium	May 1946
Maurice I. Hutton	United Kingdom	June 1946—May 1947
Fernando Illanes	Chile	May 1946—October 1948
Mario Illanes	Chile	May 1946
Edgar Jones	United Kingdom	December 1949—July 1950
J. V. Joshi	India	September 1946—February 1947
Gunnar Kjolstad	Norway	January 1950—April 1951
Mihailo Kolovic	Yugoslavia	February 1948—October 1948
Willem Koster	Netherlands	January 1947—October 1948
Alois Kral	Czechoslovakia	August 1946—July 1947
Emmanuel Lamy	France	July 1948—December 1949
B. K. Madan	India	February 1947—October 1948
Joaquin E. Meyer	Cuba	April 1947—October 1948
M. Naficy	Iran	October 1946—March 1947
Taghi Nasr	Iran	January 1949—July 1949
		October 1949—February 1950
Ali Asghar Nasser	Iran	November 1952—September 1953
W. R. Natu	India	November 1951
M. Nemazee	Iran	July 1949—September 1949
F. Noury-Esfandiary	Iran	July 1947—October 1948
J. F. Parkinson	Canada	September 1946—August 1951
Maurice H. Parsons	United Kingdom	June 1947—November 1947
Felipe Pazos	Cuba	May 1946
Arnost Polak	Czechoslovakia	December 1948—May 1950
Nenad D. Popovic	Yugoslavia	December 1952—May 1953
Reino Rossi	Finland	November 1952—October 1953
Eduardo Salazar	Ecuador	March 1951—December 1951
Javier Salazar	Peru	November 1948—April 1950
D. S. Savkar	India	November 1948—October 1951
Fernando Schwalb	Peru	May 1950—October 1950
B. R. Shenoy	India	November 1951—November 1953
Karl Skjerdal	Norway	March 1952—October 1952
Bohumil Sucharda	Czechoslovakia	June 1950—October 1950
Thoralf Svendsen	Norway	May 1951—February 1952
Geoffrey H. Tansley	United Kingdom	March 1949—November 1949
L. Waight	United Kingdom	May 1953—October 1953
Roland Wilson	Australia	March 1948—June 1949
Harry L. Wolfson	Canada	August 1951—March 1952
Boonma Wongswan	Thailand	March 1951—October 1953
Peter Wright	Canada	June 1946—August 1946
Kuo-Hwa Yu	China	December 1947—January 1951

L

Articles of Agreement of the International Bank for Reconstruction and Development

The Governments on whose behalf the present Agreement is signed agree as follows:

INTRODUCTORY ARTICLE

The International Bank for Reconstruction and Development is established and shall operate in accordance with the following provisions:

ARTICLE I

PURPOSES

The purposes of the Bank are:

(i) To assist in the reconstruction and development of territories of members by facilitating the investment of capital for productive purposes, including the restoration of economies destroyed or disrupted by war, the reconversion of productive facilities to peacetime needs and the encouragement of the development of productive facilities and resources in less developed countries.

(ii) To promote private foreign investment by means of guarantees or participations in loans and other investments made by private investors; and when private capital is not available on reasonable terms, to supplement private investment by providing, on suitable conditions, finance for productive purposes out of its own capital, funds raised by it and its other resources.

(iii) To promote the long-range balanced growth of international trade and the maintenance of equilibrium in balances of payments by encouraging international investment for the development of the productive resources of members, thereby assisting in raising productivity, the standard of living and conditions of labor in their territories.

(iv) To arrange the loans made or guaranteed by it in relation to international loans through other channels so that the more useful and urgent projects, large and small alike, will be dealt with first.

(v) To conduct its operations with due regard to the effect of international investment on business conditions in the territories of members and, in the immediate post-war years, to assist in bringing about a smooth transition from a wartime to a peacetime economy.

The Bank shall be guided in all its decisions by the purposes set forth above.

ARTICLE II

MEMBERSHIP IN AND CAPITAL OF THE BANK

Section 1. *Membership*

(a) The original members of the Bank shall be those members of the International Monetary Fund which accept membership in the Bank before the date specified in Article XI, Section 2(e).

(b) Membership shall be open to other members of the Fund, at such times and in accordance with such terms as may be prescribed by the Bank.

Section 2. *Authorized capital*

(a) The authorized capital stock of the Bank shall be $10,000,000,000, in terms of United States dollars of the weight and fineness in effect on July 1, 1944. The capital stock shall be divided into 100,000 shares having a par value of $100,000 each, which shall be available for subscription only by members.

(b) The capital stock may be increased when the Bank deems it advisable by a three-fourths majority of the total voting power.

Section 3. *Subscription of shares*

(a) Each member shall subscribe shares of the capital stock of the Bank. The minimum number of shares to be subscribed by the original members shall be those set forth in Schedule A. The minimum number of shares to be subscribed by other members shall be determined by the Bank, which shall reserve a sufficient portion of its capital stock for subscription by such members.

(b) The Bank shall prescribe rules laying down the conditions under which members may subscribe shares of the authorized capital stock of the Bank in addition to their minimum subscriptions.

(c) If the authorized capital stock of the Bank is increased, each member shall have a reasonable opportunity to subscribe, under such conditions as the Bank shall decide, a proportion of the increase of stock equivalent to the proportion which its stock theretofore subscribed bears to the total capital stock of the Bank, but no member shall be obligated to subscribe any part of the increased capital.

Section 4. *Issue price of shares*

Shares included in the minimum subscriptions of original members shall be issued at par. Other shares shall be issued at par unless the Bank by a majority of the total voting power decides in special circumstances to issue them on other terms.

Section 5. *Division and calls of subscribed capital*

The subscription of each member shall be divided into two parts as follows:

    (i) twenty percent shall be paid or subject to call under Section 7 (i) of this Article as needed by the Bank for its operations;

    (ii) the remaining eighty percent shall be subject to call by the Bank only when required to meet obligations of the Bank created under Article IV, Sections 1 (a) (ii) and (iii).

Calls on unpaid subscriptions shall be uniform on all shares.

Section 6. *Limitation on liability*

Liability on shares shall be limited to the unpaid portion of the issue price of the shares.

Section 7. *Method of payment of subscriptions for shares*

Payment of subscriptions for shares shall be made in gold or United States dollars and in the currencies of the members as follows:

    (i) Under Section 5 (i) of this Article, two percent of the price of each share shall be payable in gold or United States dollars, and, when calls are made, the remaining eighteen percent shall be paid in the currency of the member;

    (ii) when a call is made under Section 5 (ii) of this Article, payment may be made at the option of the member either in gold, in United States dollars or in the currency required to discharge the obligations of the Bank for the purpose for which the call is made;

    (iii) when a member makes payments in any currency under (i) and (ii) above, such payment shall be made in amounts equal in value to the member's liability under the call. This liability shall be a proportionate part of the subscribed capital stock of the Bank as authorized and defined in Section 2 of this Article.

239

Section 8. *Time of payment of subscriptions*

(a) The two percent payable on each share in gold or United States dollars under Section 7 (i) of this Article, shall be paid within sixty days of the date on which the Bank begins operations, provided that

    (i) any original member of the Bank whose metropolitan territory has suffered from enemy occupation or hostilities during the present war shall be granted the right to postpone payment of one-half percent until five years after that date;

    (ii) an original member who cannot make such a payment because it has not recovered possession of its gold reserves which are still seized or immobilized as a result of the war may postpone all payment until such date as the Bank shall decide.

(b) The remainder of the price of each share payable under Section 7 (i) of this Article shall be paid as and when called by the Bank, provided that

    (i) the Bank shall, within one year of its beginning operations, call not less than eight percent of the price of the share in addition to the payment of two percent referred to in (a) above;

    (ii) not more than five percent of the price of the share shall be called in any period of three months.

Section 9. *Maintenance of value of certain currency holdings of the Bank*

(a) Whenever (i) the par value of a member's currency is reduced, or (ii) the foreign exchange value of a member's currency has, in the opinion of the Bank, depreciated to a significant extent within that member's territories, the member shall pay to the Bank within a reasonable time an additional amount of its own currency sufficient to maintain the value, as of the time of initial subscription, of the amount of the currency of such member which is held by the Bank and derived from currency originally paid in to the Bank by the member under Article II, Section 7 (i), from currency referred to in Article IV, Section 2 (b), or from any additional currency furnished under the provisions of the present paragraph, and which has not been repurchased by the member for gold or for the currency of any member which is acceptable to the Bank.

(b) Whenever the par value of a member's currency is increased, the Bank shall return to such member within a reasonable time an amount of that member's currency equal to the increase in the value of the amount of such currency described in (a) above.

(c) The provisions of the preceding paragraphs may be waived by the Bank when a uniform proportionate change in the par values of the currencies of all its members is made by the International Monetary Fund.

Section 10. *Restriction on disposal of shares*

Shares shall not be pledged or encumbered in any manner whatever and they shall be transferable only to the Bank.

ARTICLE III

GENERAL PROVISIONS RELATING TO LOANS AND GUARANTEES

Section 1. *Use of resources*

(a) The resources and the facilities of the Bank shall be used exclusively for the benefit of members with equitable consideration to projects for development and projects for reconstruction alike.

(b) For the purpose of facilitating the restoration and reconstruction of the economy of members whose metropolitan territories have suffered great devastation from enemy occupation or hostilities, the Bank, in determining the conditions and terms of loans made to such members, shall pay special regard to lightening the financial burden and expediting the completion of such restoration and reconstruction.

Section 2. *Dealings between members and the Bank*

Each member shall deal with the Bank only through its Treasury, central bank, stabilization fund or other similar fiscal agency, and the Bank shall deal with members only by or through the same agencies.

Section 3. *Limitations on guarantees and borrowings of the Bank*

The total amount outstanding of guarantees, participations in loans and direct loans made by the Bank shall not be increased at any time, if by such increase the total would exceed one hundred percent of the unimpaired subscribed capital, reserves and surplus of the Bank.

Section 4. *Conditions on which the Bank may guarantee or make loans*

The Bank may guarantee, participate in, or make loans to any member or any political sub-division thereof and any business, industrial, and agricultural enterprise in the territories of a member, subject to the following conditions:

241

(i) When the member in whose territories the project is located is not itself the borrower, the member or the central bank or some comparable agency of the member which is acceptable to the Bank, fully guarantees the repayment of the principal and the payment of interest and other charges on the loan.

(ii) The Bank is satisfied that in the prevailing market conditions the borrower would be unable otherwise to obtain the loan under conditions which in the opinion of the Bank are reasonable for the borrower.

(iii) A competent committee, as provided for in Article V, Section 7, has submitted a written report recommending the project after a careful study of the merits of the proposal.

(iv) In the opinion of the Bank the rate of interest and other charges are reasonable and such rate, charges and the schedule for repayment of principal are appropriate to the project.

(v) In making or guaranteeing a loan, the Bank shall pay due regard to the prospects that the borrower, and, if the borrower is not a member, that the guarantor, will be in position to meet its obligations under the loan; and the Bank shall act prudently in the interests both of the particular member in whose territories the project is located and of the members as a whole.

(vi) In guaranteeing a loan made by other investors, the Bank receives suitable compensation for its risk.

(vii) Loans made or guaranteed by the Bank shall, except in special circumstances, be for the purpose of specific projects of reconstruction or development.

Section 5. *Use of loans guaranteed, participated in or made by the Bank*

(a) The Bank shall impose no conditions that the proceeds of a loan shall be spent in the territories of any particular member or members.

(b) The Bank shall make arrangements to ensure that the proceeds of any loan are used only for the purposes for which the loan was granted, with due attention to considerations of economy and efficiency and without regard to political or other non-economic influences or considerations.

(c) In the case of loans made by the Bank, it shall open an account in the name of the borrower and the amount of the loan shall be credited to this account in the currency or currencies in which the loan is made. The borrower shall be permitted by the Bank to draw on this account only to meet expenses in connection with the project as they are actually incurred.

Article IV

OPERATIONS

Section 1. *Methods of making or facilitating loans*

(a) The Bank may make or facilitate loans which satisfy the general conditions of Article III in any of the following ways:

(i) By making or participating in direct loans out of its own funds corresponding to its unimpaired paid-up capital and surplus and, subject to Section 6 of this Article, to its reserves.

(ii) By making or participating in direct loans out of funds raised in the market of a member, or otherwise borrowed by the Bank.

(iii) By guaranteeing in whole or in part loans made by private investors through the usual investment channels.

(b) The Bank may borrow funds under (a) (ii) above or guarantee loans under (a) (iii) above only with the approval of the member in whose markets the funds are raised and the member in whose currency the loan is denominated, and only if those members agree that the proceeds may be exchanged for the currency of any other member without restriction.

Section 2. *Availability and transferability of currencies*

(a) Currencies paid into the Bank under Article II, Section 7 (i), shall be loaned only with the approval in each case of the member whose currency is involved; provided, however, that if necessary, after the Bank's subscribed capital has been entirely called, such currencies shall, without restriction by the members whose currencies are offered, be used or exchanged for the currencies required to meet contractual payments of interest, other charges or amortization on the Bank's own borrowings, or to meet the Bank's liabilities with respect to such contractual payments on loans guaranteed by the Bank.

(b) Currencies received by the Bank from borrowers or guarantors in payment on account of principal of direct loans made with currencies referred to in (a) above shall be exchanged for the currencies of other members or reloaned only with the approval in each case of the members whose currencies are involved; provided, however, that if necessary, after the Bank's subscribed capital has been entirely called, such currencies shall, without restriction by the members whose currencies are offered, be used or exchanged for the currencies required to meet contractual payments of interest, other charges or amortization on the Bank's own borrowings, or to meet the Bank's liabilities with respect to such contractual payments on loans guaranteed by the Bank.

(c) Currencies received by the Bank from borrowers or guarantors in payment on account of principal of direct loans made by the Bank under Section 1 (a) (ii) of this Article, shall be held and used, without restriction by the members, to make amortization payments, or to anticipate payment of or repurchase part or all of the Bank's own obligations.

(d) All other currencies available to the Bank, including those raised in the market or otherwise borrowed under Section 1 (a) (ii) of this Article, those obtained by the sale of gold, those received as payments of interest and other charges for direct loans made under Sections 1 (a) (i) and (ii), and those received as payments of commissions and other charges under Section 1 (a) (iii), shall be used or exchanged for other currencies or gold required in the operations of the Bank without restriction by the members whose currencies are offered.

(e) Currencies raised in the markets of members by borrowers on loans guaranteed by the Bank under Section 1 (a) (iii) of this Article, shall also be used or exchanged for other currencies without restriction by such members.

Section 3. *Provision of currencies for direct loans*

The following provisions shall apply to direct loans under Sections 1 (a) (i) and (ii) of this Article:

(a) The Bank shall furnish the borrower with such currencies of members, other than the member in whose territories the project is located, as are needed by the borrower for expenditures to be made in the territories of such other members to carry out the purposes of the loan.

(b) The Bank may, in exceptional circumstances when local currency required for the purposes of the loan cannot be raised by the borrower on reasonable terms, provide the borrower as part of the loan with an appropriate amount of that currency.

(c) The Bank, if the project gives rise indirectly to an increased need for foreign exchange by the member in whose territories the project is located, may in exceptional circumstances provide the borrower as part of the loan with an appropriate amount of gold or foreign exchange not in excess of the borrower's local expenditure in connection with the purposes of the loan.

(d) The Bank may, in exceptional circumstances, at the request of a member in whose territories a portion of the loan is spent, repurchase with gold or foreign exchange a part of that member's currency thus spent but in no case shall the part so repurchased exceed the amount by which the expenditure of the loan in those territories gives rise to an increased need for foreign exchange.

Section 4. *Payment provisions for direct loans*

Loan contracts under Section 1 (a) (i) or (ii) of this Article shall be made in accordance with the following payment provisions:

(a) The terms and conditions of interest and amortization payments, maturity and dates of payment of each loan shall be determined by the Bank. The Bank shall also determine the rate and any other terms and conditions of commission to be charged in connection with such loan.

In the case of loans made under Section 1 (a) (ii) of this Article during the first ten years of the Bank's operations, this rate of commission shall be not less than one percent per annum and not greater than one and one-half percent per annum, and shall be charged on the outstanding portion of any such loan. At the end of this period of ten years, the rate of commission may be reduced by the Bank with respect both to the outstanding portions of loans already made and to future loans, if the reserves accumulated by the Bank under Section 6 of this Article and out of other earnings are considered by it sufficient to justify a reduction. In the case of future loans the Bank shall also have discretion to increase the rate of commission beyond the above limit, if experience indicates that an increase is advisable.

(b) All loan contracts shall stipulate the currency or currencies in which payments under the contract shall be made to the Bank. At the option of the borrower, however, such payments may be made in gold, or subject to the agreement of the Bank, in the currency of a member other than that prescribed in the contract.

(i) In the case of loans made under Section 1 (a) (i) of this Article, the loan contracts shall provide that payments to the Bank of interest, other charges and amortization shall be made in the currency loaned, unless the member whose currency is loaned agrees that such payments shall be made in some other specified currency or currencies. These payments, subject to the provisions of Article II, Section 9 (c), shall be equivalent to the value of such contractual payments at the time the loans were made, in terms of a currency specified for the purpose by the Bank by a three-fourths majority of the total voting power.

(ii) In the case of loans made under Section 1 (a) (ii) of this Article, the total amount outstanding and payable to the Bank in any one currency shall at no time exceed the total amount of the outstanding borrowings made by the Bank under Section 1 (a) (ii) and payable in the same currency.

(c) If a member suffers from an acute exchange stringency, so that the service of any loan contracted by that member or guaranteed by it or by one of its agencies cannot be provided in the stipulated manner, the member concerned may apply to the Bank for a relaxation of the conditions of payment. If the Bank is satisfied that some relaxation is in the interests of the particular member and of the operations of the Bank and of its members as a whole, it may take action under either, or both, of the following paragraphs with respect to the whole, or part, of the annual service:

(i) The Bank may, in its discretion, make arrangements with the member concerned to accept service payments on the loan in the member's currency for periods not to exceed three years upon appropriate terms regarding the use of such currency and the maintenance of its foreign exchange value; and for the repurchase of such currency on appropriate terms.

(ii) The Bank may modify the terms of amortization or extend the life of the loan, or both.

Section 5. *Guarantees*

(a) In guaranteeing a loan placed through the usual investment channels, the Bank shall charge a guarantee commission payable periodically on the amount of the loan outstanding at a rate determined by the Bank. During the first ten years of the Bank's operations, this rate shall be not less than one percent per annum and not greater than one and one-half percent per annum. At the end of this period of ten years, the rate of commission may be reduced by the Bank with respect both to the outstanding portions of loans already guaranteed and to future loans if the reserves accumulated by the Bank under Section 6 of this Article and out of other earnings are considered by it sufficient to justify a reduction. In the case of future loans the Bank shall also have discretion to increase the rate of commission beyond the above limit, if experience indicates that an increase is advisable.

(b) Guarantee commissions shall be paid directly to the Bank by the borrower.

(c) Guarantees by the Bank shall provide that the Bank may terminate its liability with respect to interest if, upon default by the borrower and by the guarantor, if any, the Bank offers to purchase, at par and interest accrued to a date designated in the offer, the bonds or other obligations guaranteed.

(d) The Bank shall have power to determine any other terms and conditions of the guarantee.

Section 6. *Special reserve*

The amount of commissions received by the Bank under Sections 4 and 5 of this Article shall be set aside as a special reserve, which shall be kept available for meeting liabilities of the Bank in accordance with Section 7 of this Article. The special reserve shall be held in such liquid form, permitted under this Agreement, as the Executive Directors may decide.

Section 7. *Methods of meeting liabilities of the Bank in case of defaults*

In cases of default on loans made, participated in, or guaranteed by the Bank:

(a) The Bank shall make such arrangements as may be feasible to adjust the obligations under the loans, including arrangements under or analogous to those provided in Section 4 (c) of this Article.

(b) The payments in discharge of the Bank's liabilities on borrowings or guarantees under Section 1 (a) (ii) and (iii) of this Article shall be charged:

(i) first, against the special reserve provided in Section 6 of this Article.

(ii) then, to the extent necessary and at the discretion of the Bank, against the other reserves, surplus and capital available to the Bank.

(c) Whenever necessary to meet contractual payments of interest, other charges or amortization on the Bank's own borrowings, or to meet the Bank's liabilities with respect to similar payments on loans guaranteed by it, the Bank may call an appropriate amount of the unpaid subscriptions of members in accordance with Article II, Sections 5 and 7. Moreover, if it believes that a default may be of long duration, the Bank may call an additional amount of such unpaid subscriptions not to exceed in any one year one percent of the total subscriptions of the members for the following purposes:

247

(i) To redeem prior to maturity, or otherwise discharge its liability on, all or part of the outstanding principal of any loan guaranteed by it in respect of which the debtor is in default.

(ii) To repurchase, or otherwise discharge its liability on, all or part of its own outstanding borrowings.

Section 8. *Miscellaneous operations*

In addition to the operations specified elsewhere in this Agreement, the Bank shall have the power:

(i) To buy and sell securities it has issued and to buy and sell securities which it has guaranteed or in which it has invested, provided that the Bank shall obtain the approval of the member in whose territories the securities are to be bought or sold.

(ii) To guarantee securities in which it has invested for the purpose of facilitating their sale.

(iii) To borrow the currency of any member with the approval of that member.

(iv) To buy and sell such other securities as the Directors by a three-fourths majority of the total voting power may deem proper for the investment of all or part of the special reserve under Section 6 of this Article.

In exercising the powers conferred by this Section, the Bank may deal with any person, partnership, association, corporation or other legal entity in the territories of any member.

Section 9. *Warning to be placed on securities*

Every security guaranteed or issued by the Bank shall bear on its face a conspicuous statement to the effect that it is not an obligation of any government unless expressly stated on the security.

Section 10. *Political activity prohibited*

The Bank and its officers shall not interfere in the political affairs of any member; nor shall they be influenced in their decisions by the political character of the member or members concerned. Only economic considerations shall be relevant to their decisions, and these considerations shall be weighed impartially in order to achieve the purposes stated in Article I.

Article V

ORGANIZATION AND MANAGEMENT

Section 1. *Structure of the Bank*

The Bank shall have a Board of Governors, Executive Directors, a President and such other officers and staff to perform such duties as the Bank may determine.

Section 2. *Board of Governors*

(a) All the powers of the Bank shall be vested in the Board of Governors consisting of one governor and one alternate appointed by each member in such manner as it may determine. Each governor and each alternate shall serve for five years, subject to the pleasure of the member appointing him, and may be reappointed. No alternate may vote except in the absence of his principal. The Board shall select one of the governors as Chairman.

(b) The Board of Governors may delegate to the Executive Directors authority to exercise any powers of the Board, except the power to:

(i) Admit new members and determine the conditions of their admission;

(ii) Increase or decrease the capital stock;

(iii) Suspend a member;

(iv) Decide appeals from interpretations of this Agreement given by the Executive Directors;

(v) Make arrangements to cooperate with other international organizations (other than informal arrangements of a temporary and administrative character);

(vi) Decide to suspend permanently the operations of the Bank and to distribute its assets;

(vii) Determine the distribution of the net income of the Bank.

(c) The Board of Governors shall hold an annual meeting and such other meetings as may be provided for by the Board or called by the Executive Directors. Meetings of the Board shall be called by the Directors whenever requested by five members or by members having one-quarter of the total voting power.

(d) A quorum for any meeting of the Board of Governors shall be a majority of the Governors, exercising not less than two-thirds of the total voting power.

(e) The Board of Governors may by regulation establish a procedure whereby the Executive Directors, when they deem such action to be in the best interests of the Bank, may obtain a vote of the Governors on a specific question without calling a meeting of the Board.

(f) The Board of Governors, and the Executive Directors to the extent authorized, may adopt such rules and regulations as may be necessary or appropriate to conduct the business of the Bank.

(g) Governors and alternates shall serve as such without compensation from the Bank, but the Bank shall pay them reasonable expenses incurred in attending meetings.

(h) The Board of Governors shall determine the remuneration to be paid to the Executive Directors and the salary and terms of the contract of service of the President.

Section 3. *Voting*

(a) Each member shall have two hundred fifty votes plus one additional vote for each share of stock held.

(b) Except as otherwise specifically provided, all matters before the Bank shall be decided by a majority of the votes cast.

Section 4. *Executive Directors*

(a) The Executive Directors shall be responsible for the conduct of the general operations of the Bank, and for this purpose, shall exercise all the powers delegated to them by the Board of Governors.

(b) There shall be twelve Executive Directors, who need not be governors, and of whom:

> (i) five shall be appointed, one by each of the five members having the largest number of shares;
> (ii) seven shall be elected according to Schedule B by all the Governors other than those appointed by the five members referred to in (i) above.

For the purpose of this paragraph, "members" means governments of countries whose names are set forth in Schedule A, whether they are original members or become members in accordance with Article II, Section 1 (b). When governments of other countries become members, the Board of Governors may, by a four-fifths majority of the total voting power, increase the total number of directors by increasing the number of directors to be elected.

Executive directors shall be appointed or elected every two years.

(c) Each executive director shall appoint an alternate with full power to act for him when he is not present. When the executive directors appointing them are present, alternates may participate in meetings but shall not vote.

(d) Directors shall continue in office until their successors are appointed or elected. If the office of an elected director becomes vacant more than ninety days before the end of his term, another director shall be elected for the remainder of the term by the governors who elected the former director. A majority of the votes cast shall be required for election. While the office remains vacant, the alternate of the former director shall exercise his powers, except that of appointing an alternate.

(e) The Executive Directors shall function in continuous session at the principal office of the Bank and shall meet as often as the business of the Bank may require.

(f) A quorum for any meeting of the Executive Directors shall be a majority of the Directors, exercising not less than one-half of the total voting power.

(g) Each appointed director shall be entitled to cast the number of votes allotted under Section 3 of this Article to the member appointing him. Each elected director shall be entitled to cast the number of votes which counted toward his election. All the votes which a director is entitled to cast shall be cast as a unit.

(h) The Board of Governors shall adopt regulations under which a member not entitled to appoint a director under (b) above may send a representative to attend any meeting of the Executive Directors when a request made by, or a matter particularly affecting, that member is under consideration.

(i) The Executive Directors may appoint such committees as they deem advisable. Membership of such committees need not be limited to governors or directors or their alternates.

Section 5. *President and staff*

(a) The Executive Directors shall select a President who shall not be a governor or an executive director or an alternate for either. The President shall be Chairman of the Executive Directors, but shall have no vote except a deciding vote in case of an equal division. He may participate in meetings of the Board of Governors, but shall not vote at such meetings. The President shall cease to hold office when the Executive Directors so decide.

(b) The President shall be chief of the operating staff of the Bank and shall conduct, under the direction of the Executive Directors, the ordinary business of the Bank. Subject to the general control of the Executive Directors, he shall be responsible for the organization, appointment and dismissal of the officers and staff.

(c) The President, officers and staff of the Bank, in the discharge of their offices, owe their duty entirely to the Bank and to no other authority. Each member of the Bank shall respect the international character of this duty and shall refrain from all attempts to influence any of them in the discharge of their duties.

(d) In appointing the officers and staff the President shall, subject to the paramount importance of securing the highest standards of efficiency and of technical competence, pay due regard to the importance of recruiting personnel on as wide a geographical basis as possible.

Section 6. *Advisory Council*

(a) There shall be an Advisory Council of not less than seven persons selected by the Board of Governors including respresentatives of banking, commercial, industrial, labor, and agricultural interests, and with as wide a national representation as possible. In those fields where specialized international organizations exist, the members of the Council representative of those fields shall be selected in agreement with such organizations. The Council shall advise the Bank on matters of general policy. The Council shall meet annually and on such other occasions as the Bank may request.

(b) Councillors shall serve for two years and may be reappointed. They shall be paid their reasonable expenses incurred on behalf of the Bank.

Section 7. *Loan committees*

The committees required to report on loans under Article III, Section 4, shall be appointed by the Bank. Each such committee shall include an expert selected by the governor representing the member in whose territories the project is located and one or more members of the technical staff of the Bank.

Section 8. *Relationship to other international organizations*

(a) The Bank, within the terms of this Agreement, shall cooperate with any general international organization and with public international organizations having specialized responsibilities in related fields. Any arrangements for such cooperation which would involve a modification of any provision of this Agreement may be affected only after amendment to this Agreement under Article VIII.

(b) In making decisions on applications for loans or guarantees relating to matters directly within the competence of any international organization of the types specified in the preceding paragraph and participated in primarily by members of the Bank, the Bank shall give consideration to the views and recommendations of such organization.

Section 9. *Location of offices*

(a) The principal office of the Bank shall be located in the territory of the member holding the greatest number of shares.

(b) The Bank may establish agencies or branch offices in the territories of any member of the Bank.

Section 10. *Regional offices and councils*

(a) The Bank may establish regional offices and determine the location of, and the areas to be covered by, each regional office.

(b) Each regional office shall be advised by a regional council representative of the entire area and selected in such manner as the Bank may decide.

Section 11. *Depositories*

(a) Each member shall designate its central bank as a depository for all the Bank's holdings of its currency or, if it has no central bank, it shall designate such other institution as may be acceptable to the Bank.

(b) The Bank may hold other assets, including gold, in depositories designated by the five members having the largest number of shares and in such other designated depositories as the Bank may select. Initially, at least one-half of the gold holdings of the Bank shall be held in the depository designated by the member in whose territory the Bank has its principal office, and at least forty percent shall be held in the depositories designated by the remaining four members referred to above, each of such depositories to hold, initially, not less than the amount of gold paid on the shares of the member designating it. However, all transfers of gold by the Bank shall be made with due regard to the costs of transport and anticipated requirements of the Bank. In an emergency the Executive Directors may transfer all or any part of the Bank's gold holdings to any place where they can be adequately protected.

Section 12. *Form of holdings of currency*

The Bank shall accept from any member, in place of any part of the member's currency, paid in to the Bank under Article II, Section 7 (i), or to meet amortization payments on loans made with such currency, and not needed by the Bank in its operations, notes or similar obligations issued by the Government of the member or the depository designated by such member, which shall be non-negotiable, non-interest-bearing and payable at their par value on demand by credit to the account of the Bank in the designated depository.

Section 13. *Publication of reports and provision of information*

(a) The Bank shall publish an annual report containing an audited statement of its accounts and shall circulate to members at intervals of three months or less a summary statement of its financial position and a profit and loss statement showing the results of its operations.

(b) The Bank may publish such other reports as it deems desirable to carry out its purposes.

(c) Copies of all reports, statements and publications made under this section shall be distributed to members.

Section 14. *Allocation of net income*

(a) The Board of Governors shall determine annually what part of the Bank's net income, after making provision for reserves, shall be allocated to surplus and what part, if any, shall be distributed.

(b) If any part is distributed, up to two percent non-cumulative shall be paid, as a first charge against the distribution for any year, to each member on the basis of the average amount of the loans outstanding during the year made under Article IV, Section 1 (a) (i), out of currency corresponding to its subscription. If two percent is paid as a first charge, any balance remaining to be distributed shall be paid to all members in proportion to their shares. Payments to each member shall be made in its own currency, or if that currency is not available in other currency acceptable to the member. If such payments are made in currencies other than the member's own currency, the transfer of the currency and its use by the receiving member after payment shall be without restriction by the members.

ARTICLE VI

WITHDRAWAL AND SUSPENSION OF MEMBERSHIP:
SUSPENSION OF OPERATIONS

Section 1. *Right of members to withdraw*

Any member may withdraw from the Bank at any time by transmitting a notice in writing to the Bank at its principal office. Withdrawal shall become effective on the date such notice is received.

Section 2. *Suspension of membership*

If a member fails to fulfill any of its obligations to the Bank, the Bank may suspend its membership by decision of a majority of the Governors, exercising a majority of the total voting power. The member so suspended shall automatically cease to be a member one year from the date of its suspension unless a decision is taken by the same majority to restore the member to good standing.

While under suspension, a member shall not be entitled to exercise any rights under this Agreement, except the right of withdrawal, but shall remain subject to all obligations.

Section 3. *Cessation of membership in International Monetary Fund*

Any member which ceases to be a member of the International Monetary Fund shall automatically cease after three months to be a member of the Bank unless the Bank by three-fourths of the total voting power has agreed to allow it to remain a member.

Section 4. *Settlement of accounts with governments ceasing to be members*

(a) When a government ceases to be a member, it shall remain liable for its direct obligations to the Bank and for its contingent liabilities to the Bank so long as any part of the loans or guarantees contracted before it ceased to be a member are outstanding; but it shall cease to incur liabilities with respect to loans and guarantees entered into thereafter by the Bank and to share either in the income or the expenses of the Bank.

(b) At the time a government ceases to be a member, the Bank shall arrange for the repurchase of its shares as a part of the settlement of accounts with such government in accordance with the provisions of (c) and (d) below. For this purpose the repurchase price of the shares shall be the value shown by the books of the Bank on the day the government ceases to be a member.

255

(c) The payment for shares repurchased by the Bank under this section shall be governed by the following conditions:

(i) Any amount due to the government for its shares shall be withheld so long as the government, its central bank or any of its agencies remains liable, as borrower or guarantor, to the Bank and such amount may, at the option of the Bank, be applied on any such liability as it matures. No amount shall be withheld on account of the liability of the government resulting from its subscription for shares under Article II, Section 5 (ii). In any event, no amount due to a member for its shares shall be paid until six months after the date upon which the government ceases to be a member.

(ii) Payments for shares may be made from time to time, upon their surrender by the government, to the extent by which the amount due as the repurchase price in (b) above exceeds the aggregate of liabilities on loans and guarantees in (c) (i) above until the former member has received the full repurchase price.

(iii) Payments shall be made in the currency of the country receiving payment or at the option of the Bank in gold.

(iv) If losses are sustained by the Bank on any guarantees, participations in loans, or loans which were outstanding on the date when the government ceased to be a member, and the amount of such losses exceeds the amount of the reserve provided against losses on the date when the government ceased to be a member, such government shall be obligated to repay upon demand the amount by which the repurchase price of its shares would have been reduced, if the losses had been taken into account when the repurchase price was determined. In addition, the former member government shall remain liable on any call for unpaid subscriptions under Article II, Section 5 (ii), to the extent that it would have been required to respond if the impairment of capital had occurred and the call had been made at the time the repurchase price of its shares was determined.

(d) If the Bank suspends permanently its operations under Section 5 (b) of this Article, within six months of the date upon which any government ceases to be a member, all rights of such government shall be determined by the provisions of Section 5 of this Article.

Section 5. *Suspension of operations and settlement of obligations*

(a) In an emergency the Executive Directors may suspend temporarily operations in respect of new loans and guarantees pending an opportunity for further consideration and action by the Board of Governors.

(b)   The Bank may suspend permanently its operations in respect of new loans and guarantees by vote of a majority of the Governors, exercising a majority of the total voting power. After such suspension of operations the Bank shall forthwith cease all activities, except those incident to the orderly realization, conservation, and preservation of its assets and settlement of its obligations.

(c)   The liability of all members for uncalled subscriptions to the capital stock of the Bank and in respect of the depreciation of their own currencies shall continue until all claims of creditors, including all contingent claims, shall have been discharged.

(d)   All creditors holding direct claims shall be paid out of the assets of the Bank, and then out of payments to the Bank on calls on unpaid subscriptions. Before making any payments to creditors holding direct claims, the Executive Directors shall make such arrangements as are necessary, in their judgment, to insure a distribution to holders of contingent claims ratably with creditors holding direct claims.

(e)   No distribution shall be made to members on account of their subscriptions to the capital stock of the Bank until

   (i)   all liabilities to creditors have been discharged or provided for, and

   (ii)   a majority of the Governors, exercising a majority of the total voting power, have decided to make a distribution.

(f)   After a decision to make a distribution has been taken under (e) above, the Executive Directors may by a two-thirds majority vote make successive distributions of the assets of the Bank to members until all of the assets have been distributed. This distribution shall be subject to the prior settlement of all outstanding claims of the Bank against each member.

(g)   Before any distribution of assets is made, the Executive Directors shall fix the proportionate share of each member according to the ratio of its shareholding to the total outstanding shares of the Bank.

(h)   The Executive Directors shall value the assets to be distributed as at the date of distribution and then proceed to distribute in the following manner:

   (i)   There shall be paid to each member in its own obligations or those of its official agencies or legal entities within its territories, insofar as they are available for distribution, an amount equivalent in value to its proportionate share of the total amount to be distributed.

(ii) Any balance due to a member after payment has been made under (i) above shall be paid, in its own currency, insofar as it is held by the Bank, up to an amount equivalent in value to such balance.

(iii) Any balance due to a member after payment has been made under (i) and (ii) above shall be paid in gold or currency acceptable to the member, insofar as they are held by the Bank, up to an amount equivalent in value to such balance.

(iv) Any remaining assets held by the Bank after payments have been made to members under (i), (ii), and (iii) above shall be distributed *pro rata* among the members.

(i) Any member receiving assets distributed by the Bank in accordance with (h) above, shall enjoy the same rights with respect to such assets as the Bank enjoyed prior to their distribution.

Article VII

STATUS, IMMUNITIES AND PRIVILEGES

Section 1. *Purposes of Article*

To enable the Bank to fulfill the functions with which it is entrusted, the status, immunities and privileges set forth in this Article shall be accorded to the Bank in the territories of each member.

Section 2. *Status of the Bank*

The Bank shall possess full juridical personality and, in particular, the capacity:

(i) to contract;
(ii) to acquire and dispose of immovable and movable property;
(iii) to institute legal proceedings.

Section 3. *Position of the Bank with regard to judicial process*

Actions may be brought against the Bank only in a court of competent jurisdiction in the territories of a member in which the Bank has an office, has appointed an agent for the purpose of accepting service or notice of process, or has issued or guaranteed securities. No actions shall, however, be brought by members or persons acting for or deriving claims from members. The property and assets of the Bank shall, wheresoever located and by whomsoever held, be immune from all forms of seizure, attachment or execution before the delivery of final judgment against the Bank.

Section 4. *Immunity of assets from seizure*

Property and assets of the Bank, wherever located and by whomsoever held, shall be immune from search, requisition, confiscation, expropriation or any other form of seizure by executive or legislative action.

Section 5. *Immunity of archives*

The archives of the Bank shall be inviolable.

Section 6. *Freedom of assets from restrictions*

To the extent necessary to carry out the operations provided for in this Agreement and subject to the provisions of this Agreement, all property and assets of the Bank shall be free from restrictions, regulations, controls and moratoria of any nature.

Section 7. *Privilege for communications*

The official communications of the Bank shall be accorded by each member the same treatment that it accords to the official communications of other members.

Section 8. *Immunities and privileges of officers and employees*

All governors, executive directors, alternates, officers and employees of the Bank

(i) shall be immune from legal process with respect to acts performed by them in their official capacity except when the Bank waives this immunity;

(ii) not being local nationals, shall be accorded the same immunities from immigration restrictions, alien registration requirements and national service obligations and the same facilities as regards exchange restrictions as are accorded by members to the representatives, officials, and employees of comparable rank of other members;

(iii) shall be granted the same treatment in respect of travelling facilities as is accorded by members to representatives, officials and employees of comparable rank of other members.

Section 9. *Immunities from taxation*

(a) The Bank, its assets, property, income and its operations and transactions authorized by this Agreement, shall be immune from all taxation and from all customs duties. The Bank shall also be immune from liability for the collection or payment of any tax or duty.

(b) No tax shall be levied on or in respect of salaries and emoluments paid by the Bank to executive directors, alternates, officials or employees of the Bank who are not local citizens, local subjects, or other local nationals.

(c) No taxation of any kind shall be levied on any obligation or security issued by the Bank (including any dividend or interest thereon) by whomsoever held—

(i) which discriminates against such obligation or security solely because it is issued by the Bank; or

(ii) if the sole jurisdictional basis for such taxation is the place or currency in which it is issued, made payable or paid, or the location of any office or place of business maintained by the Bank.

(d) No taxation of any kind shall be levied on any obligation or security guaranteed by the Bank (including any dividend or interest thereon) by whomsoever held—

(i) which discriminates against such obligation or security solely because it is guaranteed by the Bank; or

(ii) if the sole jurisdictional basis for such taxation is the location of any office or place of business maintained by the Bank.

Section 10. *Application of Article*

Each member shall take such action as is necessary in its own territories for the purpose of making effective in terms of its own law the principles set forth in this Article and shall inform the Bank of the detailed action which it has taken.

ARTICLE VIII

AMENDMENTS

(a) Any proposal to introduce modifications in this Agreement, whether emanating from a member, a governor or the Executive Directors, shall be communicated to the Chairman of the Board of Governors who shall bring the proposal before the Board. If the proposed amendment is approved by the Board the Bank shall, by circular letter or telegram, ask all members whether they accept the proposed amendment. When three-fifths of the members, having four-fifths of the total voting power, have accepted the proposed amendments, the Bank shall certify the fact by formal communication addressed to all members.

(b) Notwithstanding (a) above, acceptance by all members is required in the case of any amendment modifying

    (i) the right to withdraw from the Bank provided in Article VI, Section 1;

    (ii) the right secured by Article II, Section 3 (c) ;

    (iii) the limitation on liability provided in Article II, Section 6.

(c) Amendments shall enter into force for all members three months after the date of the formal communication unless a shorter period is specified in the circular letter or telegram.

ARTICLE IX

INTERPRETATION

(a) Any question of interpretation of the provisions of this Agreement arising between any member and the Bank or between any members of the Bank shall be submitted to the Executive Directors for their decision. If the question particularly affects any member not entitled to appoint an executive director, it shall be entitled to representation in accordance with Article V, Section 4 (h).

(b) In any case where the Executive Directors have given a decision under (a) above, any member may require that the question be referred to the Board of Governors, whose decision shall be final. Pending the result of the reference to the Board, the Bank may, so far as it deems necessary, act on the basis of the decision of the Executive Directors.

(c) Whenever a disagreement arises between the Bank and a country which has ceased to be a member, or between the Bank and any member during the permanent suspension of the Bank, such disagreement shall be submitted to arbitration by a tribunal of three arbitrators, one appointed by the Bank, another by the country involved and an umpire who, unless the parties otherwise agree, shall be appointed by the President of the Permanent Court of International Justice or such other authority as may have been prescribed by regulation adopted by the Bank. The umpire shall have full power to settle all questions of procedure in any case where the parties are in disagreement with respect thereto.

ARTICLE X

APPROVAL DEEMED GIVEN

Whenever the approval of any member is required before any act may be done by the Bank, except in Article VIII, approval shall be deemed to have been given unless the member presents an objection within such reasonable period as the Bank may fix in notifying the member of the proposed act.

ARTICLE XI

FINAL PROVISIONS

Section 1. *Entry into force*

This Agreement shall enter into force when it has been signed on behalf of governments whose minimum subscriptions comprise not less than sixty-five percent of the total subscriptions set forth in Schedule A and when the instruments referred to in Section 2 (a) of this Article have been deposited on their behalf, but in no event shall this Agreement enter into force before May 1, 1945.

Section 2. *Signature*

(a) Each government on whose behalf this Agreement is signed shall deposit with the Government of the United States of America an instrument setting forth that it has accepted this Agreement in accordance with its law and has taken all steps necessary to enable it to carry out all of its obligations under this Agreement.

(b) Each government shall become a member of the Bank as from the date of the deposit on its behalf of the instrument referred to in (a) above, except that no government shall become a member before this Agreement enters into force under Section 1 of this Article.

(c) The Government of the United States of America shall inform the governments of all countries whose names are set forth in Schedule A, and all governments whose membership is approved in accordance with Article II, Section 1 (b), of all signatures of this Agreement and of the deposit of all instruments referred to in (a) above.

(d) At the time this Agreement is signed on its behalf, each government shall transmit to the Government of the United States of America one one-hundredth of one percent of the price of each share in gold or

United States dollars for the purpose of meeting administrative expenses of the Bank. This payment shall be credited on account of the payment to be made in accordance with Article II, Section 8 (a). The Government of the United States of America shall hold such funds in a special deposit account and shall transmit them to the Board of Governors of the Bank when the initial meeting has been called under Section 3 of this Article. If this Agreement has not come into force by December 31, 1945, the Government of the United States of America shall return such funds to the governments that transmitted them.

(e) This Agreement shall remain open for signature at Washington on behalf of the governments of the countries whose names are set forth in Schedule A until December 31, 1945.

(f) After December 31, 1945, this Agreement shall be open for signature on behalf of the government of any country whose membership has been approved in accordance with Article II, Section 1 (b).

(g) By their signature of this Agreement, all governments accept it both on their own behalf and in respect of all their colonies, overseas territories, all territories under their protection, suzerainty, or authority and all territories in respect of which they exercise a mandate.

(h) In the case of governments whose metropolitan territories have been under enemy occupation, the deposit of the instrument referred to in (a) above may be delayed until one hundred and eighty days after the date on which these territories have been liberated. If, however, it is not deposited by any such government before the expiration of this period, the signature affixed on behalf of that government shall become void and the portion of its subscription paid under (d) above shall be returned to it.

(i) Paragraphs (d) and (h) shall come into force with regard to each signatory government as from the date of its signature.

Section 3. *Inauguration of the Bank*

(a) As soon as this Agreement enters into force under Section 1 of this Article, each member shall appoint a governor and the member to whom the largest number of shares is allocated in Schedule A shall call the first meeting of the Board of Governors.

(b) At the first meeting of the Board of Governors, arrangements shall be made for the selection of provisional executive directors. The governments of the five countries, to which the largest number of shares are allocated in Schedule A, shall appoint provisional executive directors.

If one or more of such governments have not become members, the executive directorships which they would be entitled to fill shall remain vacant until they become members, or until January 1, 1946, whichever is the earlier. Seven provisional executive directors shall be elected in accordance with the provisions of Schedule B and shall remain in office until the date of the first regular election of executive directors which shall be held as soon as practicable after January 1, 1946.

(c) The Board of Governors may delegate to the provisional executive directors any powers except those which may not be delegated to the Executive Directors.

(d) The Bank shall notify members when it is ready to commence operations.

DONE at Washington, in a single copy which shall remain deposited in the archives of the Government of the United States of America, which shall transmit certified copies to all governments whose names are set forth in Schedule A and to all governments whose membership is approved in accordance with Article II, Section 1 (b).

SCHEDULE A

SUBSCRIPTIONS

	(millions of dollars)		*(millions of dollars)*
Australia	200	India	400
Belgium	225	Iran	24
Bolivia	7	Iraq	6
Brazil	105	Liberia	.5
Canada	325	Luxembourg	10
Chile	35	Mexico	65
China	600	Netherlands	275
Colombia	35	New Zealand	50
Costa Rica	2	Nicaragua	.8
Cuba	35	Norway	50
Czechoslovakia	125	Panama	.2
* Denmark		Paraguay	.8
Dominican Republic	2	Peru	17.5
Ecuador	3.2	Philippine Commonwealth	15
Egypt	40	Poland	125
El Salvador	1	Union of South Africa	100
Ethiopia	3	Union of Soviet Socialist	
France	450	Republics	1200
Greece	25	United Kingdom	1300
Guatemala	2	United States	3175
Haiti	2	Uruguay	10.5
Honduras	1	Venezuela	10.5
Iceland	1	Yugoslavia	40
		Total	9100

* The quota of Denmark shall be determined by the Bank after Denmark accepts membership in accordance with these Articles of Agreement.

SCHEDULE B

ELECTION OF EXECUTIVE DIRECTORS

1. The election of the elective executive directors shall be by ballot of the Governors eligible to vote under Article V, Section 4 (b).

2. In balloting for the elective executive directors, each governor eligible to vote shall cast for one person all of the votes to which the member appointing him is entitled under Section 3 of Article V. The seven persons receiving the greatest number of votes shall be executive directors, except that no person who receives less than fourteen percent of the total of the votes which can be cast (eligible votes) shall be considered elected.

3. When seven persons are not elected on the first ballot, a second ballot shall be held in which the person who received the lowest number of votes shall be ineligible for election and in which there shall vote only (a) those governors who voted in the first ballot for a person not elected and (b) those governors whose votes for a person elected are deemed under 4 below to have raised the votes cast for that person above fifteen percent of the eligible votes.

4. In determining whether the votes cast by a governor are to be deemed to have raised the total of any person above fifteen percent of the eligible votes, the fifteen percent shall be deemed to include, first, the votes of the governor casting the largest number of votes for such person, then the votes of the governor casting the next largest number, and so on until fifteen percent is reached.

5. Any governor, part of whose votes must be counted in order to raise the total of any person above fourteen percent shall be considered as casting all of his votes for such person even if the total votes for such person thereby exceed fifteen percent.

6. If, after the second ballot, seven persons have not been elected, further ballots shall be held on the same principles until seven persons have been elected, provided that after six persons are elected, the seventh may be elected by a simple majority of the remaining votes and shall be deemed to have been elected by all such votes.

Index

Index